ALFRED E. SMITH
A Critical Study

ALFRED E. SMITH
A Critical Study

by

Henry F. Pringle

with a portrait frontispiece
by WILFRED JONES

MACY-MASIUS : PUBLISHERS
1927

PUBLISHED, SEPTEMBER 22, 1927
SECOND PRINTING, SEPTEMBER, 1927

DEDICATED
WITH AFFECTION
AND GRATITUDE
TO
MY MOTHER

Table of Contents

In Explanation

It would be indiscreet, not to say cruel, for the writer to express publicly his gratitude to certain of the gentlemen who have assisted in the preparation of this critique of the career of Alfred E. Smith. Being politicians, they will understand, for it is the custom of their profession to talk frankly when they are confident that their names will not be used. They will gladly forego any immortality which might result from prefatory recognition.

It is possible, however, to acknowledge herewith gratitude to the following: The New York *World's* Biographical Department staff for furnishing newspaper clippings dating back to 1904; George Graves and James J. Mahoney of Governor Smith's executive staff, who gladly let me see public and private papers because it is their unshakeable belief that nothing their chief has said or done can do other than redound to his credit.

Also to Julian Harris, editor of the Columbus (Ga.) *Enquirer-Sun*, for invaluable assistance in learning the viewpoint of the South toward Smith.

In Explanation

To Henry Collins Brown, whose volumes, "The Last Fifty Years in New York" and "New York in the Elegant Eighties", have been constantly drawn upon. To the *Atlantic Monthly* and to Charles C. Marshall for permission to use the Smith-Marshall correspondence. To Mrs. Henry Moskowitz, who, if she does not approve of some of the conclusions I have drawn, will, I hope, believe that the purpose was honest.

And lastly, and more than to all the others combined, to Helena Huntington Smith, my wife, who risked domestic strife by reading the manuscript page by page.

H. F. P.

NEW YORK, August 1, 1927.

BOOK ONE

Outgrowing the Brown Derby

Chapter One

A FEW DAYS AFTER JUNE 1, 1923, AT WHICH TIME the nation had been theoretically dry for some four years, the white-coated host of a speakeasy down near the Manhattan end of the Brooklyn Bridge hung, with due ceremony, a large portrait of Alfred E. Smith behind his bar. Over the smiling photograph of the Governor of the State of New York he draped an American flag in rigidly artistic folds and under it tacked a neat card bearing the words:

HE MADE GOOD!

It was a tribute from the heart. For on June 1 the Governor, after untold mental anguish, unanimous advice to the contrary from recently acquired unofficial advisers with their eyes on the Democratic National Convention, and frenzied affirmative pressure from Tammany Hall, had finally signed a law which invalidated the State's liquor enforcement act. Approving this repealer was a duty that Al Smith would have evaded, had it been possible, with the greatest of pleasure. Already a candidate for the Democratic presidential nomination, he knew that the moistness of his past was causing delegates in the land of corn whiskey and mint julep to favor the arid McAdoo. But there was, unhappily, no alternative; so, after protesting for almost a month that he had an open mind, he signed the bill. In a lengthy and carefully worded memorandum issued simultaneously, he genuflected toward the drys and said that "there will still rest upon the peace officers of this State the sacred responsibility of sustaining the Volstead Act with as much force and as much vigor" as "any State law or local ordinance".

"—warning to that effect," he added solemnly, "is herein contained as coming from the Chief Executive of the State of New York."

This, of course, was what Al himself, in the bygone days when he was more careless in his public utterances, would have branded "boloney and applesauce". It was exactly the sort of perfectly futile gesture less able politicians are always making. Certainly it did not fool the militant and well-paid leaders of the Methodist-Prohibition army. Nor did a single police chief, sheriff or other peace officer anywhere in the State have apprehension of a rebuke from Albany for failing to be diligent in "the sacred responsibility of sustaining the Volstead Act". And down in lower Manhattan the speakeasy owner rejoiced that no longer would the precinct police captain or special patrolmen from head-in my hands or in the hands of any other agency of this government to fix the price at which anybody can sell anything in this State, whether it is milk or shoes or houses or anything else."

It was a speech filled with tortuous involved sentences that would keep an ordinary man gasping for breath. Al, however, has stout lungs. Item by item he demolished the allegations of the Hearst papers. It was a lie that he had appointed a representative of the milk trust to office, another lie that he had interfered with the prosecution of the milk trust. In the last analysis, he said, there was nothing very remarkable about the Hearst attacks; his newspapers taught that "there has never been a man elected to office yet that has not been tainted in some way", that "no man has enough of Christian charity to do the right thing; that no man that ever held great public office had enough of respect and regard for his mother and his wife and his children and his friends to be right in office".

"Nobody that ever went up to the Governor's office went there with a graver sense of the responsibility of that office than I did," said Smith in conclusion. "What could there possibly be about me that I should be assailed in this reckless manner by this man? I have more reason, probably, than any man I will meet here to-night to have a strong love and a strong devotion for this country, for this State and for this city.

"Look at what I have received at its hands: I left school and went to work when I was fifteen years of age. I worked hard, night and day; I worked honestly and conscientiously at every job that I was ever put at, until I went to the Governor's chair at Albany. What can it be? It has got to be jealousy, it has got to be envy, it has got to be hatred, or it has to be something that nobody understands, that forces me to come down here, into the city of New York before this audience, and urge them to organize in this city to stay the danger that comes from these papers, to the end that the health, the welfare and the comfort of this people, of the people of this State, may be promoted and we may be rid of this pestilence that walks in the dark."

Whereupon the citizenry assembled, invited to attend the meeting by a committee organized several weeks previous and including many Republicans as well as Democrats, unanimously adopted a resolution urging "sound public opinion directed against the insidious and disintegrating opinions" of the journals owned by Mr. Hearst.

Chapter Three

A FRIENDLY BIOGRAPHER OF AL SMITH, RECALLING the courageous anger that had marked the Carnegie Hall speech in October of 1919, would find great satisfaction in reporting that from then on he had never faltered in outspoken scorn of the influence he had branded "a pestilence that walks in the dark", of the man he had declared "without a drop of good, clean, pure, red blood in his body". But this would be too much to expect of even the best American politicians. Many an otherwise upright man, having endangered his soul by public life, has had bedfellows who in later years peer forth like skeletons from closets he would prefer ever closed. Eventually, as I have indicated, Smith's better nature convinced him that it did not pay to compromise for long with decency. And there is this, at least, to be said for him: that from 1919 on he did not a single thing to win support for himself from the millionaire publisher. In public he was temporarily silent on the subject of Hearst. But in private he was as profanely bitter as ever and was deaf to suggestions from his more flexible Tammany confrères that the general good would be served by a few favors for his enemy.

Most difficult of all to defend, if Smith is to be judged by standards higher than those of practical politics, was his part in 1921 in bringing about the reëlection of Hylan as Mayor of New York. He knew perfectly well that Hylan was Hearst's property. He had seen him held up to ridicule by every responsible newspaper in New York and was aware that no injustice had been done. Four years later, having finally screwed up his courage and forced Tammany to reject Hylan for a third term, Al pointed out instance after instance of the Mayor's incompetency. All of this he had known since 1917. In that year he had run on the Hylan ticket for Aldermanic President and after the election had enjoyed ample opportunity to observe the Mayor in action. Both were members of the Board of Estimate and Apportionment, the city's most important governing body.

The offices at the City Hall in New York are so arranged that the Mayor and the Aldermanic President labor at opposite ends of the main corridor. Soon after Hylan was inaugurated his strangely suspicious nature caused him to decline to give interviews except to the newspaper men on the payroll of Mr. Hearst. The other reporters assigned to the City Hall soon became disgusted with him, with his personality as well as his lack of ability. Al Smith, of course, was an old friend and very popular. Often they would drift into his inner sanctum for consolation in the shape of a funny story. Often, also, they would air their grievance against the Mayor.

"Al," one of them declared on such an occasion, "that man Hylan is a fathead."

Smith chewed the end of his cigar, expectorated neatly and amended the descriptive phrase. In print, however, his characterization of his former running mate could appear only as a line of asterisks.

But another time, a few weeks later, he went out of his way to shield Hylan from the consequences of an uttered absurdity. It is one of Al's endearing traits that he frequently does this. A mind as keen as his, enlivened by a sparkling wit and a small-boy sense of humor, might easily give in to the temptation of making less agile men ridiculous. Smith's outbreak of chivalry toward Hylan occurred during a long session of the Board of Estimate, called to decide whether a bridge or a tunnel should be built to connect Manhattan with New Jersey. Various engineers, slightly patronizing, as is their custom when addressing men who do not know a logarithm from a tadpole, appeared before the board to give their views. They talked of investment costs, depreciation, operating expenses, maintenance and vehicle capacity. Several grew quite heated in their learned arguments on the virtues of tunnels as opposed to bridges. Mayor Hylan, listening to their long and technical dissertations, grew restless. He had little conception of what they were talking about, but resented their superior attitude and the tendency of one or two to ignore him, the Chief Executive of the city. At a particularly warm place in the debate he took off his glasses, tapped them on the table and broke in.

"This tunnel, now," he said with bland profundity, "is it your plan to build it by the open cut or by the bore method?"

The face of Al Smith was a study. Then he saw two of the reporters covering the meeting slip out of the room.

"Say," he said, following them into the corridor, "have a heart. The Mayor wasn't thinking when he pulled that! A tunnel built under a river by open cut; you'd have to hire fish to build it! If you print anything about that he'll be the laugh of the town. Can't you forget it?"

And such was Smith's popularity that the reporters, although they would have relished a chance to get back at Hylan for repeated incivilities, agreed to pass up the story. Smith has never mentioned the incident, even in private. He said nothing about it during the bitter primary fight in 1925, when he assisted James J. Walker to defeat Hylan for the Democratic mayoralty nomination.

It was in the fall of 1921 that Tammany again bowed its neck to Hearst and nominated Hylan to succeed himself. For the first time since he had gone to the State legislature in 1904, Smith had retired to private life. In 1920, due to the Harding landslide, he had been defeated by Nathan L. Miller, the Republican candidate. He was enjoying his period of freedom as chairman of the board of the United States Trucking Corporation and insisting, from time to time, that he had no intention of going back into politics. He consented, however, to make the principal oration at exercises on October 5 held to notify Hylan officially of his nomination. In those remote days Al still wore his brown derby and for the ceremonies at the City Hall he was a symphony in brown; suit, shoes, necktie and hat. In his mouth was a large and, as always, rather mangled cigar. Although he appeared cheerful enough, there are indications that he did not relish this task too much. For one thing, a very unusual precaution on his part, he read his speech from a manuscript prepared in advance. Possibly he feared that without this guide he might chance to speak sincerely and thereby plunge Tammany into a dreadful hole. As it turned out he got through the affair very well, paying tribute to the Mayor as follows:

"We congratulate you upon your unanimous nomination by the great party of progress in the city that by its nomination recognizes your untiring efforts for, and unselfish devotion to, the best interests of the rank and file of our people and we pledge you our earnest and faithful support. You have been Mayor of New York during four of the most difficult years in all her history. When you assumed office the country was at war—ordinary municipal business was subordinated to the great issue confronting the country. You have made a strong and vigorous fight for the right of the municipality to regulate its internal affairs. In that fight you have received the hearty support of our citizenry without regard to party affiliations."

A few days later, at the Wigwam on Fourteenth Street, Smith again spoke in behalf of Hylan. This time memory of some of Hylan's eccentricities of administration seems to have been too strong. In concluding, Al said:

"Whatever mistakes Hylan has made during the past four years were mistakes which he made with the best impulses, trying with all his heart and soul to do his best."

Hylan was elected and four years passed. Then Smith, campaigning for the nomination of Walker in 1925, at last had the opportunity to say what he really believed.

"I supported him the two times he was a candidate," he admitted honestly. "I left my private business to go to the steps of the City Hall to place him in nomination the second time—and if I say it myself, I made more intelligent speeches for his election than he was able to make himself."

"Everything the Mayor ever came to Albany to fight for he went away leaving in a more hopeless form than it was before he arrived. If he has helped the Albany situation in the slightest degree, he has helped it by going to Palm Beach for a month every winter."

"Why, everybody knows that he cannot make any decision until he hears from California. That is where his big boss is."

"Of course, a little thing like a Democratic Platform does not mean anything to the Mayor, for he does not understand it."

Chapter Four

FOR SOME TIME AFTER OCTOBER OF 1919, IT IS obvious, Smith was either unaware of his strength or did not care to exert it. He played the old game he had played at Albany for years, and the slow, gentle voice of Charles F. Murphy continued in his ears to be the voice of God. Despite himself, though, his influence was growing. Others remembered his Carnegie Hall attack on Hearst even if Al was himself content for the moment to remain passive. And all the time, even during the two years he was out of office, his reputation as an upright man with a quick, intelligent mind increased. The newspapers of the period from late 1919 to 1922 show that he was becoming known in distant places where Oliver Street and the Fourth Ward have no meaning.

In February, 1920—he was then starting his second year as Governor—a minor boom started to make him a favorite-son candidate at the Democratic National Convention to be held that year in San Francisco. He was elected a delegate-at-large by his party and a few weeks later the up-State Democrats, always enthusiastic in his support and destined to be loyal later on when Tammany was ready to betray him, began to demand serious consideration of the proposal to put forward the name of Al Smith for President. By April and May the political writers were conceding that he was a possible dark horse and from Chicago came word that the Illinois Democratic Boss, George Brennan, was favorably inclined. Al was outspokenly anti-prohibition in 1920 and benefited from the opposition of the New York delegates and other wets to William Gibbs McAdoo, seeking the nomination for the first time. On June 17 a special train filled with Tammany delegates and liquor started for the Coast. Smith, said Boss Murphy, was New York's only candidate.

In due time Bourke Cockran, whose silver-tongued and tear-squeezing orations Al Smith had as a boy carefully clipped from the newspapers, placed his name in nomination with all the proper flourishes. Two States joined in the demonstration that followed. The band played "Tammany" and even attempted "The Sidewalks of New York". But this song had as yet none of the significance it was to have at the Madison Square Garden in New York four years later. And the enthusiasm was a whisper compared to the uproar, partially synthetic, that swept through the Garden on the torrid June day in 1924 when Franklin D. Roosevelt limped on crutches to the rostrum, held himself erect with his strong arms, and called upon the delegates to cast their votes for "the Happy Warrior of the political battlefield".

The 1920 convention meant nothing. Will Rogers and Andy Gump have received votes at a national convention. Smith was smart enough to know this and later, recalling the sad fate of Charles S. Whitman, whose presidential yearnings while Governor of New York were the subject of much caustic comment, he remarked:

> "Say! You know what happened to every Governor who went to Albany and instead of attending strictly to business sat up in the dome of the Capitol with his eyes glued to a pair of field glasses trained on the White House."

This wise policy he has steadfastly pursued to the present day, and there are few more striking indications of the man's sanity and good judgment. Thought of the presidency has, of course, influenced him greatly—notably in that it has caused him to be cautious about talking on the subject of prohibition. But it can be stated as an absolute fact that he has done no overt thing to gratify his presidential ambition. In his inaugural message of January 1, 1927, and those interested in his growth will compare the polished diction with the language of the similar declaration quoted above, he said:

> "Now I have no idea what the future has in store for me. Every one in the United States has some notion

about it except myself. No man could stand before this intelligent gathering and say that he was not receptive to the greatest position the world has to give to any one.

"But I can say this, that I will do nothing to achieve it except to give to the people of the State the kind and character of service that will make me deserve it."

In 1922, unquestionably, Smith's province was the State of New York. And a great task lay ahead of him. As the year opened he was happy in his trucking job and still announcing, as though he really believed it, that he did not wish to return to public life. But an ominous shadow was spreading across the prospects of the Democratic Party. Hearst, elated over having again forced the election of Hylan, began to prepare for the gubernatorial contest in the fall. Governor Miller, an able man, had demonstrated his belief in government by the fit, if few, and had made many enemies. There were signs that it would not be difficult for the Democrats to return to power and prosperity. Smith, meanwhile, was rapidly approaching a crossroads in his life. On every side were demands that he again run against Miller. But down at Tammany Hall, it was plain, Murphy was fearful of the strength of Hearst. He was pondering the intentions of the publisher and wondering how unpleasant Hylan might be regarding city jobs held by Tammany men in the event that a reasonable request from his patron was denied.

It was Hearst's last stand. His political history, with the exception of Hylan, had been largely a series of defeats. He must have known that if this time he lost, it would be the end of his influence, that Hylan would probably be rejected for a third term in 1925 and that all then remaining would be retirement to his California estates, there to read in leisure the daily omniscience of Arthur Brisbane and news accounts of the increasing glory of a man named Smith. On January 22, 1922, the New York *World* published a prophetic description of the situation. It disclosed that agents of Hearst were organizing in up-State communities in preparation for demanding the nomination either for Governor or United States Senator. Both offices were to be filled in November and Hearst wanted one of them. The *World* summarized the possibilities as follows:

"With a few notable exceptions, Tammany district leaders in New York are holding well-paying jobs under the Hylan administration or enjoying remunerative returns from private business promoted to a large extent by their political connections. Upon all of these individuals, loyal though they are to the 14th Street Wigwam, pressure can be brought to bear through the Hylan administration.

"If Hearst determines to make himself the candidate for Senator, is there any likelihood of ex-Governor Al Smith aspiring to or even accepting the nomination for Governor? This is a question much discussed. Some

Democrats of consequence, inclined to accept Hearst as a Senatorial candidate, foresee a contingency where these two bitter political and personal enemies might run on the same ticket and brave the Republican threat to placard the State with the opinion Smith has publicly expressed of Hearst and the estimate of Smith's fitness for office Hearst has time and again published in his newspapers."

Hearst, who never permitted old wounds to interfere with current problems, neglected to bear ill will against Smith. His newspapers had already supported Al in the 1920 campaign for Governor. He was able to forget that this man had declared him "without a drop of pure, red blood". Gradually, as the weeks passed, representatives of the two wings in the Democratic Party began to drift to the Canal Street offices of the United States Trucking Corporation for a word with Smith. One group, composed of the minority element in Tammany Hall, and encouraged by anti-Hearst sentiment up-State, pleaded with him to speak out again against his enemy. The other, consisting of emissaries from Boss Murphy and organization leaders, whispered of the magnificent contributions that Hearst would make to the campaign chest and told him he was foolish to let ancient history interfere with expediency. Besides, did he not believe in regularity? Surely he was aware that a large number of Tammany men might have to work for a living in the event that Hearst was turned down and gave orders to Hylan to be nasty about city jobs held by the boys!

Smith, listening to these worthies, glanced out of his office window, nervously chewed his cigar and reflected, as he saw the lines of trucks parked in the street, that private life had many virtues. In the first place, his income was in excess of $30,000 a year. This was decidedly pleasant, he had been discovering. He was becoming attached to luxuries he had never known. His two daughters were growing up and becoming increasingly expensive. He had, in brief, duties toward his family. And besides, this obvious intention of Hearst to run for something-or-other was an unpleasant prospect. Tammany Hall wanted peace with the publisher. But for Smith to make peace, in the light of the past, was craven. So Al continued to debate the matter with himself. Invariably he came to the conclusion that it would be better to sit tight and say nothing for the present.

Alfred E. Smith, conceived in the popular imagination to be an affable man, a glad-hander, one who never hesitates to express himself and whose position on all subjects is known at all times, is actually a politician keenly aware of the virtue of silence. He finds it possible to say nothing for many weeks, even when excited demands for a statement come from all sides. In 1925, when he was

being urged to fight in the open against the renomination of Hylan, he belligerently refused to speak out. His recent silence on prohibition is reverberating throughout the land. Thus, in 1922, he was reluctant to declare himself when pleaded with to say that he was ready to accept the nomination for Governor. But at last he did so.

"I would not be entirely frank," he said, "if I did not admit that evidence has been presented to me which would indicate a desire on the part of the Democratic rank and file that I again take the post of leadership. If a majority of the delegates to the State convention desires me to accept the nomination and lead the party in the State to what seems to me to be a certain victory, I am entirely willing to accept this honor from their hands and battle for them with all the energy I possess."

By early summer the battle lines were being formed. On one side were Hearst and Hylan, a combination with wealth and with all the political patronage of a great city as weapons to force Tammany Hall into line. On the other were younger leaders of Tammany with outspoken preferences for Smith, up-State Democrats and the fervent hopes of the people of the State. The nominating convention was scheduled for September at Syracuse. Hearst grew stronger week by week and the outlook was dark indeed. For Tammany Hall was showing a yellow streak and it looked as though Hearst and Hylan might win.

Chapter Five

ON THE MORNING AND IN THE EARLY AFTERNOON of September 28, 1922, the gaudy lobby of the Onondaga Hotel at Syracuse, N. Y., began to swarm with delegates to the Democratic State Convention which, in the name of progress and good government, was to nominate candidates for Governor and United States Senator. Ostensibly, the delegates were free men and women sent to express the will of the enrolled members of their party on the floor of the convention the following night. Actually, of course, everything would be decided in advance in hotel rooms filled with cigar smoke, the odor of bad liquor and stout men in derby hats.

Nothing in the panorama of American life is as typical of its political system as a convention. And few phenomena are more depressing. The transcendent figure is the Boss. He arrives in time for vital conferences and is followed by a little train of self-important men. As he passes through the corridors of the hotel there are whispers of awe, fear, admiration and hatred. What will this great man decide? Who is to be nominated? Will he remember favors done for the organization? Will he bear malice because of infrequent gestures of independence in the past? The Boss goes swiftly upstairs to rooms reserved for him. The doors are locked; and down the hallway begins to form a line of local leaders, each with some petition. They wait patiently for hours, talking in low tones and throwing their cigar butts away as they are at last admitted to The Presence.

Next to the Boss in importance at a convention are the leaders from various communities. Like the Boss, they also are convoyed by lieutenants—mostly job-holders. It is their task to carry out the decisions of the organization. There are numerous other groups. Always present, for instance, are representatives of the "reform element"; serious gentlemen with vague blue eyes who are elbowed and pushed and shoved aside by the regulars. They are even more futile than the "rank and file" of the party or woman political leaders. The former are common delegates without influence, who merely await orders. The latter group consists of determined, middle-aged ladies who are thrilled at their proximity to what is going on, but carefully excluded from the inner councils. The rank and file and the ladies may be glorified in campaign orations, but at a convention they are less important than the Japanese vote in California.

Such, in general, was the scene at Syracuse in

1922. Charles F. Murphy, whose phrase "the convention will decide" has been one of the ironical jokes of New York political history, held forth on the second floor of the hotel. He was not in a happy frame of mind because he knew that Hearst was riding high. And, privately, he was doubtful about the willingness of Al Smith to compromise, even for the sake of Tammany, with honor. Mayor Hylan was also at Syracuse. He arrived with William A. De Ford, personal attorney to Hearst. A later arrival was John H. McCooey, white-haired and rotund like a butcher, the boss of the Democrats of Brooklyn. Rumored to have promised his support to Hearst, McCooey was soon in conference with Murphy. During the day the lesser leaders drifted in; Democrats from up-state, where the election of a local candidate is as impossible as that of a black Republican in South Carolina. Most of them hated Hearst. But they were dependent upon the State machine for partonage and knew that a Murphy-McCooey-Hearst coalition was more than probable.

Down in the lobby of the hotel, meanwhile, the boys from Tammany Hall were gathering. Transplanted from the Wigwam on Fourteenth Street, where they congregate on Tuesday afternoons to ask favors of the Boss, these men would stand out in any crowd. They wear black derbies, trousers creased to a knife-like edge and black shoes, highly polished. They have the appearance of saloon-keepers, as many of them once were, of small-time gamblers, of race-track bookmakers. They stand around pretending to look wise and talking so cautiously and mysteriously that even the loan of a match is negotiated in a whisper. At Syracuse they knew little or nothing of what was going on, and so were filled with theories and anxieties. Was Murphy going to ask Al to run with Hearst? Would he do it? Their opinion was that Smith would do as he was told. What the hell! Hadn't Al always been regular? Hadn't he supported Hylan the year before? Trust Al, he's a good guy. None of this reformer bunk about Al!

But the afternoon of September 28 wore into evening and with nightfall the boys were less optimistic. Hearst agents, smug with satisfaction that the outlook was so bright, spread word that their principal was being reasonable; he was willing to be the candidate for Governor and would be delighted to have Smith on the ticket, as the nominee for United States Senator. The Tammany regulars nodded their heads; no one could complain against so fair a proposition. The up-state Democrats were not as well pleased. Having no New York city jobs at stake, their hatred of Hearst was more vigorous. Then, an hour or so after dinner, rumors circulated that Al was holding out, that he was sitting back in a chair up in his suite and damning, cursing and spitting that never, even if it was the last act of his life, would he consent to be a running-mate with Hearst!

Before long the unbelievable rumors were confirmed. Al Smith was really defying the Code, was violating all tradition, was rejecting the law of the tribe. The boys looked at each other in dismay, their cigars cold and frayed between their nervous lips. The party would be wrecked. Disaster loomed ahead unless somebody did something. One by one, the more venturesome stole up for an audience. They urged Al to forget principles, to run for Senator and let Hearst be Governor. When had principles ever won an election or really accomplished anything? But they found Smith unyielding, stubborn, angry and hurt. Irritably he spat, half rose from his chair and turned on them.

"I'm damned if I will. I'm damned if I will!" He kept repeating it savagely. "I may be licked, but I'll lick Hearst, too, if I never do anything again."

Mournfully, the Tammany men returned to their friends in the lobby. Al had run out, they reported. He had a swelled head. He thought he was bigger than Murphy. He wouldn't take orders. "How can we elect local candidates without Hearst?" they whined. Soon they began to curse the man who had been the pride of the Wigwam. He was "throwing us all in a sewer", merely because of a personal grudge, an ancient grudge that was three years old, against Hearst! All the while Murphy remained in his suite. He knew that Smith was being crucified on the cowardice of the organization. He began to send emissaries; first the jovial appearing McCooey.

The Brooklyn leader, his apple-red cheeks more flushed than usual, knocked on Al's door. There was a growled invitation to come in.

"Al," he said, "you should help us out. Murphy is for you, but he's got to be with Hylan and Hearst. I've just left him. Why not take the Senatorship? You can win hands down. Help us out of a hell of a hole!"

"Nothing doing. Say, do you think I haven't any self-respect? You can tell Murphy I won't run with Hearst on the ticket and that goes!"

"Think it over, Al, think it over," begged McCooey. "It looks like your only chance to stay in the game. You know what Hylan thinks of you, and yet he has agreed to support you for Senator. We'll have the whole Hearst outfit with us in the campaign. And anyhow, you've been Governor. We all agree you'll make the ideal Senator."

"No bunk," said Smith, "I'm going to stick."

McCooey moved his large bulk down the hall and reported to Murphy. Another conclave of leaders of "the party of progress" took place. This time Norman E. Mack of Buffalo went up to the sixth floor, where the rebel had his rooms. Aged in the political arena, of great influence in the national councils of Democracy, Mr. Mack repeated the demand that Smith run for Senator. Mr. Hearst, he pointed out, would give full support. Al looked up in suspicion.

"Did Murphy send you?"

Mack flushed. "He suggested that I convey the message," he admitted.

"The answer is NO!" almost yelled Smith.

"All the leaders from New York are waiting for your answer."

"The answer is NO! NO! I won't run with Hearst. I won't do it for you, Murphy, McCooey or all of you together."

Once more dismay spread among the leaders. Al was licked, they told each other. But their fear, by this time, was not that the political career of Smith seemed about to end. It lay in the conviction held secretly by most of them that without Al the party could not win in the fall. They felt certain that the Republicans could defeat Hearst. And therein, partly, rested the strength of Smith whether he was aware of it or not. Tammany Hall, through Murphy; and the Democratic Party in New York because it had bowed to Murphy, were really in "a hell of a hole", as McCooey had said. But meanwhile a swing to Hearst was in progress. Even trusted friends of Smith were beginning to desert him. Some of the leaders told Murphy of the stampede.

"Go tell him," said the Boss, "what you've told me. He's entitled to know. Tell him the truth."

This time two other messengers, whose names cannot be revealed, were despatched. One was a personal friend to Smith. Ill at ease and slightly ashamed of his rôle, he was the spokesman.

"Why hold these feelings against Hearst?" he asked. "He's willing to forget. Why can't you do the same?"

This time Al jumped to his feet, tears in his eyes.

"That fellow nearly murdered my mother," he burst out, thinking back across three years to the cartoons that had been printed in the *Journal* while his mother was ill. "Hearst said I killed the babies of New York by allowing impure milk to come into New York City—me, the father of five children. And he knows it was a damnable lie. Remember those pictures of the forlorn looking children and the poverty-stricken mothers? God!"

For a moment all three men were silent. There seemed to be nothing more for either of the messengers from Murphy to say. Smith, looking at them, shrugged his shoulders. Maybe they were right, he conceded. Maybe the party had gone over to Hearst.

"If what you say about the fellows going is

right, I'm through," he said wearily. "But they've got to show me. I won't run with Hearst."

Just outside the door, as the ambassadors left, was a correspondent of the Associated Press.

"Smith's through," one of them said. The reporter dashed to a telegraph key and through the state flashed word that Smith had withdrawn and had left the field to Hearst. Other newspapermen rushed to Al's rooms. Was it true that he had given up?

Smith was astonished. "Quit?" he asked, his momentary discouragement forgotten. "Quit? Me? Who said so? Hearst'll quit, not me!"

"There's a report you've dropped out."

"I'll have something to say about that," Al snapped. "They don't vote until to-morrow night."

It was then after midnight and most of the delegates had gone to their rooms. Again, in the morning, the air was thick with rumors. Somehow, during the night, Smith seemed to have gained in strength. Perhaps it was because of those last words: "they don't vote until to-morrow night." They were printed in the morning papers, together with a denial of the Associated Press despatch that he had withdrawn. Did all this mean that he might start a rump convention? Would he go on the floor, again damn Hearst in public, say what he really thought of Hylan, fling the betrayal of Tammany in its face? What would happen if he did? Would party discipline hold against the magnetism of this man who was so clearly in the right? Possibly it was true that Al Smith actually was bigger than the organization. At all events, balloting was to start that night and it seemed impossible that Democracy had a chance without Smith on the ticket. Such were the meditations of the leaders. Timid men, hysteria again swept them. The panic which the night before had sent them running to Hearst now began to turn them back to Smith. Reports of the sudden change reached the agents of Hearst and were telegraphed to the publisher, who was in New York. Hearst, being no fighter, decided to surrender. He sent word to Syracuse that his name was to be withdrawn.

It was Alfred E. Smith's greatest victory.

Most of the above, in the case of some of the quotations, word for word, I have taken from the despatch that Charles S. Hand wrote to the New York *World* that night. The convention swiftly nominated Smith for Governor and Royal S. Copeland for United States Senator. Few newspaper stories have matched this one in vigor. No other account of a convention, probably, has equaled it in the picture that it gave and in the accuracy with which it reported what went on behind the scenes. It will long stand as a model of its kind. Beginning his story, Mr. Hand wrote:

SYRACUSE, SEPT. 29.—Alfred E. Smith not only is the Democratic nominee for Governor but is undisputed State leader of his party. He made his fight on a principle from which he never swerved. Even his foes who saw his struggle single-handed against Hearst, Hylan, Murphy and McCooey also admit his supremacy.

The whole anti-Smith combine collapsed this afternoon. First, Hearst quit cold. He wired his managers to withdraw his name. Second, Hylan packed up his duds and beat it to New York on the first train. Third, the whole Hearst outfit evacuated the town in the wake of Mayor Hylan, leaving Smith the boss of the works.

By 4 o'clock this afternoon, three hours before the first nominating speeches, there was not a Hearst boomer left in Syracuse. The Hearst bubble burst like a child's balloon that had been touched by a lighted cigarette. Mr. Hearst himself wrote the final chapter of his defeat. He sent a message to his personal representative, Mr. William A. De Ford, which said:

"Please be sure not to allow my name to go before the convention. I certainly would not go on any ticket which, being reactionary, would stultify my record and declaration of principles and which would be a betrayal of genuine Democracy.

"My nomination for public office is not important, but it is important that the party declare for progressive principles and show the sincerity of that declaration by nominating men who can be trusted to make it effective."

Thereby ended a fight so bitter that any organization but a political party would have been destroyed by it. It was out of this struggle that the new Smith emerged to discard, figuratively speaking, the brown derby that for so long had adorned the side of his head. He had proved himself, and he knew it, bigger than Tammany, bigger than the organization which even the revered Tom Foley had acknowledged as master, which from boyhood had seemed as unyielding as the piers of the Brooklyn Bridge in front of his birthplace on South Street.

Five years have passed and now, it is said, Al Smith looks back on the Syracuse convention of 1922 and is confident that he then saw the issues very clearly. He sees himself as the only man in the party who visualized what would happen in New York State if Hearst were permitted the nomination for Governor. He likes to believe that he saw written the downfall of Murphy and in the place of Tammany Hall a machine controlled by Hearst and Hylan with influence throughout the State. He thinks he then realized that his own destiny was at stake, that he foresaw his own ruin in the rise of Hearst and that unless the fight were made at once he never could be hailed as the leader of Democracy in the State or the nation.

Perhaps all this was so. But in doubting it I give Smith greater credit. In 1922, it will be remembered, he was a private citizen enjoying an excellent income from the trucking company of which he was the nominal head and for which he was, to a certain extent, window dressing. It is my theory that he far preferred risking permanent exile to a return to public life on the basis of forgiving Hearst. He hated the man fiercely, and with justice, for his accusation that milk had been denied to dying babies. He was in a position to wreak the vengeance that his Irish blood demanded, and did so. Surely, if Al Smith had been gazing into the crystal ball of the political future he could have convinced Murphy and the rest of the peril of giving in to Hearst.

But this speculation is unimportant. The significant thing is that Al Smith won the contest and that after defeating Miller in November he was ready to go back to Albany with obligations to none. Tammany Hall had forfeited the payment of any debts that he might have incurred during the years since 1904 when he first climbed Capitol Hill, an obscure and homesick Assemblyman from downtown New York. Only the professional politician with his conveniently short memory can have the audacity to complain if now Smith has become cocky, willing to think of his own future rather than the welfare of Tammany. Naturally, in the light of the past, he is cynical about advice from Fourteenth Street, and gathers about him men and women whom he can trust.

Chapter Six

VARIOUS FACTORS HAVE BEEN RESPONSIBLE FOR the growth of Alfred E. Smith from the low estate of Tammany Assemblyman to that of a man who has been elected four times to the Governorship and who is admitted by both parties to be of presidential caliber. Some of the influences that shaped the metamorphosis lie deep in his own character. Among them are his talent for hard work, an intelligence which grasps and then makes popular the complexities of government, his gift for the histrionic.

But it is highly probable that Al Smith might never have been more than an unusually able Governor, occasionally rising above partisan politics, had it not been that another woman besides the Katie Dunn whom he made Mrs. Smith in 1900 entered his life. I hint at no scandal, I hasten to add. Although she has grown older and motherly in the years that have passed, Mrs. Smith is to Al still the cherished blue-eyed Irish girl whom he had courted in the gay nineties. The second woman is Mrs. Henry Moskowitz, councilor extraordinary to his public life, whose dream is that some day he will be President, whose advice on countless subjects he values above that of all other persons, and who years ago whispered to him that loyalty to the State and to himself was a better thing than loyalty to Tammany. Disliked with cordiality by most of the Wigwam leaders, for this and because she is both a woman and an outsider, Mrs. Moskowitz earned five years ago the obvious title of "The Colonel House of the Smith Administration". To-day, with a few others whose minds also are swift and brilliant in contrast to the dull mediocrity of the average politician, she is constantly working in his behalf, managing his campaigns, cautioning him and causing him to grow. Her personal view of him seems to be a mixture of hero worship and maternal affection. Critical enough herself, it is difficult for her to fight down resentment when he is criticized by others.

"He's growing," she will volunteer one moment. "I no longer have to edit his speeches and messages as carefully as I did."

"It's not true," she will deny somewhat frigidly the next, "that Al was subservient to Tammany Hall when he was in the Assembly."

It was chiefly Mrs. Moskowitz who, early in 1922, prevailed upon him to break his silence, announce that he would accept the Democratic nomination for Governor if it was offered and fare forth to battle with Hearst. It was unthinkable to her that he should remain in the trucking business. And during the darkest hours of the Syracuse Convention she remained serene and unshaken in her conviction that he would eventually be nominated, and refused to haul down her flag as man after man, trained in political warfare, announced surrender and turned toward Hearst. In the campaign against Miller that followed, she was secretary of "The Alfred E. Smith Citizens' Campaign Committee", a modest title in the face of the fact that she was in almost sole command. Few of the issues upon which the campaign was made were born outside of her keen mind. Hardly an important address was drafted without her assistance. She had been influential to a lesser degree during the contests in 1918 and 1920. And each year since her power has increased.

So it is that the story of Smith cannot be told without telling the story of Belle Moskowitz, who was born Belle Lindner, the dark-eyed and beautiful daughter of a Harlem watchmaker with Russian and German and Polish blood in his veins and who was a Jew. The family was well enough off; at about the same time that young Al Smith was working in the office of the City Commissioner of Jurors, the daughter was graduated from Teachers College of Columbia University. She had specialized in literature, psychology and logic with the definite purpose of entering social welfare work.

Her first position was with the Educational Alliance on East Broadway, where she assisted the members of the Boys' Club to stage amateur theatricals.

Her settlement work was the basis of her continued interest in social problems and the experience of those early years proved invaluable when, later on, such matters as child labor, the 48-hour week, mothers' pensions and the minimum wage were part of the program of Governor Smith. It was while she was so occupied that she met Dr. Henry Moskowitz of the Madison Street Settlement, now her husband. She was first married, in 1903, to Charles H. Israels, an architect of aristocratic Jewish forebears. He died after eight years, leaving his widow with two sons and a daughter.

It was in 1912, a year when Smith was leader of the minority in the State Assembly, that Mrs. Israels first became actively interested in politics. She was one of the many attracted by the high character of Oscar Straus, who had been persuaded to run for Governor of New York on the Progressive Party ticket by his friend, Theodore Roosevelt. It was at about this time, also, that she threw her then nebulous influence to the woman suffrage movement.

Nor did she, because or her growing interest in politics, allow her devotion to the solution of social problems to lapse. She organized a committee which delved into the causes of delinquency among working girls and became convinced that undesirable dance halls were among them. She appealed to Mayor Gaynor and in planning remedial legislation was initiated into the mysteries of how laws are drafted, lobbied for and passed. Between 1912 and 1916 she managed the labor department of the Dress and Waist Manufacturers' Association and adjusted hundreds of disputes in the industry. Here, again, her experience was to be of untold value, for she was to act as the representative of Governor Smith on many boards of arbitration.

In 1914 she was married to Dr. Moskowitz, a union that had seemed inevitable, since the two had many tastes in common and had been thrown much into each other's society since the death of Mr. Israels. Obscure, perhaps, in comparison to the position of great influence that his wife now holds, Dr. Moskowitz is a man of experience both in social work and in governmental matters. He has held several city posts of importance.

Mrs. Moskowitz, it will be seen, is of uncertain political allegiance, another of the reasons for the distrust of Tammany Hall. A Bull Moose follower with Roosevelt, she watched with interest the campaign that Al Smith was making in 1918, his first for the Governorship. Abram I. Elkus, whose reputation for progressivism she knew, was managing the drive to defeat Charles S. Whitman and it was he who urged Smith to ask Mrs. Moskowitz to organize the woman voters. He did so, and she became chairman of the Women's Division. Not for a moment since that day has she ceased her energetic and untiring labors in his behalf.

Until Al Smith came into contact with Mrs. Moskowitz his attitude toward women had been the conventional one of the environment from which he was beginning to rise: that they were meant to be wives and mothers and that they graced the kitchen better than the district club or the campaign headquarters. During his years in the Assembly he had seldom been actively cordial toward woman suffrage, although he had been wise enough to realize that it was coming and had not been its enemy. The women of New York State voted for the first time in 1918 so that Smith, running in that year for Governor, found himself faced with the duty of addressing numerous organizations of new, excited, eager feminine voters. He had decided, privately, not to burden their more or less pretty heads with heavy stuff, but to speak to them in a superficial and entertaining way, not bothering much with facts or with issues.

Probably the first official business between Mrs. Moskowitz and the candidate was when, being in charge of the women, she informed him that he was to speak before the Women's University Club. Smith did not take the assignment very seriously, believing the organization to be a "high-brow" one with members more likely to remain at home drinking tea than turn out at the polls on Election Day. He indicated that his remarks would be perfunctory: a funny story, perhaps, and some hot air about how glad he was that the women had received the vote and how certain he was of the gravity with which they were accepting their new responsibility of a voice in the management of the great State of New York and of the greatest of all nations, America! Following this, he suggested, he would shake a few hands and, if it was absolutely necessary, juggle with a cup of tea and a lettuce sandwich.

Mrs. Moskowitz, however, told him frankly that he would win few feminine supporters, at least among intelligent women, by a talk leveled at morons. He took her advice this time, as he was to do fairly consistently from that point on, and spoke for over an hour on the issues of the campaign. These he analyzed with the clearness, force and lucidity which, above almost all other men in public life, he can bring to bear on involved subjects. After the meeting was over many of the women pressed up to congratulate the candidate and to promise allegiance. By their remarks they made it clear, to the astonishment of the unconsciously anti-feminist Al, that he had by no means spoken over their heads. Not that Mrs. Moskowitz herself is a feminist as the word is understood to-day, it should be remarked in passing. No woman who, from the background, devotes her own career to advancing that of a man is a feminist. She is despised by the more thorough of them.

As the campaign wore on Smith leaned more and more heavily on this placid Jewish woman who differed from other political advisers in that she preferred facts to rumors, inferences to hunches. The average politician is a timid soul. He constantly trembles at the ghosts in the surrounding fog. He is eternally afraid of taking one course because he knows that many will disapprove. He believes in political platforms that say nothing and candidates whose personalities stand for less. He is forever filled with horrid dreads that make him decline to please any one by attempting to mollify every one. Are women more realistic as a sex? Mrs. Moskowitz is, at all events. She had none of these weaknesses, and the sound logic of her mental processes made a profound impression on Smith.

The victory accomplished in 1918, Mrs. Moskowitz continued in her rôle of councilor. She consented to serve as secretary to Governor Smith's Reconstruction Commission appointed early in 1919 to study the complicated social and economic problems arising from the World War. Again in 1920, when the landslide to Harding elected Miller, she was an outstanding figure in his campaign, and during the two years that Smith was with the trucking company she never faltered in her determination that he return to the Executive Mansion at Albany in 1922 and from there eventually to higher places. Just when she persuaded herself that Alfred E. Smith, a Roman Catholic with an anti-prohibition record, could become President of a nation where the majority is Protestant and professedly dry is known only to herself. Probably it was after the San Francisco convention of 1920. Certainly she has never lost sight of that objective, and it is her influence and that of a few others that now causes him to remain as quiet as possible on the subject of prohibition. One of the few times when he has ignored her advice, it is said, was when he consented to the repeal of the State liquor enforcement act in 1923. She would then have preferred a stand for prohibition.

Mrs. Moskowitz has had the wisdom to refuse any office at the hands of Smith, although she might have had any appointment in his power. She owes him nothing and therefore is free. Her only official position is Director of Publicity for the Democratic State Committee, which pays the small sum of $4,000 a year. The duties of this are but a microscopic part of her activities. Daily she sits in a tiny office on Madison Avenue, a few hundred yards northwest of the Grand Central Terminal. To her desk come high state officials, influential politicians and many others anxious to know how the Governor feels about various matters. Almost every Friday night she goes to Albany for long conferences with Smith. The telephone on her desk is constantly linked with that in the Executive Office.

"This is Mrs. Moskowitz," she says quietly. "May I speak to the Governor, please?"

Always the answer is affirmative. With her invariable calm, she tells him of the reaction to some legislative message, informs him of an invitation it would be wise to accept, assures him that she has collected the data needed for an important address. To her office, also, come numerous magazine writers seeking information regarding the Governor and his policies. She makes available to these most of her records and is patient when they lack understanding, willing to set them straight if they are critical. In some instances she personally writes articles that appear later as the work of others. Infrequent magazine and newspaper articles signed by Smith are usually, but not always, her work. When they are she insists that the Governor read and approve them before they are published.

All great men in public life have some figure such as Mrs. Moskowitz, whose task it is to prevent "unfortunate" news stories, to broadcast subtle propaganda, to see that the newspaper correspondents are given correct impressions. They are, in a sense, super-public relations counsel, whose first duty is to create and then preserve a legend around their principals. It must not be thought, in this instance, that Mrs. Moskowitz is attempting to give the public an extravagant conception of Al Smith. It is more that she wishes him to be known as the man she would like him to be, one fit in every way to be President of the United States, interested deeply in national problems, always independent of partisan politics. Thus she plays down his weak points and builds up the many strong ones. Lately, for example, she has become convinced that water power is an excellent issue for the reason that New York's problem is similar to that at Boulder Dam in the West.

"It's going very well," she says of water power with satisfaction. "We intend to keep at it."

Being highly intelligent, Mrs. Moskowitz sees all too clearly the defects in this man in whose behalf she has labored for almost a decade. She knows that his grammar is sometimes unconventional, that his pronunciation still lives on Oliver Street and causes "first" to become "foist" and "hospital" to sound for all the world like "horspital". Publicly she professes to admire the verdancy of his speech. Actually, she is somewhat apprehensive about it, and once in awhile during a campaign fellow-strategists have brisk arguments with her when she begins to edit a speech and is on the verge of deleting most of its charm in return for what she conceives to be statesmanlike phrases. It is then that she comes perilously close to destroying characteristics unique and valuable in Al Smith, great vote-getting qualities for all the shuddering that well-bred people may do at the thought of such a man in the White House.

But the chief significance of the entrance of Belle Moskowitz in the life of Al Smith is that here was an intellect his own could meet as an equal. Whatever his other faults, there is nothing crude about Smith's mind. Somewhere in his dim and unchronicled past, if heredity means anything, he had ancestors who thought for themselves, swiftly and accurately. Despite his Irish blood he has ever been slightly alien to ward politics, to foggy thinking, to extreme sentimentality. These, it is true, have been and are still all in him, now to a lesser degree. But when he began to meet people of this type he must have felt quite suddenly that he was at home for the first time.

Unless it is true that the best type of Jew is, above all other men, sensitive, keen, alert, there is probably no such thing as the "Jewish mind". But for the lack of a better label it is sometimes said by those who know him well that Smith has such a mind. His former Tammany playfellows insult him less than they think as they sneer that, having moved uptown and deserted the Fourth Ward, he has surrounded himself with Jews. Certainly, to an increasing degree, his closest advisers have been of that race. One of the first was Mr. Elkus, who managed his 1918 campaign. A later one was Joseph M. Proskauer, now a justice of the Supreme Court and one of the ablest legal minds in the country. Among his present close associates, in addition to Mrs. Moskowitz, are Clarence M. Lewis, another lawyer, and Robert Moses, his Secretary of State. But Mrs. Moskowitz, whose talent it is that she can dream the dreams of an idealist and labor for their realization as a pragmatist, is the most important of them all.

In 1906 or 1907, when Smith was beginning to feel his oats as a young and bright Assemblyman, he would have laughed at these people as "highbrows, reformers and crack-pots," whose approbation meant nothing because they could produce no votes. Over many an Albany bar, in those days, he made smart cracks about such folk, to the enthusastic applause of his fellow legislators in both the Democratic and Republican parties.

BOOK TWO

A City Boy Begins a Career

Chapter One

In 1873 new york was a collection of scraggly villages and thought itself a city. About 1,000,000 people made up its population, the great majority living south of 59th Street and the rest traveling to their suburban homes in Yorkville, Harlem and the Bronx by stage, horse-car, river steamer or the new and somewhat dangerous elevated railroad on top of which wheezed steam locomotives that belched smoke and ashes. Visitors from the country, awed by the noise and confusion and harassed by transportation facilities almost as bad as they are now, thought the town a magnificent if bewildering place. Visitors from abroad shuddered at the filth in the streets, at buildings either grotesque or hideous that lined them and at the inhabitants who expectorated freely. They sailed for home to report that America was still barbarian.

Their criticism was not inaccurate. The Post Office just below the City Hall, now the object of lamentation, had just been built and was widely admired. Telegraph poles heavy with wires lined the principal streets. Few of the avenues were decently paved and the din of iron-rimmed wheels, the clanging of horse-car gongs and the cursing of stage drivers would send even a modern taxicab chauffeur to a psychoanalyst for treatment. Politically, the Irish ruled the city. Promotion for merit was virtually unheard of in the police department. Six years previous, 1867, Tammany Hall had laid the cornerstone of its new Wigwam on 14th Street, with the reading of an ode written for the occasion by an editor of the New York *World* as a feature of the ceremonies. The building is still in use, a reminder of the perverted architecture of the '70's, as Tammany itself is a reminder of perverted government.

But there was, of course, much that was beautiful and much to fascinate in the New York of those days. Clipper ships furled their sails along the wharfs and the inland sea that is the Upper Bay touched softly the walls of the Battery. If there was not yet the startling outline of the Woolworth Building against the sky nor the cubistic block of the Telephone Building further west, there were frequent vistas of flagstone walks and gardens seen through the iron gates of Old Chelsea. Below Canal Street all was noise, dust and confusion. But a few blocks to the north leisurely houses slumbered behind trees and men had homes with wide porches instead of grandiose apartments on Park Avenue. There was poverty in the '70's, but no slums as they are known to-day. The Bowery was really the

Bowery, a place to be shunned at night and not a midway for rubberneck guides to show the gullible at a dollar a head. And at dusk throughout the city small boys and girls pressed their noses against windowpanes to watch the lamplighter shuffle along leaving in his wake the cheerful glow of gas-lamps to dispel the gloom.

The newspapers of December 31, 1873 are, for the purpose of this narrative, not without interest. There does not seem to have been a great deal of vitally absorbing news. The New York *Herald* of that date, for instance, devoted several columns to a despatch from a correspondent at Havana. Indignation was being expressed in some circles over slavery conditions in Cuba and the *Herald* man described a futile movement toward independence. Another story in this issue reported that army men, veterans of the Civil War, were being used as servants at the White House in Washington. President Grant was taking steps to end this abuse of the military. At Gloucester, Mass., an obscure item stated, memorial services had been held for the 174 fishermen lost off the banks during the year.

Advertisements describing what the town afforded in the line of amusement were plentiful. Mr. Augustin Daly was the star of "The Parricide" at Daly's Fifth Avenue Theater. At both the Bowery Theater and Wallach's the attractions were billed, simply, "A Galaxy of Stars". Two Shakespearian productions were going on: "The Merchant of Venice" at Wood's Museum at 13th Street and Broadway, and "Much Ado About Nothing" at the elegant Academy of Music. At Niblo's Garden, near Houston Street, the offering was "A Grand Fairy Spectacle", obviously a bid for Christmas vacation children's parties. The famous Gus Williams was causing side-aches at Tony Pastor's on the Bowery.

But nowhere in the paper, such being not infrequently the unnoticed première of the great, was there mention of the fact that on the day previous a male child had been born on the third floor of a tenement at No. 174 South Street. The parents of the boy were Alfred Emanuel Smith, an unsuccessful truckman, and the former Catherine Mulvehill, a lady of Irish ancestry. Both were native New Yorkers, both Roman Catholics. They named the child after his father. Two years later to a day, on December 30, 1875, a girl arrived. There were no other children.

Smith, the truckman, is now a vague figure. He died while comparatively young, and not a great deal about him is remembered. His wife, it is known, was Irish-American. But the genesis of the blood that flowed in his own veins is not known. It is now recalled by the family that he had dark hair and eyes, as well as a dark complexion. They think it possible that far back there may have been

Italian forebears. It is asserted with emphasis by the Smiths, however, that he was not partly German. There is still in existence a certificate showing membership in a volunteer fire company. Dated 1857, it is made out in the name of Alfred E. Smith. In this way is refuted a canard published by the *Gaelic-American* last year, which set forth that the father of the Governor of the State of New York was really a Teuton named Schmidt who had later called himself Smith. This cruel charge caused terrific excitement among the Irish members of Tammany Hall. Al, himself, thought it rather funny.

Both parents of the boy destined to typify city streets as other Americans in public life have typified log cabins, farms and sap buckets, were born in the immediate vicinity of South Street. They were childhood sweethearts and were married in 1871. The truckman's father was also named Alfred Emanuel Smith and died in New York. And beyond these sparse facts nothing is available about Al Smith's family tree. The trail to the past is easier to follow in rural districts, where landmarks remain and memories are longer. In New York the scene changes swiftly and there are no village sages to sit in the sun and spin the recollections from which histories are fashioned. In 1873 the house on South Street where Al Smith was born was a presentable dwelling, although the neighborhood was looked down upon by the more prosperous residents of Cherry Street and Chatham Square. The piers of the Brooklyn Bridge were just beginning to rise. To-day No. 174 South Street, having passed from tenement to warehouse to decay, has been transformed into a filling station. But over it is the bridge that grows old gracefully and is still the most beautiful of all the four structures that rise above the river.

Chapter Two

THERE CAN HAVE BEEN FEW DULL MOMENTS IN the life of a boy whose home was on South Street in the late '70's. Alfred Smith—he was not called Al until he was well into manhood and had dabbled with politics—suffered none of the boredom that settles like a pall over most small boys when the weather is gloomy and orders for a day indoors are issued. He had only to go to a window and look out upon a scene that changed from minute to minute and was continually exciting. Directly across from the house at No. 174 South Street were the wharfs of the East River. Tied to them were the clipper ships, their bowsprits extending ten yards or more across the street. Queer tattooed sailors climbed high into the rigging of these vessels, and nearly every day a fussy tug would pull one of them out into the river and start it on a journey to Timbuctoo or the Canary Islands. And always in the air on South Street were the odors of spices and tar and turpentine.

The clipper ships were beginning to vanish as Alfred Smith grew older. Possibly they had gone before he could appreciate their beauty or their fascination. At all events the sea never called to him, and far places or dim horizons had no more allure for the boy than since they have had for the man. Now over fifty, Smith has never been abroad nor has been anxious to go. He rarely travels except between Albany and New York City. The boy preferred the fire headquarters near his home and the man is satisfied with the boundaries of New York State for his intellectual outlook as well as for his dwelling place. Rather than to the ships at his feet, the boy turned toward a city miracle—the Brooklyn Bridge—which was to rise almost directly above his home.

"The Brooklyn Bridge and I grew up together," he remarked many years later. "It attracted my infantile attention and I spent a lot of time superintending the job in my boyhood. I have never lost the sense of admiration and envy I felt for the men who swarmed like flies stringing the cables and putting in the roadways as the bridge took shape. Ten years after I was born, and nine years after the New York tower was finished, they opened the bridge."

In his informative book, "New York in the Elegant Eighties", Mr. Henry Collins Brown recalls that this historic event took place on May 24, 1883. This happened to be the birthday of Queen Victoria and the unhappy coincidence, Mr. Brown writes, brought strenuous objections from the Irish population. They were afraid that the bridge opening might be construed as a subtle tribute to the British, a race responsible for most of the evils of mankind. It is remarkable that their protests went unheeded.

During the weeks before the bridge was declared officially finished every one was eager to walk across it. Only a few had been able to obtain permission, or had the nerve, to make the journey by the dizzy footpath which swayed in the wind and had been used by the workmen. Despite the assurances of the engineers there was wide distrust of the firmness of the structure. The thread-like cables, it was said, ought first to be tested by a weight comparable to that of Jumbo the Elephant, Mr. P.T. Barnum's most famous exhibit at the time. These apprehensions, together with the belief that vast crowds would be on hand, made the opening day rather a fizzle. But on May 30, Decoration Day, it seemed as though the whole town had turned out.

The promenade of the bridge was jammed with beauty and fashion, as well as with the less decorative common people. Gentlemen in top hats, known as plugs, adjusted their manly stride to the mincing steps of the ladies on their arms, ladies wearing bustles and long skirts that fluffed out from mechanically slim waists. They walked in the warm spring sunshine and turned back to look at Manhattan and marvel at the swift growth of the city toward the north. The tallest object on the island was the slender spire of Trinity Church; for the golden dome of the Pulitzer Building, later to be visible for miles, had not yet risen. Toward the south were the waters of the Bay, but no Statue of Liberty, and further still the green slopes of Staten Island.

All in all, the trip across the Brooklyn Bridge was well worth making, as the crowds on Decoration Day in 1883 discovered. The structure seemed safe enough, too, despite the early gloomy predictions that it might collapse. It was these, however, that were suddenly remembered when late in the afternoon some one slipped on a flight of steps on the promenade and screamed. A panicky idiot, hearing the scream, yelled that the bridge was falling. In the stampede those on the bridge rushed to the Manhattan end and into a crowd just starting out. A dozen people were killed and many others hurt. Word of the disaster spread along South Street and boys and men from the district hurried to Park Row. Among the boys was Alfred Smith.

"They were taking away bodies of wounded people," he remembers. "Policemen were piling up great quantities of clothing and hats that had been torn from the victims. That was my first view of a great calamity. I didn't sleep well for nights."

A City Boy Begins a Career

Before he was ten years old Alfred was debating whether the career of a postman or a fireman offered the maximum in excitement and interest. He soon decided that the fireman's was a vastly higher calling, and in preparation for it he began to hang around the engine house on John Street and to ingratiate himself with the firemen by running errands. Nearly all the other small boys of the neighborhood were doing the same thing, of course. Competition for favor from On High was keen. But Alfred won out because he was bright and talkative. His talents as a parlor entertainer were budding even at that tender age and he would dance a jig or sing—if asked. The secret of his success, undoubtedly, was that he did not do so when he was not asked.

If the sea and clipper ships did not attract the boy Smith, the river did. It was cleaner in those days, and as soon as the weather was moderately warm the wharfs along South Street swarmed with small boys who had learned to swim and dive almost as soon as they had learned to walk. The boy of the '80's, and for decades afterwards, was glorious in the consciousness of the superiority of the male. His was the privilege of swimming without clothes, of going barefoot, of running in gangs, of holding mysterious secret rites in vacant lot shanties. No small girl was feminist enough to join him. Had she done so, and perhaps it is as true to-day, she would promptly have been chased by irate conservatives and probably paddled by her shocked mother. Woman's place was on the front stoop playing jackstraws, or with her dolls.

Chapter Three

BOYHOOD POVERTY IS ALWAYS AN ASSET TO THE American in public life. This is because the United States, being a young country, takes its Democracy very seriously and cultivates the snobbery of poverty. Many an able man, having been born to wealth and refinement and lacking the vote-getting background of adolescent deprivation, has been ruled out as unavailable for high office. The politician who will boast from the stump that in his youth he carried a handkerchief, enjoyed bathing and wore a clean shirt every day has yet to appear in this enlightened Republic. All this accounts, in part, for the number of log cabins once sheltering rising statesmen. It accounts for the fact that the popular conception of Alfred E. Smith's boyhood is that he was a lad out of a Horatio Alger tale, who roamed the streets at night for a place to sleep, and who worked feverishly during his waking hours. His honesty, it is the theory, was equaled only by his industry in sorting fish at the Fulton Market and his sole recreation was dancing to the bleat of a hurdy-gurdy on the sidewalks of New York.

Not that Smith, himself, has encouraged this fantastic conception; it has been the inevitable outgrowth of a grain of truth, years in the political arena and the romanticizing of campaign press agents. The truthful part is that as a boy he worked as hard as any youth; at least after the death of his father. To a certain extent he really has risen from the pavements of the bewildering city. His language and pronunciation to-day, his complete lack of interest in books or the cultural things of life, are the best indications of the nature of his youthful environment. But if his home was barren in this respect, it was an excellent one insofar as necessary material things of life were concerned. So now, in 1927, the Executive Mansion at Albany has a private motion picture machine and virtually no books. Young Alfred Smith's education may have been woefully neglected, but his mother always contrived to provide enough food. Rigid training in the Roman Catholic Church instilled in him principles of honesty and also the unquestioning obedience to authority which made it possible for him to be subservient for many years to the mandates of Tammany Hall. It is not true that his home was of the slums, of the type where everything is drab and there is no hope of better days to come. It was respectable, moderately comfortable, decent—and common.

South Street and the lower East Side of the '80's, before the tide of immigration reached its flood and carried in a dozen different races, were far different from now. On many of the streets in the district grew shade trees. There was hardly a tenement of the type that Smith, as Governor, has been trying to abolish by means of forward-looking State assistance. The wharfs on the river had not yet been roofed over, and it was the custom of the Irish mothers of the neighborhood to gather there to enjoy the evening breezes; not infrequently flavored with the scent of fish from the Fulton Market. They were joined, in time, by their husbands who had stopped off at a saloon for a mixture of beer and Tammany Hall political gossip. On Saturday afternoons entire families took horse-car excursions to Harlem.

Very little, as I have said, is remembered about Alfred E. Smith, the truckman. He is reported to have been politically inclined, but his activities must have been either feeble or slight, or Tammany Hall would have rewarded him with either contracts or a job. He was not very successful in his business in late years because of poor health, and when he died his widow faced life with two children, almost destitute. Smith Sr. was a truckman in the old-time sense, and would have been astonished could he have known that some day his son would hold the resounding title of Chairman of the Board of the United States Trucking Corporation, a vast affair with whole fleets of trucks. Probably he would have predicted that business on so large a scale would never pay. He was content, himself, with one or two teams which he drove personally through the streets of the city. He saw little of his son and daughter except on Sundays, for he started his labors at 6 o'clock in the morning and did not return until dusk. Then he was so weary that he went to bed almost immediately.

It was the mother rather than the father who was the dominating influence in the lives of the children. Mrs. Smith was an unusual woman for her time and place; not one of the ample, comfortable, rather stupid Irish women who gossiped over back fences until, in New York, these vanished and the dumbwaiter took their place as a means of conversational exchanges. She was small, intelligent, active. It is not to be wondered that her son, in the years of his greatness, literally worshiped her and devoted nearly every Sunday morning to visiting her on Brooklyn Heights, where she then lived. Quite naturally, too, her viewpoint toward him was that he could not do a mean or dishonest thing, that he was good beyond all men. Her faith in him was comparable only to her faith in the Catholic Church.

But if the closing years of Mrs. Smith's life were tranquil, many of the early ones had been all too turbulent. In 1886 her husband died. He had not been well for several years and his earnings, never large, had steadily dwindled. It was necessary for both young Alfred, only thirteen, and his mother to become providers. Mrs. Smith was not unprepared. Unusual among women of that day, she had already been a wage-earner, having been a maker of hoopskirts some years before her marriage. These had now gone out of fashion, but she adapted her skill to covering umbrellas. This she carried on at home, doing the housework at the same time.

Alfred had been working, but only after school hours, for two or three years before his father's death. He had contributed several dollars a week by selling newspapers. And he did not shirk his new responsibility upon becoming masculine head of the family. He did not greatly mind, it is probable, giving up his studies at the parochial school connected with the neighborhood church, St. James'. He was in the 8th grade but only a fair student, and far more interested in the discovery of talents as an elocutionist and actor than in his books. There were other sacrifices that really mattered. No longer was there time to spend hours at the engine house and provide coffee and sandwiches for his firemen friends. He had to forego the refreshing sport of swimming in the river. And, having arrived at his new dignity, he could not tease and annoy his younger sister as is the privilege of brothers. Instead he had to treat her with dignity and reserve;

at least the sister herself, Mrs. John Glynn, recalls that this change took place.

On the whole, there seems to be slight doubt, Alfred Smith was an attractive youngster. One family photograph, taken when he was about seven years old, shows that he had a slim but sturdy build, a rather sober face and a sweet mouth. Perhaps it was the ordeal of being photographed that made him look solemn. He rarely was involved in the usual boy fights because of his talent for talking himself out of difficulties. Before she died, his mother testified that for the most part he was a model small boy. He never had to be spanked, and this in an age when the hairbrush was more used than the tooth brush. Most remarkable of all, he did not object to wearing his rubbers when the weather was wet. A child of the slums? The theory is untenable in the face of the facts. Alfred Smith was well dressed, even if his shirts were fashioned from those cast off by his father and even if his first suit was tailored by his mother. This was no street arab bred in vice, running with East Side gangs, dodging the law, lucky if he had enough to eat. Had the inclination been in the boy he could have found time for self-education after it became necessary for him to leave school. Poorer youths with less leisure have delved deep into the written word.

"I never read books," he admitted in later life. "I never have read books. In all my life I have never read for amusement or to pass away the time. Life furnishes me with all the thrills."

But he was a man of responsibilities from the time he was thirteen years old, a support and prop to his mother, a youth in whom sudden reverses dimmed but did not extinguish impulses to laughter and loquaciousness. The only legacy left by his father was the creaking trucking business and a horse or two. For a time Alfred attempted to keep it going, and even managed to get some new business. But he soon decided that no money would be made that way and gave it up for a job with the oil supply house of Clarkson & Ford on Front Street. Then came the famous post at the Fulton Fish Market where he worked as a checker and where he became so familiar with the various members of the fish family that he was able, when in the legislature, to confound his rustic colleagues by his knowledge when some debate on conservation of fish in state waters was in progress.

Out of this job, too, grew the story which has been the delight of so many toastmasters and has been told and printed so many times that Smith must often regret that he ever made the wise-crack. One evening, when the State legislature was in session at Albany, a young Assemblyman burst into the chamber delirious with joy over the news that Cornell had just won another boat race. He demanded that this important event be entered on the record and even intimated that a long yell for old Cornell would not be out of place. Al Smith, sitting back and grinning, listened. Then he stood up.

"I hold a degree, too," he said.

The collegiate Assemblyman was all courtesy.

"And what, if I may ask, is your alma mater?"

"I'm an F. F. M.," said Al. "Fulton Fish Market."

Smith has changed since those days. It is not likely that he would now make good-humored jokes about his educational shortcomings. During his early years in politics these were not conspicuous. His first associates were not, in the main, better educated; nor had they Al's saving grace of an aggressive mind. But to-day his intimates in his official life are usually university trained. He cannot but sense his limitations and so, when occasionally he cannot ignore them, he becomes sardonic rather than witty and falls back on the defense of overstatement.

Once, for instance, a lady interviewer persisted in asking him about his disinclination toward reading. Already this subject, although Smith would even to-day deny that this is so, had become highly irritating; as much so as his stand on the Volstead Act was to be later on. He was not overcordial.

"Is it true, Governor," asked the interviewer, "that you have never read a book through in your life?"

"No indeed," he replied, without the shadow of a smile. "That is a lie. I've read 'The Life and Battles of John L. Sullivan' through from cover to cover."

More recently, the presidential bee having settled under his brown derby and started its work, Smith began to face the criticism that his outlook did not extend beyond the limits of New York State, that he was, in the unkind words of William Allen White, "a town-lot Sir Galahad who never fared afield." Numerous solemn people started to demand his views, if he had any, on the tariff, the League of Nations, international debts. There were two reasons why Al did not look with favor on these queries: the first was that he was still Governor and had promised that he would devote all his time to the job instead of seeking the presidency. The second reason was that he had really not thought about these weighty matters at all.

So, again he was bland and suave with an undernote of hostility when a serious soul journeyed to Albany with a questionnaire in his brief case. One by one Al evaded the questions on national issues. Finally, exasperated, the visitor lost his temper.

"But, Governor," he demanded, "tell me just one subject you think is important to people living in states west of the Mississippi."

"What states *are* west of the Mississippi?" asked Smith, as if for information.

But to return to the story of the boy, now laboring from 4 o'clock in the morning until 5 o'clock in the evening at the fish stalls. Fulton Market on the East River was a busy spot in the New York of the day. It served most of lower Manhattan and a large part of Brooklyn's population as well. The stalls where Smith worked were its most pungent section. His task was to stand on the wharf and check the cargoes deposited by fishermen and when he returned home at night he was tired, dirty, and smelled to Heaven. But it paid $15 a week, which was almost enough, in the '80's, to support a family. He stayed at the market for seven years. Then, having grown stronger as well as older, he left it to work as a laborer in a Brooklyn pumping station.

Chapter Four

Our elegant era was lavish in that curious biped known as a "parlor entertainer".

—*New York in the Elegant Eighties.*

AND SO THE TOWN GREW OLDER AND STEVE BRODIE jumped lightly from the Brooklyn Bridge, opened a saloon, died and became a myth. And the boy Smith, working at his malodorous trade in the fish market, found time to cultivate in the evening the black art of parlor entertainer. He was, in fact, more than the average indoor elocutionist of the day all agog to recite "Cohen on the Telephone" or "The Face on the Bar-room Floor", although these two, and a third now forgotten, were his specialties. His talents included great histrionic skill, as they still do, and he was the villain or the hero of many a piece played in front of sputtering gas footlights at local halls.

A flair for the dramatic, the ability to put life and vigor for night after night into old issues, as an actor can vitalize a moth-eaten drama, are happy assets to the American publicist. Theodore Roosevelt had them; and William Jennings Bryan, whose "terrible drum", wrote Thomas Beer, "sounded from city to city, and his beauty towered in the flare of torches while bands played 'El Capitan.' " Al Smith, the politician, has been outlined against far more spotlights than ever he was as a youth down in the Fourth Ward, and always his old talents have been there to give him grace. And this is why, artistically, his nomination is imperative.

Lately even a song has become his own; a *leitmotiv* to mark his emergence from the wings and destined, if he is nominated, to be sung in distant places and by men who had viewed with suspicion everything connected with the sidewalks of New York. There will be many, if this man runs for the presidency, who will bristle at the thought of his Catholicism. Spellbinders of the Republican Party will view with alarm for hours on end the perils of Rum and Romanism. It may be that the ludicrous hobgoblins of the Ku Klux Klan will dust off their robes and hold solemn rallies under the banners of intolerance. But vast throngs will crowd into the halls where he speaks, to laugh at his jokes and be won by the first real personality in politics since Roosevelt. And the melody of a city song will sweep the prairies.

The first public appearance of Alfred Smith was when he was ten years old and still a student at St. James' Parochial School. A scrapbook started by his mother and later carried on by Alfred—but which gives little information of his youth except with respect to his social and dramatic triumphs—contains a newspaper clipping showing that on the program of the school's closing exercises on June 26, 1883, was "Recitation—Master Alfred E. Smith". No one recalls, though, whether this was "The Curfew Shall Not Ring To-night" or some other of the favorites rendered noisily and moistly by nervous small boys and girls in front of proud parents.

Young Smith was not nervous—quite the contrary. Recitations soon became small-time stuff, although they continued to be his offerings at neighborhood jollifications. One of his favorites, and it must have been strangely impressive when flavored with an East Side pronunciation, was Edgar Allan Poe's clanging classic, "The Bells". It was while his father was still alive that Alfred delved into the dramatic by organizing a little theater movement among the members of the youngest set. From this he graduated to more pretentious performances held at the church.

Many a ham actor, it has been profoundly remarked, might have become nationally famous had he been able to win his way to Congress where his art would be most useful and appreciated to the greatest degree. Alfred Smith, however, would have been more than a third rate trouper had he decided to go on the professional stage. Until long after he had started his climb to the political Olympus he was the star of the St. James' Players, as the amateur stock company of the church was called. He played such tear-jerking rôles as "Corry Kinchella" in *The Shaughraun*, "Bardwell Slote" in *The Mighty Dollar* and "Jim Dalton" in *The Ticket o' Leave Man.* So vivid were his impersonations that he had at least one tentative offer which would have meant the end of his amateur standing. He was saved from a career on Broadway, though, by the opposition of a young Irish girl whom he wanted to marry and whose family thought actors to be worthless creatures. His love for the stage has never died, however. Almost twenty years afterwards, when he was Sheriff of New York, he played in a revival of *The Shaughraun.* There was to have been a second revival as recently as the spring of 1927, but it had to be abandoned for the reason that no hall large enough to accommodate the crowds could be found. Al was to have been in his old rôle, while Mayor Jimmy Walker and other celebrities were to have had lesser parts in a performance for the benefit of St. James'.

It has for many years been the custom of the political writers in New York City, as well as of the legislative correspondents at Albany, to give annual dinners similar to the more widely known Gridiron Dinner at Washington. Sketches reflecting the political events of the past year are the chief attractions at these affairs. In 1926 the Albany writers offered to put on a stunt at the dinner in New York and were welcomed with enthusiasm. This part of the program, when the night of the dinner arrived, was surrounded with mystery. When the number was called the stage setting proved to be that of the outer room of the executive offices at the Capitol. Two or three reporters were standing about, obviously waiting for something. Their conversation revealed that in his private office Governor Smith was in conference with the Republican legislative leaders.

The reporters were disconsolate. They pointed out that for years Al had been able to force the G. O. P. into line by appealing to the people, only to have the Republicans attempt to take credit for his program with the boast that they had cooperated with the Governor. Could Al lick them again? The reporters seemed dubious. At this point in the skit loud crashes off-stage were heard.

"Looks as though Al's having a bad time," said one. "Maybe we'd better go in and help."

"Oh, let him alone," replied a second.

The sound of rioting continued, however, and the reporters lit cigarettes nervously. As they did so, the door to the Governor's office burst open and the Republican leaders, extremely bedraggled, catapulted out. No, they said with emphasis, they had nothing to say. As they slumped off the door opened again. This time Al Smith appeared, in person. He had assisted the Albany men in getting up the act and now he was having a huge time playing the part of himself. His hair was rumpled. His coat was off, his collar over one ear and his sleeves were rolled up. He grinned his gold-toothed grin at the men on the stage and at the diners out in front.

"The Republicans have agreed to coöperate," he reported.

Very occasionally this flair of Smith's for the dramatic has led him in the heat of a campaign to conduct which in the light of retrospect seems to have been hardly fair to his opponent. Such an instance occurred toward the close of the bitter fight against Ogden L. Mills in the fall of 1926. To everyone's surprise Congressman Mills had been making an energetic and effective campaign; effective because it was based on the old and false Hearst issue that the milk supply in New York was below standard and that the Governor was responsible. Until the charges blew up a few days before the election it had seemed not impossible that Smith might be defeated. Irritated by this and knowing that his presidential chances were gone if he could not win his own state, the Democratic gubernatorial candidate lost a measure of his customary poise. Then, one afternoon, he was shown a newspaper containing a statement attributed to Mills.

"He (Smith) cannot be trusted either in public or private life," the quotation said.

Smith was scheduled to speak that night in the Bronx. As he appeared at the rally he was a picture of outraged virtue. Brandishing a copy of the newspaper in his hand, he charged to the front of the platform and read the quotation to the audience. Red of face and with his voice even harsher than usual, Al said that he had read the statement several times, unwilling to believe that his first impression was correct. He demanded a retraction and intimated that if Mills did not apologize forthwith he would take legal action.

> "For five solid weeks," he said, "I have been obliged to put great pressure on the men and women of my organization to keep them from speaking about the private life of Ogden L. Mills. If he has anything against my public or private life, I defy him to produce it.
>
> "Twenty-seven years ago I knelt beside the altar in St. Augustine's Church and in the presence of God Almighty promised to care for, honor and protect the woman of my choice. And if I suddenly was ushered to-night before the Great White Throne I would be prepared to establish that I had kept that promise. Let the Congressman lay his own private life beside my own."

It was, of course, very effective indeed. The audience screamed its approval and Mills seemed not only a villain but an ass, for the fact that Smith's private life is above reproach is as much of an established truth in New York as that there is something funny about living in Flatbush. I do not question that, once on the platform, Al was just as sincere as he appeared to be. His acting was consummate art, for he lived and breathed the part of the outraged husband. His unfairness lay in permitting his emotions to run away with him when, if he had really taken the time to read the statement carefully, he must have seen that Mills cast no such aspersion. The Republican candidate had been talking about Smith's record and together with other denunciations, had said:

> "There is no truth in him and men who cannot tell the truth are not to be trusted in public or private life."

The next day he apologized, protesting that he had not had the remotest intention of reflecting upon Smith's family life. This would have been clear, he said, had Al read the whole statement instead of a single sentence from it. Well, the statement in whole or in part was a silly one and an untrue one, it might be added. Perhaps Mills deserved, in part, the tongue lashing he had received and to lose the votes that the incident must have cost him.

Chapter Five

A MIDDLE-AGED HOUSEWIFE WHO ONCE LIVED on Oliver Street but who moved years ago to an up-State city has devoted her spare time, in recent years, to booming Al Smith for President. In the interval between lunch and dinner she hustles around among the neighbors of the countryside and dwells at length on his virtues. She has assisted in three of his campaigns for Governor. And occasionally she grows reminiscent of the old Fourth Ward and the Smith who was growing to maturity.

"He used to wear," she recalls, "fancy vests, a red necktie and tight trousers. I can't remember whether he wore a brown derby or not. Probably he did; one of those funny ones with a narrow brim and a high crown that you see now only on the vaudeville stage. But I do remember that when he was nineteen or twenty, maybe a little older, he was quite pleased with himself. He was talking all the time, at parties, or reciting or dancing. He was quite a boy at jigs and he thought he could sing, too. One day some of us girls were making plans for a picnic. For some reason we hadn't invited Alfred —no one called him Al in those days—but while we were talking it over he happened along and chimed in.

"'You haven't been asked to go,' one of us said.

"'Oh, you'll ask me,' he answered. 'You won't be able to get along without the talent.'"

The Fourth Ward and particularly the section of it that worshipped at St. James', this lady remembers, was very much like a small village as the century drew to a close. Oliver Street, which runs due west from Chatham Square to the river, was then considered one of the most desirable streets in the district. Its first block, between Henry and Madison Streets, where Smith was to reside at No. 25, was particularly select. It was not until long after he was married that Al could afford to live there.

"Every one knew nearly every one else in those days," his up-State booster also recalls. "On summer evenings the boys and girls would sit on the stoops of the houses until Father Curry rapped on the window of St. James' Parish House as a signal for them to go to bed. Looking back, life seems to have been simpler then and, maybe, happier than now. You didn't hear so much about intolerance. Why I remember that we never thought about whether a family was Catholic or Protestant, and it wasn't because we were all Catholics together either. Several Lutheran families lived near where I did and if there had been any feeling against non-

Catholics I'd have known about it. All we asked was that people go regularly to *some* church."

It would seem to have been inevitable, if all this evidence is accepted, that Alfred Smith would drift into politics. He was, primarily, a sociable sort who preferred people to books, and whose most noticeable early characteristic was a gift for gab. Living where he did, it was impossible for him to enlist with any hope of success under any banner other than the stained one of Tammany Hall, a flag not infrequently lowered to the mandates of dignitaries of the Catholic Church. Should this accusation arouse indignation among Tammany men I ask them only to recall the action of the local police department some years ago in suppressing, quite without legal authority, a birth control meeting.

If the history of Tammany Hall is not entirely honorable it is at least lengthy. Originally it was known as the Society of St. Tammany or Columbian Order, and was a patriotic organization to which members of all political parties were welcome. In a vague way it sought to agitate against the desires of the Federalists to centralize the national government at the expense of the States. Its first meeting was held in May of 1789 at the City Tavern on Bowling Green.

It was founded, then, with a high purpose; and had it continued along its original path most of its members would now be listed in the Social Register and wear white braid on their vests. For a time, at its inception, Tammany had branches in a number of other cities, but these dropped off when the organization turned from patriotism to politics. The fiction is still maintained, though, that the Society of St. Tammany lives, and as such 14th Street holds a rally each year on Independence Day, at which the sachems indulge in old-fashioned oratory and explain the virtues of the Democratic Party.

Some incautious member recently made the suggestion that it would be well, particularly since Al Smith might be a presidential candidate, to revive the once flourishing branch wigwams. These, it was tacitly understood by those who were present at the birth of this idea, could do valuable missionary work. But the plan was vetoed by general agreement after several editorial writers had jeered at the idea that Tammany, wise as it is, could teach anything in the line of practical politics to such Republican machines as those which dominate Philadelphia and Chicago. Tammany will, in short, remain the Democratic machine of Manhattan; sometimes better, as at present, than its reputation, and often worse. The latter may be the case again, if Al Smith goes into retirement and none arises to take his place. No one remembers, now, and no one cares, that its name is that of a somewhat nebulous Indian, Chief Tammany, who was unofficially sanctified because he was a jewel among red men. He is supposed to have signed a treaty with William Penn in 1681 which gave large grants of land to the whites.

The continued power of Tammany lies in its devotion to service. Once it was so inartistic as to buy votes. Now it earns them. It provides jobs for men out of work and city contracts for those likely to contribute to campaign chests. Distress among the poor is relieved through gifts of money and food. From the Boss himself to the lowest district captain its workers are continually on the job and on Election Day it reaps its reward, to the annual distress of the local Republican organization.

"I will give any Republican ladies some advice," said Miss Elisabeth Marbury, one of the few women politicians close to the seats of the mighty, not long ago. "Do not be afraid to know the voters. We Democrats get as close to them as possible. For instance, if Jim comes to one of our clubs and says he is in danger of losing his job we try to help him out. We don't ask Jim whether he is a Democrat or not. If he isn't, and we help him along, the chances are good that he henceforth will be. It's just a clever way we have."

Smith, beginning at the bottom, was among those who did the odd jobs always done by the privates in the political army. He was a watcher at the polls, addressed postcards to be mailed to voters or scurried around with a bag of coal for the family of some local supporter temporarily detained in jail. Tammany does not desert its own when they run afoul of the law. If their offense is not too heinous, the organization is sometimes able to whisper in the ear of a friendly magistrate and in a twinkling justice becomes undiluted mercy.

The entrance of Smith into politics, I have said, was natural. By the time he was eighteen or nineteen he began to realize that he would not go far working with his hands. Having labored for seven years in the fish market, and for some months in the Brooklyn pumping station, he decided to realize on his gift for loquacity and tried real estate. He dabbled in this for a number of years and had an office on Center Street. But probably it was too dull a trade to hold his interest to the exclusion of other things. To an increasing degree he devoted his time to politics, becoming a regular at the Democratic clubhouse on Madison Street where Tom Foley was beginning to rise in power. At no time, although his knowledge of the laws of New York State might indicate it, did he delve into Blackstone. What he knows of this subject is chiefly the result of his experience at Albany as an Assemblyman.

Smith was, in those days, a good-looking youth. His nose was not the prominent feature that it is now. His mouth was softer and his smile did not have the touch of cynicism that developed from the decades spent among the disillusionments of politics.

His novitiate in Tammany was served in a day when few voices were raised in its defense. The Tweed scandal was still fresh in the minds of the public. Richard Croker was the Boss. Charles F. Murphy was becoming influential. But the men who rule to-day were insignificant. Olvany, for example, was never heard. James J. Walker was a boy in Greenwich Village and up in Harlem a young German named Robert F. Wagner was debating whether the profession of teaching offered any real rewards. Nor had Hearst, giving New York its first taste of the queer sort of journalism he was later to perfect, any political power.

Tammany soon learned that the youth named Smith was worth watching. Already popular in his district, famous for his talents as an elocutionist and actor, he developed rapidly as a campaign spellbinder. He could be counted upon to take orders and to make fervid pleas for the candidates of the organization, whether he knew anything about the capabilities of these gentlemen or not. He was safe, sane and regular; so his political star began to rise, along with his general popularity in the Fourth Ward. From time to time he pasted clippings indictative of this in his scrapbook. A few of them are:

A number of prominent young Democrats of the Second Assembly District will spend Saturday and Sunday at the Lenox Hotel, Far Rockaway. They will be under the leadership of Alfred E. Smith, one of the most prominent Democrats in the district. Mr. Smith is an amateur actor of no mean ability and is the leading man of the St. James Company.

Alfred E. Smith, the orator of the Seymour Club of the Second Assembly District, was a hard worker during the last two campaigns. He is ambitious to become a member of the legislature and is looking for the nomination in his district. He has announced that he will take the stump for Timothy J. Campbell next year if he is not engaged in a personal canvass.

Coasting is now the proper thing among the cyclists. The New York Athletic Club set the fashion a few weeks ago when it held its coasting contest among the hills of Weschester. New York clubs are taking an interest in the sport and the chances are that before the season is over this new phase of wheeling will be as popular as cycling itself. The metropolis has already many crack coasters. Among them is Mr. Alfred E. Smith, an active member of St. James Union and the president of the St. James Wheelmen.

Friends of Alfred E. Smith, secretary of the Seymour Club of the Second Assembly District, are quietly nursing his boom for the nomination for the Assembly.

Chapter Six

THE PATH TO POLITICAL GLORY IS DEVIOUS AND long. By 1895, twenty-two years old and growing familiar with the problems of the city and the district in which he lived, Smith was amply qualified to go to the lower house of the State legislature, a body where even a limited intelligence stands out like a clean neck in a primary grade classroom. But the fact that a young man is qualified is not an important consideration to Tammany or to any other political organization. No place was available at the time and Tom Foley, whose man Smith was generally known to be, had not yet attained the height of his influence. Consequently Smith had to smother his Albany ambitions for the time being. He was, however, entitled to some reward for the work that he was doing in the Second Assembly District, and so was appointed an investigator in the office of the Commissioner of Jurors.

The job paid only about $800 a year, but as in most political posts the work was not arduous and the hours were short. Certainly it was the easiest thing that had come Al's way since the day his father died and it had been necessary for him to leave school. He entered into it with considerable zest and scurried around the town chasing jury shirkers with a diligence exceptional in men holding public offices. He seems, in fact, to have been singularly hard-boiled in listening to excuses.

The present Commissioner of Jurors, Frederick O'Byrne, was Al's immediate superior in those remote days. And now, like every one else who knew Smith then, he is fond of telling what a promising youth he was. His exceptional intelligence caused him to be placed in charge of other investigators. But despite this responsibility he was the life of the office, Mr. O'Byrne recalls. He was devoting many hours at night to his work at the district clubhouse, to acting with the St. James Players and to courting a girl whom he was anxious to marry. He would frequently stagger in to work with his eyes heavy from lack of sleep. But even under these circumstances he found energy to stick a feather-duster in his hat and bellow, in some back room of the offices, the "Toreador Song" from *Carmen*.

Mr. O'Byrne has preserved some of the notes kept by Smith in connection with his jury work. On one occasion a member of the New York Stock Exchange, called as a talesman, submitted a doctor's certificate as evidence that he was deaf and therefore unfit for service. Al, assigned to check on this, went to the Stock Exchange and located his man. Explaining that he had a cold, he spoke in a whisper and asked some questions relative to the purchase of securities. To his delight the supposedly deaf man heard him without difficulty. In the end, though, the broker won out, as the report in Smith's handwriting shows:

"Called on him in the Stock Exchange and found his claim was of no use and put him back in the wheel. His attorney called and threatened to mandamus myself and O'Byrne to show cause why we should go behind a doctor's certificate. The Commissioner allowed the exemption —that put the boots to us."

Regarding another artful dodger, with whom he had greater success, Al reported:

"Swore he was not worth $250. Investigated at house and found a swell apartment furnished in luxury. His wife admitted she was the owner of everything in there and when I showed her the affidavit her husband swore to she said they were all wedding presents to her and he had nothing to do with them. They must of talked it over that night as he appeared a little later and brought a judge of the District Court and asked as a favor of O'Byrne the return of the affidavit. We put him on the District Court list."

It was while thus employed, growing stronger in political influence and with increasing reason to hope that in time he would be sent to the State legislature, that Smith plunged into his first, and quite definitely his only, love affair. Katherine Dunn, the ample and motherly Katie who has lived at the

Executive Mansion at Albany for seven years as though it were a house on Oliver Street, had formerly resided in the Fourth Ward, but had moved when she was ten years old to the wilderness of the Bronx. The Miss Dunn of the '90's, it is recalled, was a dark-haired, slender girl with blue eyes; a character out of one of the magazine stories in which Kathleen Norris has detailed the lives of honest Irish families. Fairly well educated, at all events better than the youth who was to be her husband, marriage was the only career open to one of her environment and generation. And she has devoted her life to this alone, despite the growing activities of suffragists, feminists and militant workers for equal rights and equal liabilities. Unlike the wives of some other public men, she has played no part in his rise to eminence but that of a wife and mother within the walls of her home. Like Al, she reads very little and cares nothing for society. She shares his pleasure in motion pictures and the simpler forms of the drama.

Alfred Smith, despite his neighborhood popularity, was no all-conquering male when he set out to woo the charming Katie. In the first place her family were slightly above his own on the social scale, a distinction due to their comparative prosperity. They were not too cordial toward his advances for several reasons. Their chief objection was that when he started to call he was still working in the fish market. But they viewed him with suspicion, also, because he had tendencies toward the stage which, as any good Irish family knew, was the hotbed of licentiousness and vice. For this reason, although Al soon told Katie herself that he intended to marry her, the subject was not mentioned to her parents immediately. But after a year or so, having been rewarded with political appointment, he felt confident enough to call several times a week and his honorable intentions soon became obvious. The labors of love were not light, for transportation between the Fourth Ward and the Bronx was bad enough to daunt any but a stout heart bound to win a fair lady. The first part of the journey was made on the smoky Third Avenue Elevated, and a trolley was the only alternative to walking the rest of the way. Often it was 2 o'clock in the morning before Al got back to the lower East Side. It was fortunate that during most of the courtship he had a political job and was bossed by Irishmen, of all races most sentimental about lovers.

Katie Dunn, in addition to her personal charms, had other social assets which caused her to be something of a Bronx belle and to have many beaus who made competition rather keen. She could sing most of the mushy ballads which were popular in the '90's. Among these must have been numbered, my source of information is again the reminiscent Mr. Henry Collins Brown, such favorites as "Sweet

Violets", "Only a Pansy Blossom", "Say au Revoir but Not Goodbye", "After the Ball" and "Let Me Dream Again". Other selections probably included "Little Annie Rooney" and "The Sidewalks of New York". But this last was a new song when Al Smith, resplendent in his best suit, called with a bouquet of flowers clutched in his hand.

Eventually the obstacles consisting of wealthier suitors and parental objection were overcome and Katie became Mrs. Alfred E. Smith. The wedding was held on May 6, 1900, at St. Augustine's Roman Catholic Church at 167th Street and Franklin Avenue, the Bronx. Al would not listen to suggestions that he live in the Bronx with his bride, being aware that it would be political suicide for him to leave the Fourth Ward at that time. So he turned down offers of three or four rent-free months held out by the landlords of some of the newer tenements and took a flat on Madison Street. Life did not prove too difficult, for the cost of living was low and Mrs. Smith was a gifted cook and an excellent manager. Their first child, Alfred E. Smith, Jr., was born a year after their marriage. A daughter, Emily, was also born on Madison Street, but before the arrival of Catherine a larger apartment on Peck Slip was taken. Arthur and Walter, the other two of the brood of five, were born in the famous house at No. 25 Oliver Street. Thus all began their lives in the Fourth Ward, as had their father and mother.

The Smith children were happy in their selection of a father. He is good-natured, tolerant and easy-going. When they were small he entertained them with such songs and recitations as he remembered from his parlor-trick days, and during their younger years the bond was very close. Now, it is said, Emily is closer to her father than any of the others. Her picture is on his desk at the Executive Office in the Capitol at Albany. A dark-haired girl, she is attractive despite the handicap of her father's nose. Her mind is unusually keen. Some years ago she went to Europe and when she returned her father, then the Governor of New York, went down the harbor on a tug to meet the steamer. After he had clambered aboard they embraced and Emily, confident of the reply, asked her father whether she had been missed.

"Missed! Not by me," grinned Al. "Say, I haven't had such a rest from arguing in years."

Back of this joking remark, intimates of the Smith family say, stood a singularly close relationship between father and daughter. It has included long and heated disputes on politics and on the wisdom of courses of action that the Governor was considering. Smith likes to play jokes on his family and Emily has had more than her share; another indication, perhaps, of the cordiality of their friendship. During one of the State conventions at Syracuse the family had a suite at the hotel. Early one morning, while Smith was out, the telephone rang and a masculine voice asked for Miss Emily Smith. Going to the phone, the girl heard the voice identify itself as that of a news-reel camera man.

"We're very anxious to have some shots of the pretty daughter of the Governor," he said. "Won't you come downstairs and let us take a few?"

Delighted and flattered, Emily hurried to get into her best dress. But as she turned to go into her own room her father appeared. The snicker which escaped him as he looked at her flushed cheek betrayed him. It had been he who had telephoned from the lobby.

Until Smith became Governor in 1918 and during all the years that he was in the state legislature, his family continued to live on Oliver Street. Moving to the Executive Mansion at Albany made very little difference in their mode of living, although the butler was long regarded with a mixture of awe and ridicule by the Smith offspring. Despite urgent recommendations by some of his advisers, who thought that it would be well to permit them a broader vision, the children attended parochial schools.

Smith was momentarily disappointed in the marriages of his two older sons, for they startled the family with elopements. But he was frankly delighted when Emily announced her choice of Major John Adams Warner, Superintendent of the State

Police. He is a young man of background, has a moderate income and is connected with the State Police more because the work fascinates him than for any other reason. The Governor had never heard of Warner when, some years before, a head for the department had to be appointed and recommendations from both Republicans and Democrats suggested that he was best qualified.

The wedding took place on June 5, 1926, and was an affair out of one of the twisted dream-plays that have been popular on Broadway in recent years. The ceremony was held at the Cathedral of the Immaculate Conception at Albany with Cardinal Hayes officiating. Fifteen hundred guests were invited; ranging from Owen D. Young, chairman of the General Electric Company, to Louis Fook, the "Mayor of Chinatown". The boys of Tammany were all present, stiff and red in their top hats and cutaways. The gifts were appalling in their profusion: a truckload of silver, many gold dishes, twenty clocks, desk sets, candlesticks, pictures, ash trays, vases, jewelry and $20 gold pieces. There were scores of books, among them such serious ones as Amy Lowell's "Keats", Boswell's "Life of Johnson" and Carl Sandburg's "Lincoln", for Emily does not share her parents' distaste for reading. On the day of the wedding a railroad car crammed with gifts was still to be unloaded. The whole affair could be compared only to that other famous wedding when Alice Roosevelt became the bride of Nicholas Longworth at the White House years ago.

Through it all Al Smith was not too happy and at times his smile was forced. Even though he highly approved of the match, particularly as he watched the poise and bearing of the young bride and groom, he knew that the closest of all his children was leaving him. But he grinned with determination, danced at the reception and was red and perspired in his usual fashion. After the ceremony was over he looked at the department store collection of gifts and swore under his breath.

"Guess I'll have to run again in the fall," he muttered. "Emily's going to live in a four-room house. She'll have to have the basement of the Executive Mansion to store this junk in."

BOOK THREE

Sent Up the River

Chapter One

ON THE MORNING OF OCTOBER 17, 1911, WITH Election Day near enough so that the time was opportune for a warning, the New York *World* published an editorial listing a number of Democratic Assemblymen and called upon the Best People of the city to hurl them forthwith into the lasting darkness of political oblivion. Of them it said:

> "These Democratic members of the present Assembly from New York who have been renominated should be defeated at the polls.
>
> "Every man in this list voted for the Murphy charter for New York City despite and in defiance of the most positive and manifest opposition of his constituents. These men preferred the commands of a boss to the welfare and the interests of the people. They cannot complain if the people in turn prefer new men to those who have been tried and proved faithless."

Among the legislators on this blacklist was Alfred E. Smith, the member from the Second Assembly District in lower Manhattan and by now the leader of the Democratic majority in the lower house of the State legislature. Another was a dark-haired youth named James J. Walker, who enjoyed wide popularity as a song writer and whose home district was in Greenwich Village. If, in 1911, their careers were in peril because of the *World's* indignant demand for their heads, there is no record of that fact. The warning, as such warnings usually are, was futile. Al and Jimmy were overwhelmingly reëlected and preserved for happier days; the former to become in 1924 the *World's* candidate for the Democratic presidential nomination, the latter to rise to eminence as the most charming Mayor in the history of New York City.

It would be pleasant to think that the electorate in New York had pre-vision and realized that the sins of Smith and Walker were but temporary; that before a decade had passed they would be hailed as outstanding members of the "new Tammany Hall". The truth is, of course, that Tammany in 1911 was mightier than the editorial pen. It could win in the face of unified newspaper opposition. It can, if necessary, do so again to-day, for the citizen who cares enough about government to follow the advice of his favorite journal is vastly outnumbered by the voters who do not read at all or who are controlled by the machine. Tammany holds no monopoly in this; it is characteristic of the politics of the American municipality.

By 1911 Alfred E. Smith, elected for the first time in the fall of 1903, was a veteran at Albany. For eight years he had climbed the hill leading to the building that houses the State government. It is one of the peculiarities of the men who build State capitols that often they choose a commanding site on a hillside and nearly always erect a building that is an architectural monstrosity. Such is the Capitol at Albany. It has a really magnificent location, with the city sprawled before it and with the dim outline of the banks of the Hudson River in the distance. The structure cost millions of dollars and is a jumble of renaissance turrets and jimcracks that must cause a young legislator of artistic bent to meditate on the mysteries of democracies, if not on suicide. Fortunately the death rate among legislators is kept down by the fact that almost none is a gentleman of sensibilities. There is nothing, at all events, to indicate that Al Smith had ever been depressed by his physical surroundings. During the first year or so at Albany, it is true, he was homesick and fearful that he would never amount to much. But by 1911 he was a cocksure, hard-boiled, practical politician whose blind regularity was an insult to a native intelligence of which he was only partially aware.

It has been said of Smith, again I quote Dr. White, the Kansas sage, that he "took orders until he could give them." This leads, possibly, to the impression that early in his career Smith was aware that Tammany was less than perfect, that he was even then intellectually independent and was waiting for the day to come when he could break away and yet survive the wrath of the organization. I cannot believe, though, that in 1911 he was this type of idealistic Machiavelli, willing to play the organization game so that in the future he could listen to persistent inner voices and battle for good government. It is axiomatic, though, that any man starting a political career and brimming with the most lofty purposes would accomplish very little unless, for a time, he was regular. This is a lesson which the reform element never learns.

In 1911 Al Smith had already been rewarded for his services to Tammany. The Democrats, that year, had the remarkable luck to win control in both houses of the legislature and Smith was made the leader of the Assembly. It was a long and weary session filled with diableries, many of them guided by Smith. In supreme command, but usually out of sight, was Charles F. Murphy. The New York *World*, aware of this fact, had asked the Tammany boss for his position on a pending law and had been told that he was "not a member of the legislature" and therefore had nothing to say. This tickled the funnybone of some editor who telegraphed to Albany for comments on this statement from several of the law-makers. Was it true that Murphy played no part in their deliberations? Some of the answers that came back were:

Robert F. Wagner, then Democratic leader in the Senate and now United States Senator from New York:—"Adhering closely to his long-established policy, Mr. Murphy has not attempted to influence the legislature in any way."

Alfred E. Smith:— "Mr. Murphy is quite correct in his statement. I do not believe he is any more concerned in the deliberations of the legislature than any other good Democrat."

Franklin D. Roosevelt; in 1911 an insurgent Democratic State Senator, in 1924 manager of Smith's campaign for the presidential nomination:— "Mr. Murphy's declaration is very interesting. I thought he was said to be without a sense of humor."

The legislative system in New York, whether Democrats or Republicans are in the ascendancy, is both cumbersome and unwieldy. The massed intelligence of almost any group of law-makers is pitiful to view. Smith, as Governor, has materially lightened the burdens by accomplishing the consolidation of State departments and by forcing through a more liberal grant of home rule for the cities of the State. It ought now to be possible for the legislature to function without being entirely absurd. But even Al Smith seems to be growing discouraged and lately he has been recommending sessions every two years instead of annually as is at present the case. He has not, of course, allied himself with less friendly critics who have suggested permanent adjournment as of the greatest benefit to the commonwealth.

The forty-eight State legislatures in the nation grind out an appalling number of laws each year, a high proportion of them utterly silly. Legal enactment has become the American cure-all. Governor Smith has quoted statistics to show that in a single year in this great land of independence 49,141 new laws were proposed by its busy legislative bodies and 16,298 of them actually passed. In New York during five years 3,469 bills became law. The time is ripe for the organization of a "Fewer and Better Law" society. Some of the enlightened measures under consideration recently in the so-called Empire State were: An amendment to the game laws making it legal for an extra hook to be used on fishlines dipped into Keuka Lake, a law to enumerate and pension couples who have celebrated their golden wedding, a law authorizing the compilation of lists of bee and dog owners in Nassau County, one to collect a doctor's bill on an Indian reservation, another to punish a fraud in letting seats in theaters, and a mysterious statute to regulate the puzzling practices of cosmetology, astrology and bandagery.

Recent delegation of additional legislative powers to the cities, I have said, has improved the situation at Albany slightly. Not long ago the legislature was annually flooded with bills providing reinstatement for New York City policemen fired by the commissioner for intoxication, assault, robbery and other high crimes, but later found innocent by juries under the spell of a hypnotic defense counsel. Law-makers from Horseheads, N. Y., and other rustic centers were required to pass on garbage disposal regulations in cities they rarely visited, and then only to see the latest leg shows. Similarly, members from Harlem or the Bowery were given opportunity to debate on the necessity for a bridge over some creek near Wappinger's Falls. What all this led to, naturally, was a system of bargaining. The hayseed Assemblyman agreed to reinstate a New York cop if, in turn, his village mudhole was drained at the expense of the State. A vast amount of this still goes on. On really important matters the average legislator takes orders from the floor leader of his party. He drifts through the session in a mental fog, not infrequently thickened by liquor. During the closing hours, with the hands of the clock halted to preserve the fiction of adjournment at the previously specified hour, he votes, parrot-like, as he is told. The only check on the possible deviltry is the vigil of the newspaper correspondents who take turns at sentry duty and prevent many raw deals.

Occasionally, of course, there is a member with brains. He may follow instructions from the Boss and probably does. But he knows the reasons that lie behind what is done and may even, in private, protest once in awhile against the commands of the party dictators. He understands the meaning of bills under consideration. He has at least a working knowledge of the State government. And being intelligent he is likely, in time, to be promoted from the Moronia that is the State legislature of New York.

Alfred E. Smith was one of these exceptions.

Chapter Two

In 1903, my readers have now doubtless forgotten, Al Smith was by day an investigator in the office of the Commissioner of Jurors and by night both an amateur actor and a zealous worker under Leader Tom Foley at the Madison Street clubhouse. He had been married for three years, was fatuously proud of his two-year old son and lived in a flat a few doors away from the club. Thirty years old, he looked younger and the cares of life seemed to dissolve in the laughter with which he appreciated his own jokes and his singing of funny songs.

Tammany Hall, tipped off by Foley, did not permit so gifted a man to decay in a city bureau. The leader is dead now and his own opinion of Al in those days is a matter for conjecture; it was not his custom to talk a great deal. His friends, though, have advanced the theory that Foley had moments when he was more than merely an organization leader, when he craftily suggested for nomination a man in whom he saw the seeds of greater things than medium intelligence, a gift for spell-binding and the quality of obedience. It is a warming thought, quite without evidence in substantiation, that Foley, old himself, gazed deep into this newcomer and hoped that young Al Smith might do the things that he himself had never been big enough to do. If he did, and if the ghosts of politicians retain their interest in legislative matters, the spirit of Big Tom must now and then give a grunt of satisfaction.

But this is metaphysical. One day, late in the summer of 1903, as he was about to quit work at the Commissioner of Jurors' office, Smith was approached by a minor dignitary from 14th Street.

"That the only suit you got?" he is said to have asked.

Al nodded, a little surprised at the notion that he would have many suits.

"Well, hurry home and get it pressed. To-night you're going to be nominated for the Assembly."

Such is the legend. The truth is that Al had long been angling for the nomination to the State legislature and the designation was not unexpected. For several years he had been advancing the notion that he was well qualified; modestly when among the elders at the clubhouse, but with considerable confidence when talking to men of his own age. He could boast with convincing force that there were few more widely known politicians in the Fourth Ward, that his long and successful career as an actor would give added publicity value to his candidacy. His regularity, he could say, was not open to question. Nor could it be declared that any other youthful member of Tammany had worked more laboriously doing odd jobs for the machine. All of this Foley had acknowledged to be true, and the leader's opinion that Smith should be given the nomination was shared by Henry Campbell, a Vesey Street grocer, who was one of the organization's unofficial advisers and a frequent contributor to campaign chests.

Newspaper clippings are not always entirely reliable sources of information, since there is always an outside chance that a reporter has done his subject the injustice of imagining just a little of the story that he writes. But with this reservation, an article that appeared in the New York *Morning Telegraph* may be offered in evidence to show that Al Smith, having defeated a gentleman named Paul Kamisky for Assemblyman from the Second District in Manhattan, was jubilant about this, his first victory. The swagger behind the words is obvious:

"You see it's this way," Al is quoted in the interview. "Acting is a lot harder work than helping make the laws. That's why I'm booked for Albany for the season. The footlights for your Irvings and your Mansfields, but the comfortable and cozy seats of the State Capitol for mine.

"The fact is, politics pays better than the wig-paste profession, and, if I'm not exactly a star in the House as yet, this is my first venture, I guess I'll get the center of the stage and bask in the political limelight before I get through.

"Yes, I'm dead stuck on acting. Always have been, and my friends say that I'm a corker at the game. There are lots of comedy men with big names now acting who might not be able to hold a candle to me, and if I hadn't been elected to a seat in the Assembly, some of the top-liners in the Broadway bills might have been occupying a back seat. But it's all over now.

"I'm a politician now, and it would not be good form to brag, but you can just mention in that respect that I defeated Kamisky, my opponent, by 3,500 votes—more than twice as many as he got. It was like rolling off a log. I could have sat at home and been elected, but I took the stump a bit and did a bit of talking. I like it, you see."

This effervescence soon subsided, though, when Al got to Albany, on a cold winter day in the first week of January, 1904. Icy winds sweep down from Capitol Hill to the Union Station at the river. But their breath is no more chilly than the reception accorded verdant legislators by the veteran members. The first term Assemblyman is made to feel more unsophisticated than a college freshman, more insignificant than a second lieutenant at a staff officers' mess, more unkempt than a husband who has been cleaning the furnace and blunders into a tea being given by his wife upstairs. He searches, if he is from a large city, the newspapers for months in the vain hope that he has been mentioned in an Albany despatch. He very nearly swoons from gratitude when, for the first time, a legislative correspondent greets him in the cloakroom.

Al Smith arrived at Albany toward dusk with Tommy Caughlan, another Tammany novitiate who came as the honorable representative of the First Assembly District. They felt lonely and woe-begone and turned up their coat collars as they trudged on foot to a cheap hotel. They found that their room was heated only by a wood stove and the hotel so ramshackle that a fire seemed more than possible. Terrified, the two Assemblymen decided to take turns keeping watch during the night and this they did, each telling himself as he sat huddled in a chair that never again would he consent to run for the legislature.

During the years that have passed since then the usual stories have been told of that first night in Albany. One favorite is that as Al and his friend began their walk to the hotel a magnificent sleigh swept to the front of the station, impressive with its prancing horses, bells, lap-robes and footman. Into it was tucked, as the two Assemblymen and other travelers gaped, an important looking gentleman who had arrived on the same train. Some one explained that the opulent figure was Benjamin B. Odell, Governor of the State. Al turned to Tommy.

" 'At's the job for me," he is supposed to have said.

It is an artistic story and Smith has been artist

enough to tell it occasionally, with variations that harmonized more definitely with the particular function at which he was speaking. He was among those on the dais at the Gridiron Dinner at Washington in 1924 when the opportunity presented itself. President Coolidge had just been elected by a tremendous majority over John W. Davis, whose intelligence on all matters except politics had been considered a menace by the people. Al had never before been present at one of these famous affairs of the Washington correspondents, so he adopted an air of modesty.

"It's pleasant to have a seat at the head table," he said in the brief address that guests of honor at Gridiron Dinners make. "I remember when I first went up to Albany and the newspaper correspondents had their legislative dinner. A friend of mine got me in, but I had a seat way over on one side of the room, under the gallery. After awhile Governor Odell came in, accompanied by a staff all trimmed out in gold lace, and was taken up to the best table. 'That's the way,' I told my friend who was with me, 'to come to these dinners.' "

At this point Smith revealed that he is capable of subtleties.

"And there's the way," he concluded with a grin in the direction of Cal Coolidge, "to attend a Gridiron Dinner."

Just what the youthful Smith did during the

1904 session of the legislature must remain unknown since, unhappily, no record is kept of the deliberations of that body. In 1915, when a member of the Constitutional Convention, Al debated in favor of preserving for posterity the orations of the Assembly and the Senate. Forgetting, apparently, the bilge that appears in the *Congressional Record*, he remarked:

"—it will be a kind of automatic valve on the hot air, and if there is anything needed in this room (the Assembly Chamber) it is said valve. There is a good deal said here that when it gets into print won't look very good, and this may restrain some people from saying it."

In the absence of a record it is safe to say that Al did very little at the inception of his Albany career and that little under party commands. He held no important committee posts and was seldom, if ever, consulted. His name did not appear in the daily despatches of the correspondents. He was, however, reëlected in the fall and found life at the Capitol rather more pleasant during 1905. This was largely because Robert F. Wagner had been sent to the Assembly from a Tammany district on the upper East Side of New York City. A German by birth, Bob Wagner was inclined to be slow and thorough in his mental processes where Al was swift. A law school graduate, he was well educated in comparison to Smith's grammar grade training. He is a Lutheran whereas Al, of course, is a devout

Catholic. But the two became fast friends despite all these differences and later did battle together in behalf of Boss Murphy. Smith became Democratic leader of the lower house and Wagner served in the same capacity in the Senate. In 1905 Wagner, Smith and Caughlan roomed together in a third-rate tavern on State Street.

But if Albany in that year was socially bearable, Smith felt that professionally he was standing still. The salary of a legislator is $1,500 a year and he was finding that the months spent at Albany made it difficult to earn an adequate living for his family. The rules permitted him to draw $70 of his allowance each week until $250 remained to his credit. This he could not have until the end of the session and long before that day, his early associates recall, Smith was invariably broke. Financial worries and the fear that he might never master the complicated legislative processes dampened, for probably the first time in his life, his usual optimism. He often discussed with Bob Wagner the advisability of refusing to run for another term and mourned that he had no college diploma to assist him along life's troubled path.

Before the adjournment of the 1905 session he had made up his mind that he would not return the following year, and so informed Tom Foley. Albany, he said, had been too much for him. He had not been given a single worth-while committee assignment. He might as well be a Republican for all the good he was doing the organization. Besides, he had his family to think of; the salary of an Assemblyman was too small to be of much help. Foley, of course, had heard just such lamentations before. He pointed out that every new legislator became discouraged at first; so prevalent was this that it had become almost a precedent for them to quit after two years. Smith would not do a thing like that, would he? Help me out, begged Foley, and try it for at least one more session. The breaks would come in time and Tammany would not forget. So Al ran again and was again reëlected.

Chapter Three

Among the members of the lower house in the State legislature that convened in January of 1905 was a young man named James W. Wadsworth. A Republican, he differed from Al Smith in nearly every respect possible except that he, too, had brains. Smith came from an environment of truck horses, Wadsworth from one of saddle horses. He represented a country district not far from Rochester and his family was wealthy and cultured. He had graduated, not long before, from Yale, where he had been a star baseball player.

Jim Wadsworth was no idle son of the rich, dabbling in politics for a thrill. He was a hard worker with a natural gift for making a profession out of the calling that remains a trade to most of the men who are in it. And he was fascinated by the characteristics of the Tammany members with whom he came into contact. He had never before known men like these, hard in their city provincialism. His seat in the Assembly Chamber in 1905, just on the line that separated the Republicans from the Democrats, happened to be next to the chair of Bob Wagner. Through Wagner he met Al Smith and before many weeks the three men were eating dinner together occasionally.

"I learned a lot from Al," Wadsworth recalled more than a decade afterwards. "In fact, I learned a lot from a number of the city members. They had a point of view I had never encountered. They interested me. Even then Al Smith was a man of great charm, who was soon fraternizing with both sides of the house. He was a really talented story-teller and all of us looked forward to hearing the new jokes he picked up."

But this side of Smith, as I have said, was submerged for most of 1905, except infrequently when Wadsworth, Bob Wagner or a few others managed to make him feel at home. Even in 1906, having returned at the virtual command of Tom Foley and assured that better days would come, Al still felt obscure and unhappy and was well on the road to what would now be known as an inferiority complex. Meanwhile, although extremely young for the job, Wadsworth had been made Speaker of the Assembly. This post carries great power over committee assignments as well as with regard to pending legislation. Next to the Governor the Speaker is usually the most important man at the Capitol. One afternoon, busy with his new duties, Wadsworth ran into a rather disconsolate Al Smith.

"Getting any good committee jobs?" he asked

Smith replied, sadly, that he certainly was not, that his name had not been included by the Democratic leader in the lists that would make up the minority's representation. Jim was sympathetic and said that he might be able to do something. Later, although a Republican and a theoretical enemy, he exercised his authority as Speaker and appointed the Tammany man to the Insurance Committee. This committee was an outstanding one that year, for Charles E. Hughes had just completed his famous investigation and a mass of insurance legislation of a reform nature was to be passed upon. From that day Al Smith seldom felt lonely or unimportant at Albany again. Year by year his activities and his influence increased until he became, in succession, Speaker himself and then Governor. Meanwhile Jim Wadsworth had been elected to the United States Senate where, in 1926, the good deed that he had done for Al Smith twenty years before returned, in violation of the Scriptures, to do him grievous injury. In that year Bob Wagner, having long since left the legislature to become a judge, was nominated by his party to run for Senator against Wadsworth, whose term was expiring. Chiefly because of the popularity of Smith, heading the ticket in his fifth campaign for Governor, Wagner managed to win, although the election of the Republican had seemed certain. Wadsworth, a lame duck, now grins a trifle bitterly as he reflects on the part that he played in launching Smith on his career.

Having thus achieved a measure of distinction in 1906, all of Al Smith's old jubilation swiftly returned. He began to act as host at corned beef and cabbage dinners at Albany restaurants, dinners that were featured by good humor and beer. His guests were other members of the legislature, Republicans just as often as Democrats, and it was not long before Al became one of the most popular members. Looking back, now, on those days, he likes to think that he absorbed much wisdom from the bucolic law-makers who attended these feasts. Undoubtedly he did gain impressions of country problems that were to be of value as Governor. But Al preferred the rôle of talker to that of listener, and it is probable that his guests benefited the more. They must have learned a great deal about city ways and city men. Some of the rustic prejudice against New York and New Yorkers—against the iniquity of Tammany—must have faded under the spell of good stories, laughter and liquor.

The chief profit to Al Smith lay in the friends he made, friends who were willing to pass a particular bill that Tom Foley desired, who could be approached to consider a compromise when a legislative deadlock made it appear that the session might drag on forever. These friendships were not merely of the moment; many a Republican to-day, denouncing Al Smith in speech or print, is gratified that his private relationship is most cordial. In 1915 the amiability of the past nine years brought to Smith a very concrete return. Tammany Hall, grateful for the work that he had done at Albany and appreciating that it had been at definite financial sacrifice, designated Al for the lucrative post of Sheriff of New York County. The office then, as is still the case in many parts of the country, was run on a fee basis and the total that went into the pocket of the Sheriff was out of all proportion to the work. In 1915, as this plum was about to fall into Smith's lap, he was still a member of the Assembly and learned to his profound distress that a bill had been introduced ending the fee system and establishing a salary of $12,000 a year, as compared with $60,000 or even more likely to be enjoyed under the existing law. In this crisis Smith turned to his friends in both houses of the legislature. He begged them to have a heart. And although the Republicans controlled each branch, the affection in which he was held was such that the bill was killed. Two years later, after Al had harvested the fees for two years, it was revived and became the law of the State.

But to return to 1906, the year of Smith's emergence from insignificance; there are indications that it did not take him many weeks to discover that the other legislators were not the austere and awesome figures he had supposed. They were inclined, he found, to appreciate a measure of horseplay and were not resentful of interference with the decorum of the proceedings. Thus Al got quite a hand one day during the session when he sent a sign decorated with Chinese hieroglyphics to the Speaker's desk when an idiotic bill proposing to regulate Chinese laundries was introduced. Nor did he confine his fondness for merriment to the Assembly Chamber. Toward the end of the session two young ladies from the Fourth Ward appeared at the Capitol late one afternoon and asked Al to get them out of a predicament. They had come to Albany to make a connection for another part of the State, they explained, but had missed their train. The city hotels had refused to jeopardize their reputations by sheltering unescorted females. Would Alfred help them out? He did, by vouching for their respectability to one of the conservative tavern keepers. Hours afterwards, while the two maidens were wrapped in slumber, they were rudely awakened by loud thumps just outside the door of their room. Investigating, they found a collection of old shoes which had been pitched over the transom. In the corridor, they swear to this day, they heard a snicker easily identified as that of the Hon. Alfred E. Smith, Assemblyman from the Second Manhattan District.

It would be unjust to give the impression that

Smith was nothing but a parliamentary playboy. On the contrary, he worked harder than almost any one else at Albany. He plodded through technical bills and managed to glean from their mysterious phraseology the problem they were attempting to solve or, which was more likely, the steal they were arranged to provide. The annual appropriation bill is a document hundreds of pages in length and containing thousands of items. It is as complicated as an income tax return filed by John D. Rockefeller, the Younger, and as difficult to understand as a railway time-table in Russia. Smith mastered even this baffler, in violation of all tradition in the Assembly. The other boys preferred to incur headaches by means of liquor and permitted committee heads and party leaders to worry about the appropriation bills. Al voted as he was told, I have said. But he knew what he was doing and therein differed from the great majority.

The first year of his new prominence, 1906, Smith introduced fifteen bills, none of them of transcendent importance. One provided for lower telephone rates in New York. His expert knowledge of fish, gained at the Fulton Market, inspired an obscure measure to amend "the forest, fish and game law as to sale of wall-eyed and yellow pike." He suggested a tax on advertising posters and provided rehearings for one New York City cop and one fireman who had, apparently, been in trouble. He wanted air brakes placed on all the cars of trains, and suggested that justices of the peace who had served for five years be admitted to the bar without attending school. As Governor, in later years, he vetoed many a bill of this type. The next year, 1907, Al accomplished the passage of a law regulating the sale of narcotics. He attempted, remembering his old friends and his former job, to increase the salaries of the members of the Jurors' Commission. He made a plea for Sunday baseball and said in a speech that it was better for boys to be at the ball park than be "driven to places where they play 'Waltz Me Around Again, Willie'." He fought, with his Tammany colleagues, the endeavors of Governor Hughes in 1908 to end gambling at the race-tracks.

But on the whole his record during 1906, 1907 and 1908 was such that even the reform element looked on him with cautious favor. The Citizens' Union of New York, which for years has handed down rulings on the virtues and sins of legislators, condescended to remark in 1906 that Smith was "intelligent and active, somewhat above average of machine men". The next year it reported that he had shown "increased ability" and was "one of the best Democratic representatives from New York". In 1908 it said of him:

"Increasingly active and aggressive; very much above average in intelligence, force and usefulness, though still inclined to follow machine in support of bad measures."

The Citizens' Union, it is clear, had hopes that Smith might be saved. But before an additional twelve months had passed these dreams were shattered. He had "disappointed the expectations of those who believed he would make proper use of his increased influence". He was one of the "most dangerous men at Albany because of his experience". Off with his head! was the civic organization's appeal to the voters.

That fall Al defeated his Republican opponent by more than two to one.

Chapter Four

It was during the next few years that Smith aroused the reform element to the highest frenzies of indignation. Probably there was reason enough for their continued denunciation of nearly everything he did. The often futile, but praiseworthy, organizations which spend money in behalf of decent government can remain more or less calm in face of perfidy on the part of the average stupid officeholder. They expect nothing else. But when an exceptional man, and Al Smith was such, becomes the slave of a machine they shriek with agony and their demand for his rejection at the polls is far more heated than in the case of the dumbbells.

The legislature of the State of New York is even to-day an unhappy place for breathless believers in the democratic form of government to behold. But its sins now are more those of stupidity than viciousness. Its internal rows are brisk and bitter, yet not more so than the clashes between fundamentalists and liberals at a Presbyterian Assembly over doctrines such as the Virgin Birth. Compared to the sessions of 1909, 1910 and 1911, the meetings are redolent with brotherly love. Albany has few of the pugilistic outbreaks that have recently caused members of Congress to wave their arms at each other, pant heavily and flock to the nearest physiotherapist. Fifteen years ago these were common. Nor were the hostile acts confined to combatants; during one debate on direct primaries in 1911 a statesman fired a book at a colleague and knocked off the hat of a woman spectator. A man of God who had come to the Capitol to lobby for race-track reform was deluged, at about the same time, by Murphy's boys with pamphlets, stationery and bulky appropriation bills.

The Assemblyman of 1910 was often familiar with that portion of Albany inelegantly known as "The Gut". Here were to be found the delights of cheap saloons and the more damnable charms of the bawdy house. The Sergeant-at-Arms of the lower house, and this duty of rounding up the sinners was enjoyed by the same official in the Senate Chamber, was a sophisticated cop who knew exactly where to find the honorable members in case they were needed for a vote or some other matter of state on the Hill. When ordered to get his man, he did so. He was not, fortunately, required to guarantee either sobriety or state of apparel.

Al Smith, though, had none of these vices. Women other than his wife were less interesting to him than the speeches of a prohibitionist. He may have been similar in appearance to his fellows. He wore the same sort of clothes and his hat was invariably over one ear. His language, too, was their kind. But the fundamental decency in the man never permitted him to indulge in red-light pleasures.

During 1909 Al's name began to figure frequently in the despatches of the Albany correspondents. He was known as "Smith, the Tammany man", and it is rumored that he was directly in line to be the Democratic leader in the Assembly. He was criticized for opposing the direct primary law being sponsored by Governor Hughes, and was known to be hostile to the dry fanatics who sought to give to advanced communities, through local option, the right to bar the sale of liquor. It was, in fact, in 1909 that one of Smith's first actions as a wet took place. This was when he gave his support to a bill amending the law which forbade a bar in any building with an entrance less than two hundred feet away from a church. This daddy of the Volstead Act had been planned, obviously, to remove temptation from the paths of gentlemen bound for morning worship. It was particularly obnoxious to the Gotham Hotel on Fifth Avenue, located near the Fifth Avenue Presbyterian Church, and forced to go to all manner of bootlegging methods to provide liquor for its guests. Its efforts to repeal the statute were unavailing, however, despite the assistance of Al Smith, so a warehouse was established down the street to which bellboys were despatched as the need arose.

But the years that followed hard upon 1909 are important chiefly for the reason that Smith, in addition to his support of partisan measures, began constructive work indicative of the genius along this line he was to demonstrate in the future. For this the reformers should have given him credit and did not. Before 1915 he had assisted in the passage of the Workmen's Compensation Law and in the ratification by the State of the federal income tax amendment. He was on a committee, unquestionably among the most worth-while of the many on which he served, which investigated the factory abuses. He worked for equal pay for women teachers. He was energetic and persistent in demands that the State take proper care of its insane and provide adequate hospital facilities for these and for other unfortunates.

The Citizens' Union cannot be blamed for not recognizing that these matters were typical of those in which Smith was fundamentally interested and that his support of machine legislation was a passing phase. Perhaps with encouragement instead of condemnation he might have emerged more swiftly. I doubt it, though. His activities in behalf of welfare laws were sanctioned by Tammany. The organization has always been interested in legislation for the poor and not from any altruistic motive, either. It is one of the best means of winning elections.

The full wrath of the many who believed Fourteenth Street a menace to good government descended upon Al Smith in 1911. It was then that the New York *World* demanded that he be retired, together with the rising Jimmy Walker, who was serving his second term in the Assembly. The reason for the uproar lay in Democratic control of both houses for the first time in years. Accustomed to being in the minority, the Democrats had proceeded to take full advantage of the situation. For a long time the Republicans had been living in prosperity under the leadership of Boss William Barnes, whose political practicality was at least the equal of Murphy's. But when word came that Tammany was to rule the roost many a beer glass was lifted in joyous anticipation.

With these alluring prospects in view Al Smith had been named majority leader of the Assembly and his old roommate, Bob Wagner, the leader of the Senate. The two became invaluable to the Wigwam. The first big job was the election of a United States Senator, those being the days before the people in their superior wisdom named these gargantuan figures at the general election. Murphy gave orders that a gentleman named William F. Sheehan was to be sent to Washington, so Al and Bob started to carry out his demand. They ran, however, into unexpected opposition from Franklin D. Roosevelt and a few other up-State Democrats and a deadlock lasting almost two months resulted. Murphy then substituted Judge James O'Gorman. The *World*, the following fall, recalled the events in an editorial calling for the defeat of the Democrats in the Assembly. It said, in part:

"Early on the morning of March 31 Murphy took a milk train for Albany, where he called about him Senate Leader Wagner, Assembly Leader Smith, Senator Sullivan, sub-boss of the lower East Side; McCooey, the Brooklyn sub-boss; Boss Fitzpatrick of Erie County, and Senator Frawley. The Federal Constitution says that Senators from each State shall be 'chosen by the legislature thereof'. Since Murphy owned the legislature he saw no impropriety in announcing in advance to the six statesmen that O'Gorman was to be the man.

"Murphy's coming cleared the situation. Wagner was sent to postpone a caucus until orders were given out. Later O'Gorman's name was presented and received 63 caucus votes out of 101. The legislature was immediately called in joint session and O'Gorman was chosen, only one Democrat voting against him. Murphy's choice in the end prevailed.

"Holding no office in the State, Murphy had laid his heavy hand upon the deadlocked legislature of 9,000,000 people. When he nodded the deadlock was broken; and he named the Senator.

"The election of a Democratic Assembly next month would mean Murphy's vindication. It would be a vote of confidence. It would mean another year of Murphy government."

It was a long, wearisome session that dragged its way, with several adjournments, almost to October. Smith, it would seem, enjoyed thoroughly his rôle of majority leader. Certainly he was efficient at the job, as even those who demanded his defeat admitted. He was thirty-eight years old and was developing a gift for neat phrasing that deserted him only in times of great emotion and was a constant refutation of his lack of education. Almost always, speaking in public, he used grammatical English, although he did not know, probably, how it was that he did so. He had an innate sense of the right word, particularly when some other subtly changed the meaning of a bill. It was often, though, difficult for him to explain his reasons for an objection. This got him into a momentary jam while Democratic leader when he attempted to correct the grammar of a Buffalo Assemblyman who had used "or" instead of "and" in the phraseology of a measure under discussion.

The up-State man, who had been graduated from high school with honors, resented this pedagogical rebuke from the alumnus of the Fulton Fish Market. Why, he demanded in a voice heavy with sarcasm, was "and" right? What authority had the gentleman from the Second Manhattan for his assertion? Perhaps he could quote the rule?

For a second Al was baffled. Then he got up from his seat.

"I will refer the gentleman from Buffalo," he said nasally, "to the grammatical rule that says 'When a pluperfect adjective precedes a noun, insert a plus'."

Murphy may not, as Smith had asserted so blandly, have been "any more concerned in the deliberations of the legislature than any other good Democrat". But he was enough interested so that he was frequently at Albany during 1911 and the measures he desired to have passed received the energetic support of Smith, Wagner and the rest. Some of them are hard to defend and I have a suspicion that Al, himself, would now condemn them as heartily as anyone. The passage of the so-called "Murphy Charter" for New York City was one of the worst. This was the outgrowth of an investigation in which Smith had taken part a year or so before. The charter finally adopted is declared to have deprived the members of the Board of Estimate, the city's principal governing body, of vital powers. It is said to have weakened the civil service system and to have made plunder on the part of a political machine easier in numerous ways. Several Democrats fought it during the session, among them Roosevelt, Loring Black, now a Congressman, and John Godfrey Saxe, who was for years chairman of the Law Committee of Tammany Hall.

The Democratic Party in 1911, declared that industrious critic, the Citizens' Union, "devoted much attention to the pursuit of patronage and to bills legislating out of existence Republican officeholders and providing for the appointment of their successors by the Democrats". Here, I am sure, the Union was a little fussy. All parties do that, once they are in power. It added, however, the more damning indictment that the 1911 session increased by at least $350,000 annually the payroll of New York City. This was done in violation of all theories of home rule, now a sacred precept of Tammany Hall.

Nor is the list of the evils done or led by Al Smith yet complete. He assisted in the repeal of the Hughes edict against gambling at the race-tracks. He fought a direct primary law. But in the light of history, I submit, it is not difficult to offer a defense of at least the theory of his position on these matters. Betting on the ponies was not, of course, halted by legislation. As for the direct primary, to which Smith has long since been won over and which has been partially emasculated by the G.O.P., it is excellent in principle but works very badly. For the average citizen in New York State declines to bother with a primary election. The political machine, at an "unofficial convention", designates or "suggests" the man who is to receive the nomination. There is small doubt that he will win when primary day comes around. If, for instance, Mayor Hylan had received the benediction of Tammany in 1926, and Walker had run as an independent in the primaries, the former would still grace the City Hall in New York. The reverse being the case, Walker won by an overwhelming vote.

Chapter Five

Even the might of Tammany Hall was not powerful enough to overcome the righteous wrath of the populace that followed the Democratic field day in the 1911 session. Smith and most of the other veterans of the legislature were personally so popular, and represented such anti-Republican strongholds, that they were retained in office. Their party even managed to retain a majority in the Senate. The 1912 Assembly, however, was Republican by a safe margin and Al Smith became minority instead of majority leader. Dix, a Democrat, still had a year of his term as Governor to complete. But the transcendent figure at the Capitol was again Boss Barnes. In the place of Murphy appeared the cunning, although comparatively feeble, Samuel S. Koenig, chairman of the Republican Committee of New York County. He still holds the job, a local leader who shines in defeat and feels strange on the rare occasions when his organization wins a victory in Manhattan.

During the excitement of the previous year, I have related, the critics of Al Smith ignored the interest that he was beginning to take in such matters as workmen's compensation and legislation improving the unhappy lot of the State's insane. They also neglected to record an even more important event of 1911: his appointment to the New York State Factory Investigating Commission. This seemed, no doubt, insignificant at that time. But his work on this board and the contacts that he was to enjoy for the next four years with social instead of political minds were to have a profound effect on his career. The emergence of Smith as a man bigger than Tammany, it has been my theory, dated from his milk row with Hearst in 1919. The factory commission and its work, however, brought him his first enthusiastic endorsements outside of Fourteenth Street circles, and paved the way for still greater praise after the Constitutional Convention in 1915. The about-face on the part of those who had viewed him only with pain and sorrow is little short of amazing. In 1915, when running for Sheriff of New York County, his candidacy was endorsed by both the Citizens' Union and the New York *Tribune*, a Republican journal.

The New York State Factory Investigating Commission came into being because of the Triangle Fire in New York City on March 25, 1911. This was one of the worst disasters in the history of the many caused by the greed and carelessness of employers. It took place in a shirtwaist manufactory in the lower part of the city and trapped several hundred girl workers. More than one hundred and fifty were killed when, panic-stricken in the face of congested and inadequate exits, they jumped from windows to the street. An ordinarily placid public was aroused by the negligence which had made this possible and demands were made that the State legislature abandon its quarreling and search for plunder, so that laws preventing similar outrages could be passed. Smith, as majority leader, gave his full support to the creation of the commission and insisted upon being personally a member. It was given wide powers to make inquiry into all phases of factory perils as well as to determine the extent to which women and children were being forced to work for long hours and small pay. In all the years since then Al has never abandoned interest in these problems. He is certain to lose his temper when it is falsely charged, as by Hearst, that he has been faithless to this trust.

Senator Wagner was made chairman of the factory commission and Smith the vice-chairman. Its members included the late Samuel Gompers of the American Federation of Labor, and Mary E. Dreier, president of the Women's Trade Union League. Its counsel was Abram I. Elkus, former Ambassador to Turkey, who became so impressed with Smith that in 1918 he consented to manage his campaign for Governor. Bernard L. Shientag, a thorough student of social problems and later appointed head of the Labor Department by Smith as Governor, was assistant to Mr. Elkus. The commission was not one of the usual lethargic legislative boards of inquiry whose members slumber through public hearings while the counsel does all of the work. Wagner, too, stepped out from the cloud of Tammany domination which for years had befogged the very real ability that is in him. As chairman he took pains to see that the investigations were thorough. With Al Smith and the other members he traveled from one end of the State to the other inspecting scores of factories. Wagner, even more than Smith, was responsible for the comprehensive nature of the reports submitted to the legislature from time to time. But Smith, as leader of the Democrats in the Assembly during the next four years, exerted his growing skill as a floor strategist to force the passage of curative laws. He resorted, in doing so, to all of the expedients a practical politician knows and which he had so often used in obtaining passage of legislation ordered by Boss Murphy. He made bargains with the G. O. P., traded votes, conspired, cajoled and bluffed.

Among the objectives of the commission were laws requiring fire drills in factories, adequate staircases and fire escapes and sprinkler systems. The members had been appalled at conditions discovered in many plants, and the reports recommended statutes enforcing sanitation, provision of seats for woman workers, the abolition of labor by women in foundries and of factory night work for women. The inquiry went thoroughly into child labor abuses, here assisted by an independent investigation undertaken by the New York *World*. Manufacturing in tenements, where women and children in advanced stages of tuberculosis worked on clothing, dolls and artificial flowers, was another line of investigation. The "one-day-of-rest-in-seven" law was offered for passage. Bills were introduced reorganizing the State Labor Department and providing a larger staff. Heavier penalties were suggested to reduce violations of the labor code.

Many of these proposals were incorporated, during the years from 1911 to 1915, into the law of the State. But the good was not accomplished without vigorous opposition from business men; who are public spirited citizens except when confronted with the possibility of lowered profits. These organized powerful lobbies to kill the bills and found in the Republican Party, which had shown high virtue in its attempts to end race-track gambling, a cordial ally. Smith led the debates in favor of the suggested laws. He attended every hearing at which protests were made against their enactment. He had long since become a master of debate with a constantly growing gift for sarcasm. This proved particularly useful when the employers' lobbyists proclaimed that protective legislation was contrary to the constitutional right of a man or woman to work. The canners, for instance, asked to be exempted from the law requiring one day of rest each week. They even had the arrogance to despatch several clergymen to a hearing, and these ecclesiasts declared piously at a hearing that the men and women living near the canneries were destitute and needed seven days' wages. Smith, who was present, looked at them in disgust.

"If the good Lord were to revise the Decalogue, which He isn't going to do," he said, "I have no doubt that He would pick a committee from these gentlemen to do it and that one commandment at least would be rewritten to read 'Remember the Sabbath Day to keep it holy, except in canneries'."

Obviously, in 1912, Smith had reached a position where he deserved some reward at the hands of Tammany. The political gossip of the day was that he would certainly become Speaker when his party again controlled the lower house and it is said that Murphy had given his word that at some future time he would be permitted to run for Governor. Of this there is, however, no confirmation. For the present he was invaluable in his rôle of leader in the Assembly. The Boss might have done far worse, though, than to nominate Al in 1912. Instead he chose and accomplished the election of the grotesque William Sulzer. Before many weeks after the inauguration he was regretting with bitterness and surprise that he had done so.

Certainly no stranger figure than Sulzer has ever been chief executive of the State. For all that he is heard of now he might be dead, having vanished completely from the political picture. As a matter of fact he is practicing law in New York City. Like the present Governor of New Mexico who protested, upon being inducted into his high office, that he had never worn a dress-suit and did not intend to begin, Sulzer insisted that business clothes were formal enough for the inaugural ceremonies. The quality of his democracy was studied. He expectorated frequently, but without the spontaneity with which Al Smith does the same thing. One of his first acts was to inform the newspaper correspondents that they were the most important persons at Albany and that he would interrupt any conference to talk with them. He granted one important interview at the Executive Mansion in his nightshirt. The reporters thought him very much of an ass, but from the viewpoint of news they could not ignore him. He landed on the front pages almost daily.

In addition to electing Sulzer the Democrats gained control of both houses for the legislative year beginning January 1, 1913. Smith was made Speaker, according to schedule, and the session started harmoniously enough. The majority party trotted out an idea that the eminent Samuel Untermyer, as counsel to the Pujo money trust investigation at Washington the year before, had propounded; regulation by the State of the autocratic New York Stock Exchange. Al Smith remarked publicly on the "good sense" of the Governor in lending his support to this worthy plan and the members of the Exchange became fearfully excited. They have long since grown blasé. Countless politicians have threatened State control, but their bills have always died in committee. Relations between Sulzer and Tammany, thus cordial as the year opened, first became strained when the Governor was injudicious enough to remark with some accuracy that the organization's direct primary bill was "a betrayal of the people, a fraud and a sham". He offered a primary bill of his own which he said was far better. But toward this measure the machine proved extremely unenthusiastic.

It soon became apparent, even to the dullest of the Democrats, that Sulzer had grown heady on the wine of publicity and had formed the quaint notion that he could be independent of Tammany Hall. By May, Boss Murphy was calling him "that man at Albany", while lesser Fourteenth Street leaders invented terms more picturesque and unprintable to express their outrage. When the session ended, on May 3, 1913, the break was complete. Tammany slew the Stock Exchange bill and the rest of Sulzer's pet projects, with Al Smith wielding the snickersnee. The Republican machine, which had a fellow feeling of hatred for independence among governors, joined with Tammany in making Sulzer impotent. The Governor retaliated by denying Fourteenth Street the patronage it sorely needed.

The moral that lies in what followed—I offer it for what it may be worth—is that only men whose past is unblemished and who are truly great figures can afford to cross swords with a political organization as powerful and vindictive as the Tammany gang of 1913. Convinced that Sulzer was obstinate and would take no orders, Tammany began an investigation. It soon filed charges that Sulzer had diverted campaign funds to his own use and the Assembly swiftly voted Articles of Impeachment. And this was the end of Wild Bill. Since then the theory has been offered, heartily upheld by Sulzer himself, that the whole affair was a plot hatched in Fourteenth Street. This, however logical, is not in accord with the record. I am, though, convinced that the evidence of wrong-doing would never have been made public had it not been that Sulzer aroused the bitter anger of Murphy and Murphy's Albany hired hands. Upon his forced retirement, Lieutenant-Governor Glynn took his place and Bob Wagner became Lieutenant-Governor. The 1913 legislature, having spent so much time putting independence in its proper place, dragged on until December before its business was completed. It was one of the longest sessions in history and most of the members had to borrow carfare in order to get home.

Sulzer did not yet believe himself crushed. He ran that fall for the Assembly from the Sixth Manhattan District and told so convincing a story of martyrdom that he was elected. He felt that Smith had been in large part responsible for his impeachment and announced as he took the stump that a vital part of his campaign would be a drive against Al, who was running in the Second. The man did not lack courage. On November 11 he went down to the Fourth Ward and started to speak on a balcony a short distance from Tom Foley's club on Madison Street. The first interruption was the appearance of a dozen young women on a nearby fire escape who laughed and screamed hysterically every time he opened his mouth. Then a fife and drum corps in full blast paraded by. After these novelties a false alarm was turned in from a box on the corner and an assortment of fire apparatus clanged up. Every Madison Street car that passed disgorged a number of Tammany roughnecks who booed, yelled and set off giant firecrackers. But Bill Sulzer kept on talking throughout the riot.

During 1914, at Albany in the humble rôle of Assemblyman, he had several engagements of a verbal nature with Al and other Democrats. But his threats of wholesale investigations of Tammany departments never became more than threats and he was permitted to fade swiftly into the obscurity of private life.

Chapter Six

THE YEAR 1915 WAS A LEAN ONE FOR DEMOCRACY. Charles S. Whitman had won the Governorship by his zeal, while District Attorney of New York County, in securing the conviction of Police Lieutenant Charles Becker and the four gunmen for the murder of Herman Rosenthal, gambler and squealer. His candidacy the previous fall had been a symbol of righteousness and his strength brought substantial majorities for the Republican Party in both the Assembly and the Senate. Virtue, it was generally agreed, was to have its day at Albany. Bill Barnes, however, was still the Boss of the G.O.P. and as soon as the legislature convened the old pastime of enacting laws obnoxious to New York City began. The two major parties in the State have become the champions of country and city, respectively. Rural terror of domination by New York City, which has a majority of the population, led to a constitutional provision still in effect that the city shall not control either house. Thus, when occasionally the Democrats have a majority in the Assembly and the Senate, it is because of Republican losses in up-State municipalities.

"The minute we assemble to build a basic law, one of the first declarations of principle is that the rule of the majority is right, except when the majority is in New York City," said Al Smith in the Constitutional Convention in the summer of 1915. "And yet the commonwealth will look into the tenement for a defense of itself, just as it will look to the farm, and may receive it more readily from the city than from the country."

He had said the same thing, if less effectively, many times before. But Smith, the Republicans knew, was a city man and for all the personal affection with which they regarded him, they paid no attention to his repeated protests against the apportionment discrimination. In 1915 the Republican Party, self-proclaimed champions of Good Government, exhibited most of the vices that it attributes to Tammany Hall in campaign effusions. It lost no time booting Democrats out of office to be replaced by needy Republicans. It sought legislation increasing taxes in New York City, although the metropolis was then contributing almost 70 per cent of the funds of the State. It passed a bill providing $3,400,000 to be spent by the Republican highway department, although even its own Governor had asked for but $2,000,000. It planned a revision of the Aldermanic district boundaries in New York by an ingenious arrangement which would have vastly benefited the Republican minority in that city.

Al Smith and Bob Wagner, minority leaders in their respective houses, did work during the year of a caliber never possible when their own party was in control. It is a phenomenon not unusual in politics that leaders win their greatest distinction when they represent a minority. So, in 1915, Al and Bob devoted their time and their skill to blocking Republican steals instead of advancing the similar demands of Murphy. Not always successful, their efforts were masterly. And they found time, also, to press for passage such of the Factory Commission's recommendations as still remained to be enacted into law. For the most part, though, they hurled invective, scolded, stormed and criticized.

"Tammany Hall," said Smith in one outburst, "is a bed of roses compared to the Barren Island (a city garbage dump) of the Republican Party of New York. The intellectual giants of politics, law and business belong to Tammany Hall. The New York City Republican organization is composed of crackpots and mush-brains."

The previous year, 1914, the plight of the Democrats had not been as dire. They held the Senate and had Glynn down in the Executive Offices on the second floor completing the term of the unwept and unlamented Sulzer. Al Smith was again the Assembly minority leader, having been Speaker for but one year. It was an unimportant session, worthy of historical mention only because it witnessed the first break in nearly a decade of hostile criticism of Al Smith. There were numerous, if still half-hearted, instances of commendation for his activities in the passage of welfare laws. Both major parties were handicapped during 1914; the Democrats because of their minority and the Republicans because they were constantly annoyed by a group of Progressive Party Assemblymen.

Smith, running again for the Assembly that fall, declared emphatically that 1915 was to be his last year as a member of the legislature. Continuously since 1904 he had struggled along on the salary of $1,500 with only an occasional condemnation proceeding fee, and what he could pick up when not engaged in politics, to provide the amount necessary for his growing family. By now he had five children and was living at No. 25 Oliver Street. He told Murphy and Foley that he had done his share and was then assured that he would be rewarded with the glittering job of Sheriff. The Boss had, naturally, no intention of permitting so valuable a lieutenant to retire. And the years from 1915 to 1918 proved pregnant ones for Al. First, he was to shine with new brilliance in the Constitutional Convention. In 1917 he was elected President of the Board of Aldermen in New York. In 1918, Governor Whitman, running for a third term, was to accept with very little grace defeat at Al's hands in a gubernatorial contest.

It must have been a rather incredulous Smith who read, late in 1915, the verdict of the Citizens' Union on his part in the session that marked the close of his career as a legislator. Having berated him with monotonous regularity, the civic organization now proclaimed him an "intelligent and forceful legislator", a "strong supporter of desirable industrial and social legislation". Criticism from the Citizens' Union and similar groups had never bothered Smith a great deal. Year after year he had seen candidates survive its blasts, while those who had received its endorsement had been humbled in defeat. He had probably joked, with his Tammany playmates, over the thought that approval from such crack-pots was a hoodoo certain to bring a licking.

But he had gained a new dignity in the Constitutional Convention and if such was still his viewpoint as he ran for Sheriff he did not permit it to show when the Union said:

"Alfred E. Smith is endorsed for Sheriff of New York County. As to his qualifications for this office there can be no question. The service to the State rendered by Mr. Smith in the Constitutional Convention this year entitles him to special consideration.

"Although a party leader, Mr. Smith has in recent years been instrumental in obtaining much desirable and important legislation. We are endorsing Mr. Smith in the expectation that he will improve conditions in the Sheriff's office."

Notified that he had been thus decorated, Smith replied very politely:

"It is needless to say that it pleased me very much and I shall, to the best of my ability, endeavor to prove worthy of the great confidence you have reposed in me by your endorsement."

But words even sweeter than those of the Citizens' Union appeared in the editorial columns of the New York *Tribune:*

"The city of New York could well afford to pay Alfred E. Smith all the prospective emoluments of the Sheriff's office as a consideration for his continuing to represent a local Assembly district at Albany. In the past ten years there has been no Republican, Progressive or Democrat in the State Legislature who has rendered as effective, useful, downright valuable service to this town as ex-Speaker Smith."

During his campaign that fall, there are indications, Al Smith took himself rather more seriously than had been his usual carefree custom. It was, perhaps, not too unnatural that he did. As candidate for Sheriff his audience included all of Manhattan instead of merely the Fourth Ward. For the first time in his life he was in a contest where the vote would run into the hundred thousands instead of five or six thousand. And he could not quite forget the sweet praise from the Best People who had so recently been his critics. His speeches, those who listened now recall, were marked by a new reserve. He became, in brief, a more restrained figure than he had ever been and more stuffy than at any time since, even during his five campaigns for Governor and his close approach to winning the Democratic presidential nomination. He seemed to believe that, the old careless days of a legislator being gone forever, his new rôle demanded the qualities of a statesman.

One meeting that he addressed with some of his fellow candidates on the county ticket was held at a midtown hotel. The campaign managers had been fearful that the audience would not be large and so they recruited a flock of East Side residents. Former Judge Edward Swann, who was running for District Attorney, preceded Al on the program. A rather precise gentleman, he viewed with dismay the hastily assembled crowd. Its hands were grimy. Its cheeks needed a shave. And in the hands of each man was clutched a somewhat crumpled American flag. The chairman of the meeting knew his audience.

"Here," he said in presenting the former judge, "is the right sort of a chap to have had on the bench. He will be right as a District Attorney. Before passing sentence when he was a judge he was willing to confer with the defendant's counsel to make certain that justice was being done."

"Hurrah!" bellowed the cross-section of Democracy, waving the flags. Swann rose to address them.

"I believe," he said, "that the judge should have sympathy for the poor criminal. Ah, yes, for the poor criminal. And I believe that the District Attorney should be a prosecutor, but not a persecutor. Certainly a prosecutor, but not a persecutor."

"Hurrah!"

"And the next man who will get you when you go wrong," said the cheerful chairman, forgetting that this official no longer has much to do with criminals in New York, "is the Sheriff. I present Al Smith."

Again the flags fluttered and Al Smith buttons were hastily pinned on coat lapels. Al got up, very aloof and a little annoyed over the suggestion that as Sheriff he would send any Democrat to the hoosegow. He cleared his throat and looked at the grimy faces before him.

"The chairman, I fear," he began, "has touched on the most unpleasant part of my duties as Sheriff. But I give you my word of honor that no personal act of mine will bring the blush of shame to the cheek of any one of you."

It was difficult, however, to keep the campaign on a really high plane. Al's neighbors on Oliver Street were overjoyed at the prospect that he was to return to his old home for the entire year instead of merely between battles at Albany. A week before Election Day they held a mass meeting in front of the Smith homestead, with red fire and Roman candles and beer flowing freely in a dozen nearby saloons. Greeks, Italians and Jews, the newer residents of the Fourth Ward but as fond of Al as any, rubbed elbows with Irish first families. It was an East Side version of Old Home Week, with Al Smith and his wife sitting on their front stoop and grinning back as young blades and oldsters called "You know me, Al!" or "Hello, Katie Dunn!"

> "For those of the men whose thirsts returned with them," said the *Tribune* the next day, "the doors of the Pan-Hellenic cafe swung easily. Displayed in one of its windows was a portrait of Premier Venizelos and a no-less austere one of Mr. Smith."

Smith was elected, of course, by a comfortable margin. He received 113,791 votes to 72,590 cast for Frank K. Bowers, his Republican opponent. Once in office, he kicked out the Republican incumbents and appointed more or less deserving Democrats, many of them Irish. Two of the best jobs, paying $6,000 a year each, went to John F. Gilchrist, a boyhood friend, and George W. Olvany. Gilchrist became under-Sheriff and the future leader of Tammany Hall counsel to the Sheriff. Al quickly recovered from the air of dignity that had slightly chilled him during the campaign. He took part in a revival of *The Shaughraun* at St. James, again playing the hiss-producing rôle of "Corry Kinchella". Jimmy Walker, already among the brightest stars at Albany, was also in the cast. Others included Assemblyman Peter Hamill, now boss of the district Al has forsaken in order to live at the Biltmore, and Henry McCadden, the jovial mortician who recently took up the lease of No. 25 Oliver Street.

But that he was the same old Al of his legislative days, fond of his beer and saddened by personal discords, is best shown by an incident that took place during the summer of 1916. On the morning of a hot July day, going to his office, he was scandalized to hear that during his absence on the previous afternoon a reporter from a friendly newspaper had been ejected. There had been a row, a deputy explained, and made it clear that the reporter had been wholly at fault. This, Smith pointed out, was irrelevant in the face of the fact that he had been from a friendly journal. When the further detail was added that the city editor had telephoned to demand an explanation, he clamped his brown derby on his head and started for the newspaper's editorial room.

The editor in question had not yet arrived and to an assistant was brought the card reading "A. E. SMITH, SHERIFF OF NEW YORK COUNTY". Wondering whether some creditor had obtained an attachment, the assistant went out to the reception room in some trepidation. He found a red-faced man, with his coat off and his suspenders slipped from his shoulders, fanning himself with his hat. The visitor asked to see the editor and upon being told that he had not yet come in leaned over confidentially.

"I wanted to explain about yesterday," said Al. "They tell me one of your men was kicked out of my office. Say, will you tell him for me it was a mistake; tell your boss that. Tell him I wasn't in and that I didn't know anything about it. He called up, they told me. Say, ask him if he thinks Al Smith's *crazy!* I'm not kicking reporters *out* of my office. I *want* 'em there."

Chapter Seven

BUT BEFORE AL SMITH BECAME LORD HIGH Sheriff of the County of New York, and enjoyed a weekly income almost as large as the annual honorarium of a member of the State legislature, he returned to Albany for the sessions of the Constitutional Convention. These started in April of 1915 and lasted until September. The convention was called to frame a new draft of the State's fundamental law, which had become so bulky, involved and antiquated that the few lawyers expert in its mysteries were uniformly growing wealthy. The delegates to the sessions included many gentlemen of education and training, together with a liberal allowance of organization men despatched by both parties to see that nothing too radical in the way of reform was slipped over. The convention, in the end, accomplished little except to suggest ideas that Al Smith was to develop and bring to fulfillment a decade later. Its new constitution was rejected at the polls in the fall. But this was not, as has been so often charged, because of the wicked Tammany delegates. It was because the best minds bowed to the will of the Republican machine and consented to a draft manifestly unfair to New York City.

Smith was among the men named by Murphy to keep an eye on the proceedings. His selection was deplored by some of the high-minded gentlemen who were viewing the convention as the opportunity of a lifetime so to improve the constitution that political parties would disband and the functions of government left to writers for journals on political science. Before many days had passed, however, Smith had demonstrated that facts are superior to theories. All of the knowledge that a keen mind and a retentive memory had absorbed and stored since 1904 was at his disposal. This included not only the innumerable complexities of the constitution and the supporting statute law, but the machinations of politicians with respect to these codes. As a sleight-of-hand artist might reveal his tricks, but never does, Al stood for hour after hour on the floor of the convention and told how things are really done.

"Of all the men in the convention, Alfred E. Smith was the best informed on the business of the State of New York," said Elihu Root, its president, after the convention had adjourned. A sage of the Republican Party, Mr. Root is as different in temperament and education from Smith as a man can well be.

"He was the most useful man in the convention," admitted George W. Wickersham, who had been

Republican floor leader and was a former United States Attorney General.

Perhaps the work of Smith during those months can be explained only by the hackneyed formula that two persons were in him as he stood before the convention. One was the legislative leader, wise in the practical methods whereby laws are made or forced to die in committee, knowing that party platforms mean little, aware that governments by men operate through bargaining with principle. The other side of him was the Smith whose work with the Factory Investigating Commission during the four years that had just passed had given him insight into the social obligations of governments. He had come to believe with a sincerity quite devoid of politics that the State must, in its own interest, exercise its police powers to protect the weak and the poor. He knew that wealth and privilege, usually enlisted with the G.O.P., were ever alert to prevent the use of that power.

"Take line 12 on page 5," he would say, in substance, one moment. "You think that makes the Governor approve appropriation bills. Well, maybe, it ought to. But any man who has been at Albany for more than a couple of years knows that actually it doesn't work that way at all."

Then, with charming lack of reserve, Al would describe the inner workings of the system, would demonstrate how the amendment must be framed if it were to have any salutary effect. But the next time that he was on his feet the politician in Smith had given way to the sociologist and he was making an impassioned plea against amendments that sought to invalidate such legislation as workmen's compensation, factory safety laws and the fifty-four-hour week for women.

It was the hard-boiled politician, confident and assured, who discussed emergency messages at an early session. These, it must be explained, are authorizations from the Governor permitting the legislature to pass bills without regard to the requirement that they must be in printed form for three days. A time-honored scheme, the emergency message makes possible much of the crooked work that the legislature accomplishes. As Speaker and majority leader, Smith had often resorted to it in rushing appropriation bills. But now he declared himself heartily in favor of its abolition, in the best interests of the State. He said, in part:

"I do not say it has been done by any one party any more than the other. I was Chairman of the Committee on Ways and Means for a long and stormy session. I was the Speaker for another long and stormy session and had something to say about when appropriation bills were to pass, and I myself directed that they should wait until the last moment because it was easier. Now that is the truth about it. If you do away with the emergency message, you will compel the majority leader, you will compel the

Committee on Ways and Means, the men that are responsible for the legislation, to have their program ready and put it through; and they can do it.

"There is another class of bills that the emergency message has been very useful in passing in the last days, and those are the bills that give rise to disputes between the two houses. The Senate does not entirely agree with a little that the Assembly wants to do, or vice versa, and finally in the last days of the session, while the flags are flying from the Capitol and the band is playing and everybody feels happy over the prospect of the last $250 draw and a good time for the summer—they will patch up their differences and say 'Well, go downstairs and get a message and put it right through', and they do it, and the minority can do the best it can."

It is impossible, within the limitations of this book, to do more than mention briefly the part that Smith played in the Constitutional Convention. I commend to the attention of scholars the four ponderous volumes published by the State of New York and entitled "Revised Record, New York State Constitutional Convention, 1915". Buried in their 4,500 pages will be found an analysis of a State government as it really operates, purged of campaign oratory and free from the vaporizings that so often make the academic worthless. Most of the gold will be found in the record of the remarks of Delegate A. E. Smith. I think there is material for countless theses in the opinions of this man who had scarcely seen the inside of a schoolhouse and who had never listened to the profundities of a seminar on political science.

After the convention had been in session for some weeks, Smith focused his attention on an apparently innocent amendment which had been offered by the more reactionary Republican delegates. It sought to prevent the enactment of laws giving privileges to certain classes, and on the surface seemed in complete harmony with the American form of government. Al realized that it was utterly vicious in effect and would invalidate such cherished projects of his own as workmen's compensation and control of labor by women and children. The debate on the subject was long and windy. Orators supporting it quoted ancient statutes, told of the follies of paternalistic governments. They described deplorable lapses on the part of the Emperor Diocletian and the mistakes of Edward III and Edward IV of England. The position taken by Governor Cook of Rhode Island in 1777 was cited as relevant and even the Justinian Code was dragged into the argument. Finally it was Smith's turn to speak and Mr. Wickersham, who was also aware of the nature of the amendment, conceded twenty minutes of his own time to the former ward politician. I quote from the stenographic record of the Tammany delegate's remarks:

"We are getting away from our ideas of government. Apparently preaching for a return to the American ideal, we are ourselves, by the force of our arguments, drifting in the other direction. Now I may be entirely wrong. The gentlemen around this chamber would lead us to believe that law in a democracy is the expression of some Divine or eternal right. I am unable to see it that way. My idea of law and democracy is the expression of what is best, what fits the present-day needs of society, what goes the farthest to do the greatest good for the greatest number. After all, is not that the reason for the existence of great political parties?"

He went on to point out the necessity for the workmen's compensation enactments, for mothers' pensions. He cited a decision of the United States Supreme Court in justification of limiting working hours for women on the ground of their physical handicaps and the burdens of motherhood. He continued:

"That is equally true where labor laws are enacted for the preservation of the health of the men of the State because, after all, what is the State? Green fields and rivers and lakes and mountains and cities? Why, not at all. It is the people, all the people of the State, and anything that tends to make the members of the State strong and vigorous in turn helps to make the State so, and every one of these enactments has been for the general good and could in no way be described as a privilege."

The amendment, he said, was offered under the pretense that it was to stop the granting of privileges or immunities to certain classes. Was not, he demanded, the law which had created the State Department of Agriculture one giving special privileges to the farmers? No Department of Industry had been brought into being to give similar assistance to business men.

"By the way," he said, "it might be interesting to know why the Department of Agriculture was organized. It was organized for the very same purpose that all these labor bills have passed and become laws: It was organized to be a check upon the greed of men that had under their control the natural resources of the State. Men looked for too many crops from their land; they did not provide for the future when it should be in the fullness of its bloom. As a check on their greed the department was organized to further a campaign of education, to show them how to get the greatest possible results out of that resource that was given to them.

"So it might be said that all the labor laws, that this (amendment) seeks to prevent the legislature from enacting, are nothing more or less than campaigns of industrial education. What about the Excise Law? Written into every line of it is privilege and immunity. A man has the privilege of transacting business in this part of the State (Albany) for half what it costs in the City of New York. The very definition of a hotel in the Excise Law spells out privilege. A man with nine rooms in his hotel cannot sell a drink on Sunday, but a man with ten rooms can sell it. All he has got to do is to have a sandwich with it. This is privilege.

"Now let us get down to business and stop all this constitutional talk, and the talk about the representatives of the people and all of that, when we do not really believe in it. Let us get right down to hardpan. The question we have to deal with here to-night is this: Is this a wise thing for this convention to put its stamp of approval upon? No matter what it may prevent, no matter what it may promote, there is throughout the length and breadth of this State a general belief that the men that proposed this thing have in mind the setting of the fundamental law against—the workmen's compensation acts; the people have in mind that it is proposed to array the constitution itself against the decisions of the Supreme Court as to what is a matter of duty on the part of the State; they have in mind that it proposes to erect a wall around the representatives of the people to prevent the wholesome, beneficial change in State policy that came from the enactment of the child welfare bill.

"Whatever may be the final result of it, we are to-night by our votes to decide whether or not we are to put our stamp of approval upon a proposition which means that, so far as the fundamental law is concerned, and having in mind that the great curse in poverty lies in the utter helplessness that goes with it, reduces that basic law to the same level of the caveman's law, the law of the sharpest tooth, the angriest brow and the greediest jaw."

With the assistance of Wickersham and other Republicans the proposal was defeated. Its leading exponent had been William Barnes, the G.O.P. Boss.

It was Al's lack of pretense and refusal to indulge in subterfuge, combined with his wealth of knowledge, that made him the most impressive of all the delegates. Never since, probably, has any man in public life been so free from hokum as was Smith during the months between April and September in 1915. This caused him to be a devastating opponent in debates. He laughed to scorn the assertions of the theorists that apportionment of representatives in the legislature, one of the important matters before the convention, could be discussed without the taint of politics.

"Going back as far as you can in political history," he said, "apportionments have always spelled politics. We had a little sample of apportionment in the legislature that just adjourned (the 1915 session). Without any precedent for it, the last legislature undertook to apportion the aldermanic districts in New York City. They did not say it came from any great demand on the part of the people that there be any change in the lines of the districts. They were open and frank about it. They said it was done for the purpose of trying to select a fusion or anti-Tammany Board of Aldermen in the second two years of Mayor Mitchel's term. And following the little lessons we have learned from our constitution, and having uttered our little political prayer, we made all the Republican districts this way (hands held out a short distance apart) and then we made the Democratic districts this way (hands held a very long distance apart). The Mayor of the city said he would like to sign the bill, but it was too raw, it was more than he could stand."

Most of the delegates, half a dozen with justification, attempted to portray themselves as in attendance only in the interest of the State; great nonpartisan figures, remote from any thought of politics. But Smith was not among these. During the debate on the reorganization of State departments the friction between the Republicans and the Democrats became more heated than usual. The details are not significant; the substance of Smith's contribution to the argument was that a Republican amendment did not make for fewer State offices but additional ones. He said so at some length and thereby aroused the anger of Frederick C. Tanner, the Republican State Chairman.

"There was a great deal of uneasiness over Sunday as to what some of you gentlemen were going to do," Tanner declared in a tone out of all harmony with the usual decorum of the convention. "You had to go down to New York to find out."

"Oh, don't be too thin-skinned about these things," said Al soothingly. "We men of legislative experience do not hesitate to call a spade a spade. When we make a deal for votes we admit it."

But Bob Wagner, another Tammany delegate, could not forget Mr. Tanner's nasty remark about going down to New York to ask for instructions. It carried, of course, the insinuation that Boss Murphy was in command. He demanded that this "very unfair and insidious reflection cast upon the minority members of this body" be stricken from the record. Speaking for himself, Wagner said, he was "independent of any other man's judgment to do whatever I can to advance the welfare and the government of this State." At this point Smith flashed his familiar grin:

"I would like to have it said, speaking for myself," he remarked cheerfully, "that if there is anything to be expunged from the record, I would like to have it remain on the record as applying to myself, for this reason: I do go to New York to find out what they think about things in New York. This last week I could not go down so I went to Saratoga. I stayed over Sunday with my family and just before I left the hotel for church the telephone bell rang. I was requested to answer a long distance call, and it was from Tammany Hall.

"Somebody said to me, 'Is this you, Al?'

"I said 'Yes.'

" 'This is Tammany Hall.'

"I said, 'I know it.'

" 'What is the meaning of the printed matter on the last four lines of page 3 of that State officers' bill?'

"I answered back, 'That is a new job, that is another place.'

"Word came back, 'Who is proposing that?'

"I said, 'A gentleman named Tanner.'

" 'The Republican State Chairman?'

" 'Yes, sir.'

" 'Read him page 5 of his Governor's message.' "

Whereupon, while the delegates chuckled with delight, Smith read the passage in the last message of Governor Whitman in which that Republican Chief Executive criticized the "increase on an unprecedented scale in the number of State offices". Little may be remembered, now, of the deliberations of the Constitutional Convention of 1915. But ask any of those who attended to recall some of the high moments and it is not unlikely that he will tell of this occasion, when Smith punctured another balloon of dignity and demonstrated that the G.O.P. was through its Governor pledged against the very thing that the amendment under discussion sought to accomplish.

Chapter Eight

IF AL SMITH AND HIS TAMMANY COLLEAGUES ARE to be damned for listening to Murphy, the Republican machine delegates must admit that their own guilt was at least as bad. Murphy, as it happened, was this time on the side of right. In recent years, due principally to the long enduring hold of Smith upon the voters, the influence of the Republican party in New York has waned. Its present leaders are often ludicrous and nearly always helpless. They have the urge to be bosses, but nothing more. In 1915, though, Bill Barnes was still alive and cracked his whip at the silk stocking clad ankles of the delegates he owned. There were, of course, exceptions. Wickersham was among these and, to a lesser extent, Jacob Gould Schurman, then president of Cornell University and now Mr. Coolidge's representative at Berlin. But most of the delegates to the Constitutional Convention, having disavowed in dozens of orations any political motives, did as they were told when the voting started.

"The steam roller they used," remarked Al Smith after it was over, "was the most scientific I ever experienced. Also the chlorine gas, as they used it, was admirable."

At the final session the delegates were required to cast their vote for or against the proposed constitution as a whole. "It was difficult," said Smith when his name was called, "for a man from New York to support it", although with much he was "in very hearty accord". As a whole the new draft was out of the question.

"I believe," he said, "we have made some substantial progress in the budget article. I have no particular fault to find with the State officers article. I believe it is as near the Democratic declaration as we can expect to have it, coming from the opposite side.

"But . . . it must be admitted by every man around this circle that the Senate limitation cannot reasonably expect approval from the people of New York to-day. There are men in the State of New York who still believe that it is probably right that there be some limitation put upon the Upper House, but some men have learned by experience that the Assembly apportionment provision operates in the same direction, although it is not written into the constitution in so many words.

"We (of New York City) have a right to expect something better. We have grown in size and influence. That we have been discriminated against there can be no question. . . . It was very interesting to have the Chairman of the Taxation Committee say we are only paying 68 per cent. That encourages me to say that if we are only paying 68 per cent of the direct tax we must be paying about 90 per cent of the indirect tax.

"As for the charter for New York City, it could easily be said that when a large majority of the people have decided upon their form of charter they should be permitted to live under it, whether good, bad, or indifferent. It is their own and they have the power to change it any time, but when you say that the men from all over the State have the last say as to what New York City is to have as a charter, well, you come down and try to explain that that is home rule."

Unquestionably the draft of the constitution as it was offered to the voters that fall was unfair to New York City. It was certain to be, with the rural-minded Republicans controlling a majority of the delegates. It sought to perpetuate the discord between town and city which is stronger to-day even than in 1915 and which, it is not improbable, will reach new intensity if Al Smith, city man, runs for the presidency in a nation politically agrarian. The distrust of New York is profound in the rustic parts of the State. It is equally profound in more distant sections of the nation. On the other hand, however, the supporters of Smith can find encouragement in the degree to which he has cut in on the up-State vote. The farmers of the West, the Middle West and the South may find after all, as I have before suggested, that the menace of city things has been unduly magnified.

It was the unfair apportionment article, together with the discrimination in taxation and the denial of real home rule to New York City, that led Al

Smith to confide to the Speakers' Bureau of Tammany Hall a month later that the new constitution was "a gold brick". Orders went out from 14th Street that it was to be defeated and on November 2nd the people, 99 per cent of whom had not the remotest notion of what it was all about, turned it down at the polls.

In the decade that has passed since the convention, the part that one man played in its deliberations has done more than anything else to keep memory of it alive. The bound volumes of the proceedings are rotting to decay on dusty library shelves. Most of the men who then were leaders are heard in the council chambers of their parties no longer. But the principles for which Al Smith fought have not been forgotten. Least of all did he, himself, forget them. In behalf of a few of them he still speaks, in a voice that has become more restrained but which largely retains its old freshness and flavor. For others, a simplified government, home rule, revision of the judiciary and a short ballot he no longer is forced to fight. He has written them into the State's basic law.

On December 17, 1926, Al was a guest at a dinner at the Hotel Astor. It was in the nature of a reunion for those who had been members of the Constitutional Convention. Henry L. Stimson, a former secretary of war; Charles E. Hughes, and Mr. Wickersham were among the better known of those present. Smith, about to begin his fourth term as Governor, heard himself praised by various speakers for his activities of ten years before. An enthusiastic Democrat again predicted that he would be President and members of both parties joined in the applause.

"I am happy," he replied in a brief address, "that this reunion has been brought about. It was a great opportunity for me, that convention. You know, I never let my campaign manager forget for a moment what I did in the Constitutional Convention."

BOOK FOUR

A Prisoner at Albany

Chapter One

THE AVERAGE OFFICE HOLDER IN THIS GREAT democracy is an aloof and austere figure except as Election Day approaches and expediency demands, for the moment, sudden hospitality toward the citizenry. During these crises the attendants in the reception room become as cordial as apartment house hallboys at Christmas time. Visitors are given an oleaginous welcome and are permitted to see the Great Man toiling in an inner office in their behalf. It is more than probable, in fact, that this figure will interrupt his labors to do some handshaking.

But all of this has been signally absent from the executive offices on the second floor of the State Capitol at Albany, particularly during the years that Al Smith has been Governor. The entrance to these offices is through heavy oaken doors, always open unless a meeting of the Governor's Cabinet happens to be in progress. The outer room is long and narrow, with a red carpet on the floor. At the far end is a railing and behind this a desk where sits Willie Lambert, as remarkable a man in his rôle as any at Albany. Dark-haired, his face is cheerful and hospitable when he asks the visitor's business.

If this chances to be with the Governor he summons one of the secretarial staff. The exceptional thing about Lambert, however, is a memory which would put any of the mail order course graduates to shame. If the caller has been in the executive offices before, even if years previously, the chances are that Willie will recall his name. One begins one's business with Governor Smith with a satisfactory feeling of importance.

A measure of cynicism is not, perhaps, out of place when it is asserted by the assistants of an elected official that no one, no matter how eccentric his appearance or peculiar his request, is denied a hearing. I am entirely convinced, though, that this has been true with respect to Governor Smith's administrations. I am even prepared to believe that any person in trouble or perplexity and unwilling to reveal his problem to an attendant will, in time, be able to pour his story into the ears of Al himself. This does not mean, of course, that Smith spends much of his time listening to crazy stories. He is blessed with two able and experienced secretaries, George B. Graves and James J. Mahoney. The former is a Republican and became Governor Smith's first lieutenant because of his abilities and long service in the executive offices. Mahoney is a youthful Irishman with a sympathetic nature that would persuade even a Vermonter to confide the secrets of his soul. He is usually the first to confer with those anxious to see Al.

"No one who has valid business is refused a moment with the Governor," he has insisted. "Naturally a lot of cranks come in with impossible stuff. But George Graves or I can spot them and we ease them out. When they insist they can tell only the Governor their story, it's a cinch it's about somebody in prison; it's an appeal for clemency of some sort. Why shouldn't we be sympathetic? What I do, in these cases, is to explain how terribly busy Al is and to point out how much more chance there is of getting help if the yarn is told to me first. Then I can outline it to the Governor and put all the papers on the case before him. It saves time, I say. But if this doesn't work I tell the Governor, and I've never known him to turn anybody away unheard."

There is a definite aura of good cheer, these days, about the second floor offices at the State Capitol. As far as the clerks and stenographers are concerned, this is due to a sincere admiration for the Governor. Many of them have seen a host of chief executives. They have never, they say, known one who has worked as hard as does Al Smith, or who has understood his job half so well. But the cheer is caused also, I think, by a very distinct note of triumph in the air. It is an unusual day when Al has not taken a shot at a hostile legislature and hit the mark; when some public address or legislative message is not a subject for laudation in the morning's newspapers. All of these victories are regarded by the staff as personal accomplishments. When Smith receives a setback the gloom is but momentary and predictions are made that "he'll show 'em up". If Al's executive staff had the power to name presidents, and among them are Democrats and Republicans, Protestants, Catholics and Jews, he would, it is certain, be despatched to the White House for life.

Two of the more important events of the executive day are the conferences at 11 o'clock and 4 o'clock with the Albany newspaper correspondents, journalists who represent papers in all parts of the State as well as the press associations. About a dozen are from New York City. The morning session is normally the better attended, and for this about twenty writers report. Those who have been at Albany for any length of time are personal friends of the Governor, for Al has not lost his ability to make friends irrespective of politics. In 1915, it will be remembered, he blarneyed a Republican legislature into postponing, until he had enjoyed two juicy years in the job, its intention of slashing the compensation of the Sheriff of New York County. To-day the correspondents from the most critical Republican papers, even from the Hearst sheets, are almost always his friends. So it will be if he is a presidential candidate. Writers on the campaign trains, whatever their reaction to his policies, will find pleasure in his company. Inevitably, in the long run, this will soften intended denunciations.

The correspondents assemble for the conferences in a large outer room where executive hearings are conducted. On the walls are paintings of past Governors, several of them aristocratic appearing gentlemen who look down from their frames with a supercilious air, as though reflecting that this upstart is making a tremendous noise, but lacks their own inimitable administrative talents. Always present as the newspaper men gather is Bobby Fitzmaurice, whose title is "Executive Officer" and who is another figure without whose story that of Al Smith is incomplete. Actually slightly older than the Governor, he seems much younger. There is a note of immaturity about him which makes it inevitable that he should be universally addressed as Bobby. His rôle is that of Man Friday to Smith, and his duties include the thousand details that must be attended to when a hearing is scheduled or some trip is to be made. Whenever the Governor travels Bobby goes along as a sort of bodyguard. He has thus served Al for years, ever since the days when Smith became an officer of the Assembly and was entitled to a small staff. In his eyes the Governor is nearly divine.

At one of the recent stunt dinners given annually by the Albany correspondents a skit had a schoolroom for its set. A teacher propounded various questions, most of them ridiculous, regarding familiar figures at Albany.

"What," he asked toward the end of the act, "is loyalty?"

The actors, taking the parts of scholars, did not grin this time. One of them got up.

"Bobby Fitzmaurice," he said.

When the Governor is ready for the conference, Bobby is the one who ushers the correspondents into the inner office. It is a small room, smaller than that of Mr. Graves, which it adjoins. The chief piece of furniture is a large flat-top desk, cluttered with papers and containing bound copies of State reports, a legal volume or two and possibly some newspaper clippings. A photograph of Smith's daughter, Emily, and her husband, Major John Adams Warner of the State Police, is also there. On the mantelpiece in back of the desk is a framed copy of an editorial, "The Governor's Loss", published in a New York newspaper at the time his mother died in 1924.

It is a very sure, self-confident figure who sits behind the gubernatorial desk these days. Always this has been characteristic of Smith, save during his first two years in the Assembly. But as he has grown in distinction, particularly as he has developed his expert knowledge of the post he holds, his confidence has increased vastly. It is pleasant for any man to be secure in knowledge. The Smith of today, also, seems very fit from a physical point of view. His skin is pink and clear. His blue eyes are bright and also are clear. He no longer gnaws nervously at the ends of his spectacles as he did a few years ago, and he is less irritable when he is crossed. The irritability remains, it is true, for all his good nature. But the nervousness that prompts it is now revealed in the way he chews his cigar, which constantly goes out and is constantly relit as he talks. In this, and in his habit of expectoration, which continues to the extent that in his private office, where he feels at home, there is a cuspidor underneath his desk and another behind it. He often wears a wing collar and a black tie and his suits are usually dark. They are well tailored. Smith's appearance, I repeat, leaves little to be desired. Even those peculiar creatures, writers on male fashions, could find no fault with his clothes now that he has forever abandoned East Side eccentricities.

His personality in the high office that he holds is far more difficult to picture with accuracy. For this man, whom thousands call "Al" and believe they know so intimately, is filled with complexities and the truth is elusive. As he sits behind his desk during an interview, though, it is clear that he is no mere jovial person, anxious to agree. He has none of the difficulty experienced by his friend, Mayor

Jimmy Walker of New York, in saying "no". He plays his cards very close to his face and if he decides that he has nothing to say, the most skilled reporter on earth will leave with little information. He has no real newspaper confidants, as do so many public officials. There is no reporter to-day who can send daily despatches as the spokesman of Smith. All this hardness that is part of him is reflected in the lines of his face, lines that have settled and deepened since the day when he was the delight or the bane of so many East Side parlors. Yet despite it the general conception persists that he is a bubbling spirit, always frank and always open. It is unnecessary to point out that his career does not suffer by a combination which enables him to be taciturn as an official and talkative enough off duty to counteract any resentment that this might cause.

As a source of news the conferences with Smith are almost without value. The Albany correspondents are always discovering this fact to their surprise and forgetting it again immediately; for the reason that the sessions in the Governor's office are too enjoyable to be missed. It is now an accepted custom among politicians to take reporters into their confidence, under the pledge that they will not be quoted. President Coolidge did this, until recently, through the fiction of "a spokesman for the President". Smith occasionally uses this device, but not often.

When he does, the news stories relate that "friends of the Governor" believe that a certain thing will be done. Other governors have been far better, so far as news is concerned, than Al. Among the best was Nathan L. Miller, who defeated Smith in 1920 and was in turn defeated by him in 1922. It was Judge Miller's custom to answer nearly any question, freely and frankly, with a stenographer present to insure correct quotations. Whitman's system was somewhat like that of Smith, but provided more news. Charles E. Hughes was inclined to be direct in his answers, but seldom permitted himself to be quoted.

Al Smith tells funny stories.

A typical conference, for example, discloses the Governor behind his desk with his chair tilted back. The correspondents are draped over a lounge opposite the desk or perched on the window sills.

"What's going on?" one will ask.

"Not a thing I know of," says Al.

Then will begin a series of questions on bills pending in the legislature, on the particular fight in which the Governor happens at the moment to be involved. For the most part he evades or declares flatly that there have been no developments. The understanding is that he is never to be quoted without specific permission. But this is sometimes given as, for instance, when he was asked to comment on a somewhat absurd speech made the day before by young Theodore Roosevelt.

"If bunk was electricity," Al snapped, "the Colonel would be a power house."

The chances are great that most of the conference will be devoted to reminiscences of the East Side, changes in the style of living in New York, memories of his days as an actor. The rise of the modern apartment house caused him to snort in disgust at one recent conference.

"I know a fellow," he said, "who was invited to invest $600,000 in one of those new duplex coöperative ownership places and then pay $30,000 a year rent; 30,000 simoleons!"

"The $600,000 was for the privilege of paying the rent," suggested one of the correspondents.

"Sure," guffawed Al, "it was a cover charge!"

It would be incorrect to infer, however, that the conferences are unduly lengthy or a waste of the Governor's time. If Smith prefers to address the public by means of formal statements, prepared in advance and handed out in typewritten form, he has the right to choose his own method. Never, probably, has the business of government moved so swiftly or so efficiently as during the four administrations of Governor Smith. He works under heavy pressure, rarely doing more than snatch a bite of lunch at noon and often remaining at the Capitol until after 7 o'clock at night. The door between his own office and that of Mr. Graves is seldom closed. Constantly, as the line of visitors passes in and out, the nasal voice of the Governor resounds with a penetrating clearness that makes secrecy impossible.

"Look up Chapter 34 of the laws of 1914," he will tell a State Senator, asking for advice about a pet bill. "Maybe there's a conflict. I think there is. You better fix it. Outside of that the bill's o. k. with me."

The next man is the head of a department, complaining that some subordinate, a political appointment, is falling down on his job.

"You're the boss," Smith booms. "You tell him. You tell him if he don't work, out he goes. He's being paid good money. Make him work!"

After this there is, perhaps, an extradition hearing in the outer room. Smith strides to the chair at the head of the table and nods to the attorneys. Bobby Fitzmaurice scurries over with an armful of papers; the lawyers begin their argument in protest against the removal of their client to some other State where he is charged with crime. Smith cuts short their legalistic phraseology, gets at the root of the matter and demands that briefs be filed.

Perhaps the hearing is to afford the public an opportunity to express its views on some bill awaiting the Governor's signature. Smith has a genius for maintaining peace at these sessions, despite the presence of numerous windy citizens. At these, too, he translates legal dissertations into plain English, vivid and understandable. Once such hearing was on a bill to amend the penal law. A former district attorney held forth at length on the mental processes of criminals, on the preventive nature of punishment. What the criminal does, he said, is to ponder whether he can break the law with safety.

"If he decides that he will probably not be sent to jail," he concluded, "he goes ahead and breaks it."

"What you mean," said Al, a little bored, "is that the Ten Commandments are no good if a man doesn't believe in Hell."

Smith went to Albany in 1919 with a great advantage over previous governors. As Speaker and majority leader in the Assembly he had sat in the Governor's office for many hours, poring over State business. He was aware that the theory of the separation of the legislative and the executive did not work in practice, and as soon as he took office he demanded the creation of a system that would enable him to know just what was going on in the legislature. This was perfected by Mr. Mahoney. By means of it Smith knows, probably better than any legislator, the status of every bill in which he is interested. In addition to this he has a file of his own, kept in a cabinet in the inner office. It contains thousands of notes and memoranda, unintelligible to all except himself. But to the Governor they are filled with meaning and it is the assistance of this file that has enabled him, again and again, to confound his opponents by the simple method of knowing their stuff as well as he does his own.

Chapter Two

"I ATTRIBUTE MY SUCCESS," AL SMITH MIGHT declare in an interview, but undoubtedly never will, "to the Republican Party."

There would, however, be a large element of truth in such a statement. The G.O.P. in New York State, smug in the knowledge that it is widely heralded as the party of the educated and well-bred, has been incredibly stupid during all the years that Smith has been Governor. Always in control of at least one house of the legislature, due to the constitutional limitation on representation from New York City, it has consistently chosen the wrong side of almost every public question. It has been stone blind in its partisanship and has adopted the policy that anything desired by Al Smith is evil, extravagant, radical or unscientific. Its predicament, as a result of all this, has not been too happy a one at any time. Smith, from the start of his first term, has had a faculty for being right in his theories of government. Many of his policies were once cherished theses of the Republican Party itself. The views of this Tammany Governor have been evolved, repeatedly and frankly, from studies made by eminent

Republicans. But once he had spoken for them and they became his, the thin brains operating the Republican State machine made frantic efforts to block their fulfillment.

This much, and little else, can be said for the party of refinement: that its capacity for taking beatings is comparable only to that of a heavyweight champion's sparring partner. Year after year it has been defeated when Smith has used the newspapers, the stump and the radio to go to the people and explain what he wanted. So great is the skill with which he does this that the resulting deluge of protest received at Albany has forced Republican legislators to back down and defy their leaders. And when the time came for Al to run again all he needed to do, as the G. O. P. hastily but feebly called attention to the extent to which it had "cooperated", was to point out what he had accomplished. The most superficial examination of the years from 1919 to 1927 discloses that the Republican Party's record for doing the wrong thing is virtually unimpaired. It has opposed, to enumerate but a few of the issues, tax reduction, welfare legislation, budgetary responsibility and a plan for scientific reorganization of State departments. All these it once believed in and all were in the end forced through by Smith. At the present moment it is in the process of getting fearfully snarled up by a water-power policy which probably would mean the theft of this resource from a public that is slowly awakening to the importance of natural wealth.

Al Smith is not perfect. He has the Tammany viewpoint which sees no danger in piling up huge bonded debts to be met out of future taxes. During the last two years, his head slightly swollen by continued victories, he has verged on the cocksure. His conception of the State as a huge corporation, which must borrow for improvements as does an industrial plant, is not wholly accurate, since the State has no earnings out of which to meet payments and no income save taxes. I wonder whether he might not have gone too far in his anxiety to improve conditions had the Republican Party been bright enough to give him some rope. Certainly he would never be the nationally known figure of to-day, declared by Republican strategists, terrified of his ability to win campaigns, to be unfit for the presidency. Even during the two years in which Nathan L. Miller, a very able man, was Governor, the Republican Party showed its customary asininity. It did everything possible to antagonize New York and other cities by attempting to raise utility rates. Laws requiring loyalty tests from teachers and other of its enactments against the mildest of radical thought were insults to a democracy. There is at least evidence, even if unreliable, that the G.O.P. organization in some parts of the State knifed Miller when he opposed Smith in 1922.

The Republican boys, who differ from Tammany not in the least in this, were resentful of their Governor's economy program which had meant fewer jobs.

The obstructionist campaign of the Republicans started a few weeks after Smith began his first term in 1919. In his message to the legislature the Governor called attention to important problems arising from the war that had just ended. These, he said, included not only the care of wounded soldiers and employment for other veterans, but more permanent problems that had been aggravated by the national hysteria. Among the objectives to be attained were: taxation to be borne equally by all classes, production and distribution of the necessities of life at low cost, improved welfare legislation and housing relief. To solve these vital perplexities Governor Smith appointed, on January 20, 1919, a reconstruction commission and invited Abram I. Elkus, former Ambassador to Turkey, to act as chairman. There is not the slightest indication that Smith considered politics for an instant in selecting the members. Most of them were distinguished citizens and many were Republicans. Among those who agreed to serve were George Foster Peabody, Charles H. Sabin, Mortimer L. Schiff, Dr. Felix Adler, Michael Friedsam, the late Charles P. Steinmetz, Bernard M. Baruch, Arthur Williams and V.

Everit Macy. Mrs. Henry Moskowitz became secretary of the commission.

Announcing the personnel of this body, Smith asked the legislature, controlled by the Republican Party in both houses, to appropriate $75,000 for its expenses. The funds were available from several unspent sums previously set aside for patriotic purposes during the war. The commission swiftly demonstrated the nature of the work that it was doing and its great value to the State. The whole thing was, however, Smith's idea; so the master minds of the Republican Party refused to pass the appropriation. This meant, as a matter of fact, very little to the members of the commission. Several were men of wealth, and they paid the cost of the work out of their own pockets. Thus Smith, in the end, received sole credit for statutes that resulted in numerous reforms. The researches into taxation, alone, that the reconstruction commission completed were worth many times $75,000 to the State of New York.

The action of the majority party in this instance was repeated with regard to nearly every recommendation that Al Smith made. He urged, at about the same time, a popular referendum on the prohibition amendment, soon to be presented to the legislature for ratification. He suggested a scientific water-power policy. He asked for additional protection for child workers, for the creation of a minimum wage commission to pass upon the earnings of women and minors. Health and maternity insurance, he said, were essential to the welfare of the commonwealth. The cost of milk in New York was a menace to infant health. The State hospitals for the insane were in a deplorable condition. Candidates for public office should be required to file an accounting of their campaign receipts before, instead of after, elections, so that the public would be informed in time to take action at the polls. The prison problem needed attention.

A number of these ideas, it will be recalled, had been the subject of debate in the Constitutional Convention. Many had received Republican support at that time. Nearly all were sound. But now they had become tainted with the approval of Smith, not yet strong enough to break down the opposition, and so they died in committee without debate. In time Al forced enactment of some of these, and similar statutes. But he was, in 1919, a long way from being the figure that he has since become. Even in 1919, however, the Republican policy of obstruction had its effect in advancing the career of Smith; toward the close of the year he was editorially commended by the Springfield (Mass.) *Republican* for his management of the State government. Al used his veto power effectively from the start. He managed to slash about $2,000,000 from the general appropriation bill and vetoed most of the special measures advanced by country legislators and providing for bridges across the old mill stream. With these last he was very familiar. During his legislative days he had agreed to the passage of many similar bills in return for laws that Tammany Hall needed.

Much, it is true, of the Al Smith that was fast vanishing remained during 1919. He permitted Charles F. Murphy to come to Albany to reward organization workers who had brought about his election. A month after he took office he gave a reception at the Executive Mansion to the members of the legislature and delighted them by dancing a jig to the melody of "Tim Toolin' ". But almost at the same time he was recommending the abolition of fat counsel jobs in numerous State departments and pointing out that this work could easily be done by the Attorney General, the law officer of the State. Some of the men in these berths were his personal friends.

Early in March he was invited to preside at a meeting at the Metropolitan Opera House at which President Wilson was to speak on the League of Nations. It was the sort of function that Smith, prior to this time, had either not adorned at all or merely as a member of the audience. Former President Taft was among the platform dignitaries. Caruso was there to sing. There were as many dress shirts as at the opening of the operatic season.

But Al was superbly calm in the face of all this concentrated wealth and culture. He had the intelligence, so exceptional among chairmen, to make his introductory remarks brief. In presenting the President, who was about to sail back to France, he said:

"Whatever may be the cross-fire of opinion, there is one thing we are all agreed upon, and that is that America will not have completed her part in the great world conflict until she has done everything possible to prevent the recurrence of the death, the misery, the suffering, the waste and the devastation that from time immemorial has followed in the wake of war. At the Peace Conference to that task our President is applying his wonderful talents. He told the mothers of our country that they were giving up their sons not only that the world might be made safe for democracy but that there would never be another war. To the fulfillment of that promise he has dedicated himself with all his heart and all his soul and all his strength and all his great ability."

The 1919 session of the State legislature was not, to return to it for a moment, entirely barren of accomplishment. Summoned in special session by the Governor, the legislature ratified the suffrage amendment. It also passed several laws, upon recommendation of a legislative committee of which a Republican was chairman, to relieve the housing crisis in New York City. Meanwhile, as I have related at the beginning of this attempt to evaluate Smith, Hearst was beginning to beat his journalistic tom-toms in a war which was to bring greater luster to the name of Alfred E. Smith, with the milk situation in New York as the excuse for savage attacks. While he is meeting these attacks there will be time to relate how he came to be nominated in 1918 and the manner of campaign that he made.

Chapter Three

THE YEARS FROM 1915 TO 1917 DURING WHICH Smith was Sheriff of New York were, on the whole, uneventful. This official, it has been pointed out, no longer wears a tin badge or carries a gun. He has no police functions, but devotes his time to incarcerating miscreants who have neglected to pay lawful alimony, to making attachments in debt cases and to selling at mortgage properties that have reverted to the county because of non-payment of taxes. The chief excitement of the office until recently was tabulating the fees that poured in. Now, since it is on a salary basis, it does not provide even this diversion. Except for it Al spent his time growing accustomed to wearing a dress suit at the many political dinners to which he was invited. When he retired he is supposed to have salted away between $50,000 and $80,000.

Meanwhile Tammany was making preparations to persuade the public that Mayor Mitchel, whose term expired in 1917, had been a failure and that it would do well to elect some one else. It was at this point that Hearst stepped into the situation to support John F. Hylan, then a Brooklyn county judge. Smith might otherwise have had the nomination. Undoubtedly he would have accepted it and been elected. If this had happened, and if the history of other mayors of New York City means anything, his political career would probably have ended after a term or two in that office. For some reason it is a blind alley. Murphy, however, listened to Hearst and consented to endorse Hylan. To satisfy the growing Smith wing in Tammany he chose Al as candidate for President of the Board of Aldermen. The campaign that followed was about as low in quality as any in recent years; that is to say, it was as low as it could possibly be. The nation had been swept into the World War the previous April, with the result that patriotism became the chief issue.

"Judge Hylan," said Al Smith in one address, "is an American American who is going to lead us to an American victory."

Both the fusion group, working for Mitchel, and Tammany Hall gave orders that Liberty Bonds were to be peddled at all meetings and their forums opened to "Four Minute Men" and other patriotic talkers whose task it was to keep the home-fires burning. Hylan frequently abandoned his accusations concerning the "moneybund" that gripped the city to recall that his father had been a corporal in the Civil War. Somehow, though, the Mitchel forces were able to appear more loyal and more patriotic than Tammany and at last Murphy declared explosively that the Americanism talk was, in brief, the bunk. Besides, he said, "Al's father was killed in the Civil War in which Mayor Mitchel's father fought on the Confederate side". The next day he discovered that Smith's father had died quite peacefully in the late '80's.

It is recalled that Smith, except when he praised Hylan's Americanism, showed increasing ability as a campaigner during this contest. He was handicapped, however, by the fact that Hylan was the head of the ticket and received most of the publicity. Newspaper accounts of meetings frequently included a column of dull rambling by the mayoralty aspirant and merely a line at the end that "A. E. Smith, candidate for Aldermanic President, also spoke". Smith was opposed by Robert Adamson, now a banker and one of his supporters. Unusually able and convincing, Adamson was very effective, with the result that on Election Day Smith ran several thousand votes behind Hylan. The entire Tammany ticket was, however, elected.

Fortunately for his own happiness, for he soon discovered that Hylan was less than the great figure his own stump speeches had indicated, Smith was not required to remain a member of the administration for long. A few months after he took office, in January of 1918, up-State Democrats began to talk of him as a candidate for Governor. It is even said that Smith went personally to Murphy and demanded the nomination. The Tammany Boss, knowing that rural members of the party were suspicious of 14th Street, was wily enough to show little enthusiasm.

"Let the up-State leaders pick their man," he said in June. "Tammany Hall will help to elect him."

The State convention was scheduled for Saratoga Springs in July, and as the date drew near the decision of the up-State men to work for Smith was definite. This was largely due to rumors that Hearst was again in the field and to a justified apprehension that Tammany would again accept him, as it had done in 1906. In the end Smith was designated as the official choice of the party. The publisher abandoned his threat to run in the primaries and later gave newspaper assistance to the election of Smith. The prospects for Democratic success were moderately bright as the campaign opened. Governor Whitman had aroused antagonism by his obvious desire to run for President, while his services as District Attorney in New York, which had brought about his first term at Albany, had been forgotten. Al made an excellent campaign, drawing upon the detailed knowledge of the State machinery which he had gained during his long years in the legislature. His managers enlisted the assistance of followers of President Wilson, who had not yet fallen under the cloud of the League of Nations. Among the letters of endorsement which Al received was the following:

THE SECRETARY OF THE TREASURY
WASHINGTON

September 6, 1918.

DEAR MR. SMITH:

It gives me genuine pleasure to send you my warm congratulations upon your nomination as the Democratic candidate for Governor of the State of New York.

Your public career has qualified you, by training and experience, for this great office, and your ability and character fit you admirably for the discharge of its responsible duties.

All good wishes for your success. With kind regards, I am cordially yours,

W. G. McADOO.

Hon. Alfred E. Smith,
President, Board of Aldermen,
City of New York, N. Y.

Despite Smith's part in it, the campaign was not particularly exciting. The war made the bleatings of politicians seem even less important than usual and an epidemic of influenza kept even the most conscientious party members away from many of the campaign rallies. Smith enjoyed the opposition of the Anti-Saloon League, due to his wet record and to his platform demands that a referendum be held before the State ratified the prohibition amendment.

As to how he would conduct himself in office, he declared:

"Never in my political career have I permitted partisanship to swerve me from absolute loyalty to the people. The approval I have received from non-partisan organizations like the Citizens' Union attests this.—I will be subservient to no faction."

Which proves, of course, that Al's renown as a man with an amazing memory is exaggerated in some respects. The Citizens' Union had, it is true, endorsed him for Sheriff. But in its 1911 analysis of the members of the State legislature it said he had shown "not the slightest evidence of independence". In 1912 he had "on most issues of importance stood against the public interest". In 1913 he had "executed the orders of the machine" and had "opposed primary and election reforms".

Toward the close of the campaign, probably irritated by the cordiality with which his opponent was being featured in the newspapers, Whitman seems to have lost his head. Thinking of Smith's years on the public payrolls, he incautiously made the statement that the Democratic candidate "has never earned a dollar with his hands". Al's retort was obvious.

"When Whitman was an Amherst College student," he said, "I was working at the Fulton Fish Market, at the hardest work that any man could do. I started before sunrise and worked until dark."

Another excited assertion by Republican orators was that Smith's associations "have been among the lowest and vilest persons the nation could produce", that his appointments as Speaker of the Assembly had been crooks, that he had been friendly with thieves, pickpockets and other criminals. But the worst that Charles E. Hughes, a gentleman even when he makes a political speech, could say was:

"I distrust Tammany Hall even in its most amiable aspect."

Smith was elected by the small majority of 14,000 votes. The margin was narrow enough, considering Tammany's long reputation for dirty work, to justify a demand by Whitman for a recount. In the end, however, the Republican sent his congratulations and so far recovered from his ill-temper of the campaign to become an affable and charming host when the inaugural exercises were held. The Smith family moved to Albany on December 30, 1918, Al's forty-fifth birthday. Their arrival at the Union Station was very impressive. In addition to the Governor-elect and his wife there were five children. Walter, the youngest, was yanked along the platform by a huge Great Dane that was to be part of a constantly increasing menagerie at the Executive Mansion. As Smith stepped off the train, arriving members of the legislature rushed up to felicitate him. One or two timid new legislators looked with awe and respect at the man who, fifteen years before, had come to Albany no less forlorn than they now felt.

The Inaugural Ball, held the next night at the State Armory, was a strange function. As the Governor-elect appeared in his box the band played "Hail to the Chief" and then a series of melodies of old New York. Among these tunes was "The Sidewalks of New York", but this had, as yet, no sentimental meaning. It was the assortment of guests that made the party not a little grotesque. Tammany Hall had turned out in full force and there were hundreds of old neighbors from the East Side, many wearing dress suits which they had hired on Canal Street. Mr. and Mrs. James Colombo, Jimmy Kelly, Solly Bernstein, Michael Kuku and Dr. Paul Sarrubbi, all from the Fourth Ward, rubbed elbows with the Dutch aristocracy of Albany, which had condescended to attend in order to smile behind its hand at this roughneck who had become Governor. Mrs. William Bayard Van Rensselaer had her first close view of Charles F. Murphy, Mrs. Murphy and their daughter, Miss Mabel Murphy. Tom Foley circulated around, shaking hands indiscriminately, and beaming that the young man whom he had assisted to rise in life had already done so well. Al Smith, surrounded by his family, was magnificently at ease.

Among those seated in the box of the Governor-elect was his mother, a little old lady in black silk who was white of face and very proud. To a few intimate friends she shyly exhibited a picture post-card, now growing yellow. It was a scene of the Executive Mansion which Al had sent to her in 1904, the year when he began his duties as an Assemblyman. The message on the back read:

"Dear Mother: This is a picture of the Governor's residence. I'm going to work hard and stick to the ideals you taught me and some day—maybe—I'll occupy this house."

Chapter Four

So much has been said during the last four or five years on the expertness of Alfred E. Smith in the governmental machinery of New York that there is danger, I suspect, of forgetting facts about the man which are potentially more important. If Smith is merely to be reëlected for repeated terms to the post he now holds it is enough that he is a politician of great skill, who understands his duties far better than have most of his predecessors. But this, it can be argued, makes him little more fit for the presidency than does Henry Ford's knowledge of industry. Every department at Albany or Washington has some expert of inestimable worth in his own line, but with a horizon limited by the problems concerned with highways, taxation, agriculture or Hopi snake dances.

Certainly an appreciation of Al Smith must go behind his undoubted competency as Governor. It may be true that a mind such as his, which has so thoroughly mastered the State government, will have slight difficulty with national matters. But it is not necessary to make conjecture regarding certain facets of his mind which, it is my theory, now receive less attention than they deserve. It is these which have caused him to enunciate principles that carry weight far beyond the boundaries of New York. Among the principles in this classification are his belief in the social importance of welfare legislation and his insistence upon executive responsibility. Most striking of all, for Smith is by no means an outstanding liberal but a conservative with a liberal mind, is his consistent defense of the rights of minorities. So has he spoken in behalf of Socialists and more extreme radicals with whose views he is, himself, in utter disagreement. As head of the nation he would, I think, discourage imperialistic tendencies fostered by business men greedy for the natural resources of feeble nations. He would use his influence and his veto to prevent sporadic bursts of discriminatory legislation against aliens.

As the year 1919 began the United States was shaken by apprehensions that an appreciable part of its foreign population was in direct communication with Moscow and that overthrow of the government by Bolsheviks wearing beards and carrying bombs was under serious consideration. Big Business led the onslaught against radical, even liberal, thought. Through chambers of commerce and other service organizations it began a drive against the Red Menace. Funds poured into the National Security League and the National Defense Society. The federal government became infected and sent secret agents out by the hundred to regard with suspicion, and arrest, if possible, every one who spoke with a foreign accent.

There were, it must be admitted, a number of incidents that partially justified the general panic. Several bomb outrages occurred and the Department of Justice, in its raids, uncovered tons of inflammatory literature. Even Al Smith, in an address at Cornell University in June of 1919, dwelt on the dangers of radicalism. But the ardor of the radical chasers was out of all proportion to the actual danger, and one result of the persecution was outspoken resentment on the part of voters in the congested sections of New York City. To give voice to this they elected five Socialist Assemblymen in the fall of the year. These men were legally elected beyond any question. They represented the honest choice of their constituencies. But when they arrived at Albany for the 1920 session they were branded, by virtue of the right of the Assembly to pass on the qualifications of its members, ineligible to serve. The Republican Party, it is probably unnecessary to remark, was in control of the House. Governor Smith fought with energy to prevent the expulsion of the Socialists and indicated his own position by inviting the five men to a reception at the Executive Mansion. He was, however, powerless, although he called a special election that fall so that the five assembly districts would be represented at a special session of the legislature. All of the five so-called Reds were reëlected. In commenting on the ouster Smith voiced his own conception of a democracy:

"Although I am unalterably opposed to the fundamental principles of the Socialist Party, it is inconceivable that a minority party, duly constituted and legally organized, should be deprived of its right to expression so long as it has honestly, by lawful methods of education and propaganda, succeeded in securing representation, unless the chosen representatives are unfit as individuals.

"It is true that the Assembly has arbitrary power to determine the qualifications of its membership; but where arbitrary power exists it should be exercised with care and discretion because from it there is no appeal.

"If the majority party at present in control of the Assembly possesses information that leads them to believe that these men are hostile to our form of Government and would overthrow it by processes subversive of law and order, these charges in due form should have been presented to the legislature and these men tried by orderly processes. Meanwhile, presumably innocent unless proven guilty, they should have been allowed to retain their seats.

"Our faith in American democracy is confirmed not only by its results, but by its methods and organs of free expression. They are the safeguards against revolution. To discard the methods of representative government leads to the misdeeds of the very extremists we denounce . . . and serves to increase the number of the enemies of orderly free government."

The 1920 legislature spent most of the session, however, at the business of scotching Bolsheviks to the neglect of everything else except appropriation bills. It passed laws, ultimately vetoed by Smith, which permitted teachers to be questioned regarding their loyalty, and dismissed from the service unless they could prove themselves 100 per cent Americans. Another patriotic enactment required that private schools must submit their courses of study to State officials. A third gave the Attorney General power to initiate proceedings against radical candidates for office before the Appellate Division of the Supreme Court. No more vicious or more ridiculous measure than this last has ever, probably, been sent to a Governor for his signature. In his prompt veto, Smith again outlined his theories of government:

"This bill would place upon one particular appellate division of the supreme court of this State . . . the duty of deciding upon the validity of the political principles advocated by any party in the State. Its determination would be final and controlling. To its members would be permitted the despotic power to strike from the ballots the candidates of any party. The tests which it would be compelled to apply would, of necessity, be not legal but political tests. The bill would throw a high appellate court into the very midst of political controversy. This alone would require its disapproval, but to this one objection must be added an even more vital and far-reaching one.

"The bill would confer upon this small body of men, perhaps of one political faith, the absolute power in effect to disenfranchise hundreds of thousands of voters. It may even exercise this unheard-of power upon the faith of affidavits, without ever hearing a witness. A few judges elected in one part of the State, and assigned to the appellate division of their department, would have the power to keep from the ballot all candidates of whose parties they disapproved. . . . If unpopular minorities are to be deprived of their basic rights to representation upon the ballot they will, indeed, have conferred upon them a just claim to political martyrdom. The very evils of ultra-radicalism which are feared by the proponents of this measure would, in my opinion, be infinitely enhanced if the bill became law.

". . . In a State just as in a legislative body, the majority need no protection, for they can protect themselves. Law in a democracy means the protection of the rights and liberties of the minority. Their rights, when properly exercised, and their liberties, when not abused, should be safeguarded. It is a confession of the weakness of our own faith in the righteousness of our cause when we attempt to suppress by law those who do not agree with us. I cannot approve a bill which confers upon three judges, learned though they be, but nevertheless human, the power to disenfranchise any body of our citizens."

So with the other two bills, the loyalty tests for teachers and the proposal to regulate private schools, the veto messages were statesmanlike papers now nearly forgotten. Critics of Smith may say that he had assistance from persons more learned than himself in drafting them, that they bear marks of the polishing touch of Mrs. Moskowitz. Even if this is true, it makes no difference. This East Side politician, who has never had the desire to read, looks deeply and wisely into the principles of government. Those that are right he seems intuitively to adopt for his own.

The teachers' loyalty test, said Smith in placing his veto on it, provided that every public school teacher in the State must obtain from the Commissioner of Education a certificate showing good moral character, intention to support the State and federal constitutions and a pledge that he is "loyal to the institutions and laws thereof". The certificate can be revoked by the Commissioner without a hearing. The test, said Smith, is not what the teacher teaches, but what he believes.

"It permits," he said, "one man to place upon any teacher the stigma of disloyalty and this even without hearing or trial. No man is so omniscient or wise as to have entrusted to him such arbitrary power not only to condemn any individual teacher but to decree what belief or opinion is opposed to what he deems to be the institutions of the country.

"No teacher could continue to teach if he or she entertained any objection, however conscientious, to any existing institution. If this law had been in force prior to the abolition of slavery, opposition to that institution which was protected by the Constitution and its laws would have been just cause for the disqualification of a teacher.

"Opposition to any presently established institution . . . would be sufficient to disqualify the teacher. Every teacher would be at the mercy of his colleagues, his pupils and their parents, and any word or act of the teacher might be held by the Commissioner to indicate an attitude hostile to some of 'the institutions of the United States' or of the State. . . . The bill . . . deprives teachers of their right to freedom of thought, it limits the teaching staff of the public schools to those who lack the courage or the mind to exercise their legal right to just criticism of existing institutions."

In disapproving the proposal to license private schools, Smith said that it gave to the Board of Regents power to withdraw its approval in the event that the course of instruction was "detrimental to the public interest". Schools under the guidance of the Roman Catholic or other churches were exempted from the provisions of the law.

"It is unthinkable," he said, "that in a representative democracy there should be relegated to any body of men the absolute power to prohibit the teaching of any subject of which it may disapprove.

"This bill seeks to bring within the power of prohibition of the Board of Regents every subject, political, ethical, religious or scientific. Under its provision they might decree that it was inimical to the public interest to give instruction on the theory of the single tax, on minimum wage, on child labor laws, and on public regulation of industry. . . . The free play of public opinion, resting upon freedom of instruction and discussion within the limits of the law, would be destroyed and we should have the whole sphere of education reduced to a formula prescribed by governmental agency.

"The clash of conflicting opinions, from which progress arises more than from any other source, would be abolished by law; tolerance and intellectual freedom destroyed and an intellectual autocracy imposed upon the people. . . . . The safety of this government and its institutions rests upon the reasoned and devoted loyalty of its people."

But a large number of earnest gentlemen, most of them paid for their services, continued to batter at the Bolshevik man of straw that they themselves had erected. In 1920 the Republican Party succeeded in electing Nathan L. Miller to the Governorship and the following year the bills regulating teachers and private schools became law. In 1923 Smith returned to the Capitol. In his first message to the legislature he demanded the repeal of these statutes. By this time the hysteria had abated to a certain extent and he was successful. I quote from his message:

"I am firm in my belief that the law . . . which requires the teachers of our public schools to submit to a loyalty test is a direct violation of the letter and spirit of the laws of our State, unless you are prepared to take the stand that this great army of useful public servants is incapable of being responsible for the abuse of their rights. . . . It is wrong in principle. It is a violation of the spirit of our Constitution and it is an unwarranted interference with freedom of opinion—one of the foundation stones of democratic government. Throughout the history of the world, where people have allowed the government to think for them, the government has been unsuccessful. Part of the success of America lies in the undisputed fact that the government permits the people to think for themselves.

"Equally vicious is the law . . . which provides for licensing and supervising private schools. While ostensibly for the purpose of safeguarding the traditions of our country, its real effect is to weaken them by abridging the fundamental right of the people to enjoy full liberty in the domain of idea and speech. . . . Liberty and the pursuit of happiness cannot be said to be safeguarded in a community that delegates to anybody the absolute power to prohibit the teaching of any subject of which they may disapprove."

I have quoted at such great length from these messages and statements by Alfred E. Smith because they throw so much light on a side of his character often, as I have said, forgotten. It is far more important that he will speak out against laws that abridge freedom of thought than for him to reorganize the State departments, worthwhile as that may be. Viewed as a presidential possibility, it is well that he has sympathy and tolerance for the beliefs of those with whom he does not agree. I doubt that Al Smith has read a line of Voltaire. But with Voltaire he can exclaim: "I do not agree with a word that you say, but I will defend to the death your right to say it".

One of Governor Smith's first acts during his second term as Governor was to pardon the famous "Jim" Larkin, who had served two years in prison for advocating criminal anarchy. Larkin had joined in the promulgation of a manifesto which called for a change in the form of government to that of "a dictatorship by the proletariat". This was to be achieved by strikes general enough to force political action. In his pardon message, Smith said, in part:

"My present action in no way involves the slightest agreement with this manifesto. I condemn the dictatorship of 'the proletariat', of the farmers, of the capitalists, of the merchants or of any other section of the community. In a free democracy we know no dictatorships and we endure none. No group has any legal, social or moral right to impose by dictatorship its views or interests on any other group. Likewise I condemn the project to coerce political action by any such method as the calling of general strikes. Labor has the right to strike for the purpose of securing reasonable improvement of its own conditions, but not for the purpose of driving other groups into the acceptance of a proposed political dictatorship. I disapprove such a project just as I would disapprove a combination of capitalists or of manufacturers to constrain political action of the laborers or the farmers by withholding from them the means of procuring the necessaries of life.

"I pardon Larkin, therefore, not because of agreement with his views, but despite my disagreement with them.

"The public assertion of an erroneous doctrine is perhaps the surest way to disclose the error and make it evident to the electorate. And it is a distinct dis-service of the State to impose, for the utterance of a misguided opinion, such extreme punishment as may tend to deter, in proper cases, that full and free discussion of political issues which is a fundamental of democracy."

Chapter Five

A POLITICAL CAMPAIGN INVARIABLY BRINGS OUT the worst in even the best of men. It is a little difficult to explain why this is so, but probably it is partly because the average campaign strategist has, at heart, a very low opinion of the intelligence of the public. He directs his candidate, of course, to dwell in all his speeches upon the extrordinary brilliance of the electorate and particularly upon the super-intelligence of the section of it that belongs to the party. But when the strategist has summoned the Supreme Council to secret conference, he urges a course of action based on the assumption that those who vote are lower in mental capacity than the State legislature of Mississippi. The party platform that is laboriously drafted says nothing at all in the most obscure and elegant manner. The issues chosen are likely to be either bogus or ones about which there is not the slightest interest. The Supreme Council shies from any really vital question, such as prohibition at the present time, as does J. P. Morgan from a newspaper reporter. If the platforms they adopt are a criterion, campaign managers are confirmed pessimists who believe the electorate universally feeble-minded.

Perhaps they are not far wrong. Certainly there are incidents in the history of the land, too painful to enumerate, that give weight to their theories. I offer in rebuttal, however, the thought that occasionally the striking career of some one man shows that campaign commanders have been in error. Alfred E. Smith has demonstrated that voters of both the major parties will flock to support a candidate of character and proved worth, despite an official party platform of negation. The Democrats, for instance, are going to argue themselves into many a headache before 1928 trying to write a prohibition plank that will delight the drys as well as the west. But if they select Smith as their candidate, his own wetness will be the basis of judgment by the voters. A dry plank will, perhaps, disgust a great many people, but it will fool very few.

Exceptional among politicians as he has been, however, even Al Smith must give way to profound melancholy if he reads over some of the campaign orations that he has made in the past. In 1920, it will be recalled, he ran against Nathan L. Miller for Governor and was defeated. In 1922 he again opposed the same Republican and was elected. Miller, too, is a man possessed of intelligence. But the campaigns of both frequently descended to the level of aldermanic contests. The first contest was befogged by the fact that it was a presidential year. The Democratic state platform, in consequence, was a senseless document calling for recognition of the mythical Irish Republic, modification of the Volstead Act and endorsing the reference in the national platform to the League of Nations, but avoiding mention on its own responsibility of that obnoxious parliament.

Judge Miller, under orders from the Republican High Command, devoted most of his time to national issues and drew to his bosom those who believed the League of Nations was conceived by the Devil, the British and the selfish governments of Europe. He also won the support of the rapidly increasing number who were to cast their ballots more as a protest against Wilsonism than as indication of admiration for Harding and Coolidge, of whom they knew little and cared less. Smith's appeals for a State campaign on such State issues as welfare laws, the executive budget and the reorganization of departments were largely futile. And so, in turn, the Democratic gubernatorial candidate made long speeches defending Article X. On the whole the Republican plan appears to have been fairly smart, although the defeat that Smith suffered seems, looking back, to have been one of his greatest victories. He ran some 1,000,000 votes ahead of the national ticket in the State. The margin of his defeat was only 74,000, proof of the vast number of voters who had split their tickets to elect a Republican President and a Democratic Governor.

Nor was the 1922 campaign much more intelligent. Miller had been in office for two years and deserved a drubbing on one issue more than all the others combined; that he had sanctioned laws in mockery of freedom of thought and education. Two years previous, as I have quoted, Smith had vetoed these measures in language that was vivid in its force and that approached the profound in its understanding of the ideals of true democracy. But in his campaign he barely touched on these matters. Instead, he devoted hours to emulating Mayor Hylan and denouncing Miller as the tool of wealth, the friend of the public utility companies, a dictator and a czar who believed that the governor should be the supreme ruler of the State. My point is not so much that these accusations were untrue. Miller's subsequent connection with the United States Steel Corporation, where he was close to the late and very loquacious Elbert Gary, and his work as counsel to the New York city traction companies, are indicative of his corporation philosophy. But I think Al chose in them a lesser issue, flavored with demagoguery and calculated to be more effective in arousing the moron public.

Miller was just as bad. He called Smith's two years as governor the most expensive in the history of the State, a naïve assertion in view of the fact that a Republican legislature had controlled both houses and had approved appropriation bills from which Al had slashed several millions of dollars. He boasted of his own great works at Albany and refrained from mentioning the mysterious manner in which the amendments for consolidation of State departments, once officially approved by the G.O.P., had been permitted to die. Both men were anxious to ignore prohibition, and if Smith said anything about repealing the State enforcement act, an issue which later was to prove most distressing, his remarks on the subject are lost in the mists of time.

After his defeat by Miller in 1920, Smith was fortunate in the offer to become chairman of the United States Trucking Corporation. Discussed by some of the newspapers, but not by Tammany Hall, which planned to renominate Hylan as the next mayor of New York, Al declared that he did not intend to run again for public office. He did not, however, really mean this and few were convinced. While he was still at Albany he began to consider what he would do to make a living when his term expired. The choice of a job was a ticklish matter. He had many offers, naturally, since a former Governor of the standing and talent of Smith is a big asset to any large corporation anxious to win public approbation. Most of them were out of the question, since his private life was to be but temporary. If he allied himself with the usual financial interests, Smith knew, valuable ammunition would be placed in the hands of future Republican spellbinders. Connection with a great bank, for which he was eligible because of his knowledge of State banking matters, was obviously impossible. Thus he was delighted when some old friends approached him with the suggestion that he head the United States Trucking Corporation, which they controlled. The post was ideal, even though the company had a capitalization of over half a million dollars, owned several thousand trucks and was, by any other rule except the illogical one of politics, Big Business at its biggest. For Al Smith, whose father had been a truckman and who had dabbled in the art himself, the job was poetic in its suitability. Sam Koenig and the other mentalities of the G.O.P. could never make an issue out of Smith the Truckman, even though his work was exclusively executive and paid $30,000 a year.

Al had rather a huge time during those two years. He enjoyed the reunion with his neighbors on Oliver Street. For the first time since he had been Sheriff he was free from financial tribulations. It is in harmony with his love for action that he was not content to draw his salary for acting as window dressing, as he might easily have done. He bustled around in pursuit of new business with the energy of a young and ambitious salesman. One of his visits in this new rôle was, as it happened, to win him a measure of political support of great value during his subsequent terms as Governor.

He learned, in some manner, that there was a chance of doing the trucking for the New York *Sun*, *Herald* and *Telegram*, three newspapers captured by Frank A. Munsey and still permitted to live. He did some figuring and decided that the United States Trucking Corporation could save the publisher-grocer-capitalist some money. The job of carting the huge rolls of newsprint that must be delivered daily to a newspaper plant is a lucrative one for a trucking concern.

Arriving at No. 280 Broadway, the office of the *Sun* and the *Herald*, Smith must have sent in his card with some misgivings. Munsey had urged the election of Miller in the campaign the previous fall. His editorial policies had been contrary to nearly everything that the Democrats had fought for. Al had often heard from his Albany newspaper friends of the degree to which Munsey was despised by the profession because of his industry in destroying newspapers and for his unpleasant whims that often resulted in the discharge of subordinates who were too fat, or too young, or too old, or who were left-handed.

But on this occasion Munsey differed from the popular conception of a man cold and narrow, and the experience enjoyed by Smith indicates that there was a side to him, usually hidden, that could be gracious and broadminded. He looked up with interest as Al sat down. Just what was it that he wanted?

"We'd like," said Smith, using a trucking phrase that he had already picked up, "to ride your newsprint. We can save you money. I've got some—"

But Munsey interrupted.

"Let's talk about politics," he suggested.

For two hours they did so. Astonished for only an instant, Al launched into a dissertation on matters still far closer to his heart than trucking contracts or any other means of making a living. He told of what he had tried to do during his first term at Albany and described the theory behind State reorganization. Then he outlined the desperate needs of the State hospitals. He may have hinted that if he became Governor again he would press for huge bond issues to remedy conditions which placed wards of the State in danger of death by fire and hindered effective cures. Munsey listened attentively and with apparent appreciation. As Smith arose to leave he gave orders, without waiting for the carefully prepared cost figures, that all of his business should go to the United States Trucking Corporation.

In due time Smith went back to Albany for the three terms that caused him to become a national figure. Munsey never went so far as to recommend his election as against the Republican candidate. But he repeatedly gave assistance to the Governor's program in the face of otherwise unified Republican opposition. Then, in 1926, he died. Editorial writers, some of whom had worked for Munsey and hated him, wrote stilted columns of praise on a career that they really viewed with contempt. But Smith was able to send an appreciation to the *Sun* that was sincere, for during six years the publisher had continued the friendly attitude that had so unexpectedly resulted from the visit to obtain a trucking contract.

"Frequently," he wrote, "when I came down from Albany I had luncheon or dinner with Mr. Munsey and in many such informal meetings, with a variety of topics under discussion, it never failed to come to this point in his mind—'Is that the best thing to do and the right thing to do?' . . . I say truthfully that I have felt rewarded richly for much of my hardest work as Governor by the warm, honest, confidential friendship of Frank Munsey."

Munsey, Smith revealed, had always declined public recognition for his assistance in the furtherance of State projects. He had given his aid to the passage of the $100,000,000 bond issue for public improvements and had been largely responsible for the passage of laws which, it is now hoped, will wipe out the tenements of lower New York. In one letter that he had written, Smith said, Munsey had expressed himself as having small use for either of the two large political parties and had indicated that he remained a Republican because this organization "fits my point of view least badly".

Chapter Six

No governor in all the history of the State of New York has gone to Albany under happier circumstances than did Al Smith on January 1, 1923. That summer at Syracuse he had fought single-handed against Hearst and a Tammany Hall that had been cowed into subjection by the publisher-politician. He had emerged from the convention victorious in his defeat of the Hearst-Murphy combination and immeasurably stronger because he had demonstrated that he would never again, in all likelihood, bow to the demands of men he despised. He was unquestionably, for all the grumbling that the feeble intellects of 14th Street might do, the leader of the Democratic Party in New York; a man whose obligation was now to the people who had elected him and not to the organization which had given him his start.

It is not to be wondered that Smith, as early as 1923, was filled with justifiable pride in himself. He had received almost 1,400,000 votes in the election that fall; about 400,000 more than Miller. It was a record majority, made up in no small measure by the support of up-State residents who under normal circumstances vote the straight Republican ticket. Another happy factor in the situation as Smith began his second term was the control by the Democrats of the Senate, which meant that Jimmy Walker would become majority leader and would battle with infinite skill for the pet projects of the Governor. The majority, it is true, was but a single vote, which makes the task of a leader precarious in the extreme. But this, to so versatile a parliamentarian as the present mayor of New York, was ample. His floor leadership of the upper house during the sessions of 1923 and 1924 was a constant source of worry to the Republicans. Because of it, Smith forced through several measures which otherwise would have remained buried in committee. The G.O.P. was following its consistent policy of obstruction which was, in the long run, to prove of such great benefit to the career of Al Smith.

There was, since no one knew that the Mullan-Gage act would be repealed, only one cloud on the azure sky. One morning the legislative correspondents found a very bothered Smith, surrounded by check stubs and personal account books.

"I'm trying to figure out my income tax," he said, mournfully. "I have to pay a tax on the $30,000 I earned last year from the $10,000 salary I get as Governor. Trying to do that would give any guy a headache."

In emphasizing the new strength of Smith in

1923, it would be unfair to give the impression that he had shown no independence during his first term. He went to Albany with a profound sense of obligation. He has often said that he was determined to show that an East Side resident, a life-long member of Tammany, could be a strong executive. And if he permitted Boss Murphy to suggest many appointments, there were others of primary importance that he made on merit alone. The most striking of these, perhaps, was the selection of Colonel Frederick Stuart Greene, who had been in charge of road repair work in the American occupation areas in France, for the office of Commissioner of Highways. Colonel Greene is an engineer of ability who, although nominally a Democrat, has been extremely casual in his political allegiance. His reputation among politicians was demonstrated at the time of his appointment when pop-eyed Democrats ran to the Governor giving yelps of protest. Smith also deserves credit for making Miss Frances Perkins a member of the Industrial Commission in 1919, in the face of protests that she was somewhat radical, and for redesignating Justice Frank C. Laughlin to the Appellate Division of the Supreme Court in the First Department, although he was a Republican and the action gave that party a majority of the members of the court. Al has, it should be noted, frequently resisted Tammany pressure to throw the courts into politics. In describing the origin and cause of his quarrel with Hearst, I have detailed his refusal to take appointive recommendations from the publisher.

In 1919 and 1920, even in 1923 and 1924, Smith was not yet as concerned with fitness as he was to become in later years. His growth in the selection of men qualified by knowledge and talent for their posts has been gradual. It was at the beginning of 1927, elected for a fourth term, that the Governor wounded his former Tammany intimates most deeply by announcing that his cabinet, created by the State reorganization plan, would consist of eight Democrats and six Republicans. The so-called Republicans included George Graves, once secretary to the Governor and still serving in that capacity, but given the title of "Head of the Executive Department"; Robert Moses, Secretary of State; Commissioner Alexander MacDonald of the Conservation Department, Commissioner Byrne A. Pyrke of the Department of Agriculture and Markets, Dr. Frank P. Graves of the Department of Education, and Charles S. Johnson, director of State Charities.

The announcement of this cabinet was greeted with some skepticism by the critics of the Governor, particularly the Republican critics who are afraid that he will become the Democratic candidate for President. Their disparaging remarks about these gentlemen not being Republicans, in the pure sense, at all, but debauched "Al Smith Republicans", were almost as frequent as statements of a similar nature by the lads of Tammany Hall. Smith, they repeated, had his eye on the glories of the White House and was trying to build up the fantastic theory that he had never committed a partisan act. They concluded with the assertion that he could not boast regarding the Republicanism of Dr. Graves and Commissioner Pyrke, for the reason that these two officials are chosen by the legislature and not by the Governor.

Among all the appointments that Al Smith has made, however, there is none more worth-while than that of Colonel Greene in 1919. Even while a member of the legislature, Smith had been irritated by the ardor of the Elder Statesmen in manipulating the highway problem. When possible he had blocked Republican schemes to build satin roads to the wilderness homes of up-state legislators, or to gratify their districts by the construction of boulevards over which constituents might drive their hogs. Consequently he selected Colonel Greene to take charge and instructed him that politicians were to be viewed with a glassy eye. Ever since, through changes in his department which have annually placed heavier burdens on his shoulders, Greene has been in command. He has spent hundreds of millions without incurring, despite scholarly researches into his record, the vaguest charge of graft or incompetence. He is hated by the machine men of both parties, is not bothered by that in the slightest, and spends his leisure hours writing short stories.

Despite Republican obstruction, Smith was able to accomplish a good deal during his second term. In addition to repealing the laws inspired by fear of Bolshevism he obtained passage of statutes controlling motor traffic, limiting rents in the congested areas of the cities of the State and providing referenda by the voters on bond issues authorizing $300,000,000 for grade crossing removal, $50,000,000 for State hospital improvements and $15,000,000 for State parks. His greatest triumph was accomplished during 1924: the reduction of taxes by a total of about $17,000,000. Besides being financially sound, the Governor's action was political witchcraft of the sort that left the G.O.P. shuddering.

"I believe," he said in his January message, "that it is a very great mistake to take from the taxpayers in any one year more than is needed for the actual conduct of the government, always leaving a safe reserve in the bank in case of trouble. I am satisfied after a comparison of the State's resources, plus the clear surplus over and above commitments, taking account of fixed charges and making allowances for progressing other public work of a special nature, that there can be a substantial reduction in the State income tax, to every person paying it, for at least this year."

The amount of the reduction, the Governor recommended, should be 25 per cent. His suggestion was generally applauded, but nothing was done; for the obvious reason that the greater the sums in the treasury the more would be available for local improvements in rural districts. Besides, the Republican leaders knew, the income tax was more obnoxious to the city than the country sections. Toward the end of the session, however, the leaders were told with emphasis that their plan to use the surplus for vote-producing appropriations was futile because the Governor intended to veto all of them. They passed the income tax cut with reluctance.

Then Smith, the city man theoretically uninterested in levies on real estate, sprang a surprise that was to win for him widespread approbation in upstate communities. Still further reductions were possible, he announced. These should be in the form of a 25 per cent slash in the direct tax. To this, of course, the befuddled country cousins could offer no objection and they stampeded to approve the bill. The saving was about $8,700,000 in each case. The inability of Al's opponents to perceive when they are beaten is, I have said, amazing. The tax reduction was for the current year, only. The next year Smith found that the same lower rates were possible and he again urged them. It was not, however, until protests began to arrive in every mail that they again passed the bill. Then Al received all of the credit.

Chapter Seven

The tale of Smith as governor grows, perhaps, monotonous in its repetition of nomination by acclaim, vigorous campaigning, reëlection and then victory over an obstructionist Republican legislature. In 1924 he defeated young Theodore Roosevelt, whose chief claim to the governorship was an excellent record as a member of the A.E.F. and whose campaign meetings were featured by the presence of local veterans on the platform, Gold Star mothers, flags and bands playing the more polite melodies of the war his father had been eager to manage for America. Two years later the G.O.P. discovered most of its notables strangely reluctant to join the ranks of those who had been defeated by Al in gubernatorial contests. At last, however, it found a candidate in Ogden L. Mills, a gentleman of wealth and social position who at the moment was a member of the House of Representatives and reputed to be an intimate of the Silent Man of the White House. Now that Mr. Mills, like Whitman, Miller and Young Teddy, has joined the Licked-by-Al Smith-for-Governor Club, he is serving his party and the nation as first assistant at Washington to

Andrew Mellon, "the greatest Secretary of the Treasury since Alexander Hamilton".

"Beat Smith now and you will not have to beat him in 1928" was the unofficial slogan of the Republican strategists in the 1926 State campaign. Having failed to accomplish this laudable purpose, and aware that 1928 is rushing toward them at a fearful speed, these same gentlemen are now issuing statements to the effect that Smith is obviously the last candidate that the Democrats will nominate. They consent to frequent interviews in which they point out that no party would be so absurd as to jeopardize even a remote chance of winning the presidency by naming a man handicapped by being wet, a Catholic and a member of Tammany Hall. In the 1926 contest, however, the watchword aroused the party's workers to unprecedented heat and industry. Mills himself, there is slight doubt, would have preferred to lecture on such high class issues as extravagance, inefficiency on the part of Smith, and the dangerous evils of a water-power development program which threatened to limit the exploitation of hydroelectric projects by private interests. It must have been extremely distasteful to him, a man whose home had never been contaminated by yellow newspapers, to hear that the moribund Hearst, as a final gesture in the New York political scheme, had published another blast against Smith and had announced his support of the Republican candidate. Mills successfully suppressed, however, any urge of his better nature to reject this support. He even permitted his managers to hand him that ancient Hearst issue—Bad Milk in New York!

He stumped up and down the State making exactly the sort of speeches that he had so often heard ridiculed in the more exclusive New York clubs. He screamed that the milk in New York was "deficient in butter fats", and cited laboratory tests, made at the order of the Republican State Committee, to prove it. In the Hearst papers and in other journals appeared the old, wild headlines of "poisoned milk", although the Republican nominee had never gone that far in his accusations. This barnstorming, typical of Hearst and Hylan and the Tammany Hall of a former day, had its effect on the mass mind and toward the end of October it seemed possible that Mills might win. Then the milk issue blew up utterly when the very scientists hired by the G.O.P. were forced to admit that their tests had disclosed only that the city's milk supply was at least the equal of that in other parts of the State. Last-minute yells from Sam Koenig's men that Tammany had villainously corrupted those who had made the tests were without effect, so Mr. Mills tossed in his sleep and wondered how large would be Al's majority this time.

The Al Smith who in 1926 was, for the fifth time, the nominee of his party for the highest office in the State had grown enormously in stature from the man who eight years before had eagerly accepted designation to run against Whitman. Statesmen, who for months have pulled wires and made bargains in order to obtain a nomination, frequently deny in public that they are candidates and assert that they will consent to run only "if drafted by the people". But it was really true, in 1926, that Smith was forced to run; first by his ambitions for the presidency and second because the Democrats had no other candidate of merit. Smith, I have said, was a vastly different figure in 1926 than he had been in 1918, for the reason that in the intervening years there had been pregnant changes. The most important of these, obviously, was the death early in 1924 of Charles F. Murphy. This seemed an appalling blow to Tammany and weeks passed, filled with bitter quarrels, before his successor had been chosen. To Smith it meant the loss of a skilled manipulator; but it also meant quite definitely a step upward in his own standing. With Murphy in command he always faced the possibility that the Murphy-Hearst conspiracy of 1922 might be repeated. Al had been a young and totally obscure politician when Murphy had become the Boss, and the memory of those days could never be entirely dispelled. The selection of George W. Olvany as head of Tammany placed, of course, a different emphasis on things. Here was no figure once viewed, from the lowest ranks, as the embodiment of all power. Olvany was Smith's contemporary, already in his debt. In 1915, as Sheriff, Al had made him his counsel.

Thus it was not Olvany, but Al Smith, who was the Boss of the State convention, again held at Syracuse, in September of 1926. His was the omnipotent presence that stalked through the hotel lobby to a suite from which came peremptory orders. Behind him stretched the years of his achievement in the State. In the dim past was his work in the Constitutional Convention, with its endorsement by Republican leaders of prominence. The foundation of his might lay in his series of victories: the defeat of Whitman in 1918, his personal triumph in 1920 when he polled an amazing vote although he lost to Miller, his come-back in 1922 when he ran far ahead of this same candidate, and his victory over the flag-waving Teddy in 1924. It rested, too, in the still vivid memories of 1922, when Tammany had betrayed him for Hearst and had then retreated in the presence of courage. The boys had not forgotten that the year previous, 1925, Smith had turned against Hylan and had forced the nomination of Jimmy Walker. They knew that McLaughlin, already hated in his job of Police Commissioner of New York, was Al's man and therefore unassailable, despite his nasty attitude toward politicians seeking favors. They knew, finally, that Al Smith and no other would select this time the ticket to run with him and the platform on which Democracy would make its appeal to the voters.

All of this Smith did, harshly and arrogantly with his coat off, his collar wilted and his shirt wet with perspiration. There was a sporadic insurgent movement in the shape of two candidates for minor State offices. Buffalo, Syracuse and Albany, ruled Al sharply, must be represented on the ticket and it was the privilege of the bosses of those communities to pick their men. The insurgents slunk off. Then the wise ones from Tammany, Olvany among them, objected to a platform plank endorsing the entrance of the United States into the World Court. This, they said, smacked of the League of Nations and would bring brickbats from the Irish. But Smith, probably so advised by Mrs. Moskowitz, insisted that the plank go in. It did, and he gained thereby a talking point in the event that he runs for the presidency in 1928.

Long before the campaign against Mills in 1926, Smith had reacted from his inclination, on first becoming more than a ward politician, toward platform formality. All the old sprightliness is there, and much of the flavor of the East Side. Consciously now, instead of despite himself, he resorts to tricks of the stage. Sometimes he is effective to a degree that is startling and an address becomes as fascinating as a Broadway show. Laughter strides the boards with Al Smith; "Laughter and applause", as the hurrying stenographers who record his speeches phrase it.

He spent most of the afternoon of October 30, 1926, laboring on an address to be made that night at the Metropolitan Opera House. It was the last important speech of the campaign and those unfamiliar with Smith's present methods might have supposed that it was to be long and tedious. But preparation on the part of the Al of to-day does not mean boredom for his audience.

"I will take for my text," he said that night, grinning his old grin, "the subject of 'The Republican Dilemma' or 'Looking for an Issue'. Now what I propose to do to-night is to stage a conference for you. I am going to paint a picture in words of a Republican conference. In this I am going to have the leaders in thought in the Republican Party, familiarly referred to as the best minds. I am also going to have a few of what is known as the machine leaders, the men that are elected to deliver the goods. And the conference would certainly not be complete without a few of the legislative leaders. Picture in your mind's eye that they are right around me, here."

Standing well toward the front of the platform, he gestured in the direction of an imaginary group behind him. The audience snickered. Then Smith explained that the conference was seeking "an overshadowing issue" by which they could accomplish the election of their candidate. I quote from the stenographic report:

"One of the better minds immediately said: 'Wel-l-l, why then, take economy! We seem to be progressing reasonably well with that in the nation. Why not transfer it to the State? We will take economy for an issue!'

"The machine leader knows nothing about Economy. He hates it. He is satisfied to ride along with it for an issue, though. But we have got to hear from the legislative leader. He says:

" 'Now wait. Don't be in too much of a hurry. Don't go too far with the Economy issue It may be too difficult for us to develop. In the first place, you have to bear in mind that even the boys and girls in the public schools of the State know that Governor Smith and no part of his administration can spend a five cent piece until that piece is first appropriated by the legislature. We have been in absolute control in the last five years. Smith was chairman of the Ways and Means Committee of the Assembly for a long while. He understands these appropriation bills from good, hard, long experience and he is liable to ask you to point to something in that bill that you could take out. And if he does, you will be in bad.' "

Smith pulled a wry face and glanced around at his fictitious fellow-Republicans. He mimicked another legislative leader, pointing out that the G.O.P. majorities in the last three years had sent appropriation bills to the Governor from which $20,000,000 had been slashed by veto. This, he said, made the best minds at the conference gloomy and one of them asked:

" 'What kind of a deal could that be?'

"And one of the legislative leaders immediately fitted into the breach and says, 'Well, you know some of the boys from the interior counties and on the Canadian border go back to the legislature each year under the promise they are going to get some State money for local improvements. And we couldn't let them go back home saying they were unable to pass the bill in their own legislature. So we let it go down to the Governor and let him get the abuse that comes from the specially selected sections of the State when they are vetoed."

Al paused again, to picture the effect of this on the Republicans seeking an issue. It was unanimously agreed that economy could not be used and silence settled over the meeting. Then, said Al, some one suggested tax reduction, also an effective part of the party's national program. Why not say that if a Republican governor were elected similar tax reductions could be achieved at Albany? Smith resumed his dialogue:

"One of the leaders said, 'Now, wait. Don't go too strong on tax reduction; don't stress that because we made an awful mistake in 1925. We stood up in Albany and we bitterly opposed tax reduction. We fought the Governor. We made wild and foolish statements to the effect that the Governor's policy would impair the State's surplus'.

"Another one said: 'Wait a minute. You ain't said half of it. Tell the conference about that night we sat up until 4 o'clock in the morning trying to find things to spend money on, and tell about the list of appropriations we suggested, amounting in total to over $13,000,000, which, if adopted by the legislature and signed by the Governor, would have made tax reduction impossible. And listen, while you're at it tell the whole truth.

" 'Tell the conference what Smith said about that $13,-000,000. You remember how stupid we were about it. We put $2,500,000 in it anticipating a verdict in a damage suit that hadn't been decided yet. And above all things, don't overlook that night Smith had the General Electric Company rig a radio up in the Executive Chamber and sat talking into it up to 12 o'clock. Don't forget the advice that he gave to the people of the State to write to their Senators and Assemblymen and let them know what they thought about it. And don't forget the wagonload of mail that came up Capitol Hill the next day and saturated the post office.

" 'No, we better not crow on that too strong because we were wrong. Smith demonstrated that taxes could be reduced, that every known activity of the government could be cared for, and that there could be a safe surplus. And there was. So go easy on it.' "

For over two hours, in this fashion, Smith continued to mimic this conference. He was, beyond much doubt, close enough to the truth to be almost phonographic. He skipped from one side of the stage to the other, grinning, frowning and gesticulating while the audience in the hall pounded its applause and countless thousands listened in by radio. He showed the consternation of the Republican leaders when, discussing water power, they recalled that the family of their candidate, Ogden Mills, was financially interested in some of the power companies seeking franchises under the Republican program. One of the best minds, continued Al Smith, next offered labor as an issue, saying:

"'What is all this talk about labor? Our platform gives page after page to our devotion to the laboring man. We tell him every September and October how we love him. And what our heart is aching to do for him. Is it possible we have never carried out any of these promises?'

"All is quiet in the conference [Smith went on]. You can hear a pin drop in the conference for over five minutes. Then one of the leaders said:

"'Keep off that! Keep away from it. It is loaded with dynamite. In 1924 we made a definite promise, a specific promise, that we would enact a 48-hour law for women in industry in this State and do you remember how our candidate went around talking about the great sympathy he had with the laboring man? Lay off that! What happened? Why, two years in succession the Senate passed a 48-hour bill and when it went over to the Assembly it met the strong and overpowering force of a well organized and well-greased lobby and it went down to an ignominious death. But wait, you haven't heard half of it. Keep off labor, because we may be asked to give our candidate's record on it. He was the great driving force behind the bill that wrote the direct settlement provision into the Workmen's Compensation Act, that left the injured men and women of the State at the mercy of the insurance companies. And Smith was able to show in 1919, after a thorough investigation, that that amendment alone cost injured men and women in this State over $500,000 in a single year.'"

Smith next took up education and had his fancied conference admit that the Republican Party had resisted efforts to improve conditions in the schools and had even refused an appropriation for an independent investigation conducted by a committee of which Michael Friedsam of B. Altman & Company was the chairman. This board, as in the case of the reconstruction commission in Al's first term, paid its own expenses. The conference-in-search-of-an-issue then decided to abandon its efforts to attack the Democratic candidate and to emphasize, instead, the accomplishments of its own party:

" 'Let's talk about what we did ourselves. . . . Certainly some of the things that happened up in Albany were constructive; reorganization of the government, rehabilitation of the State hospitals, the perfection of public works, the laying out of public parks, the elimination of grade crossings—all of these are great things that affect not only the business but the human side of government. Let us take some credit for them.' "

At this point Smith paused once more and the audience, knowing the obstructionist record of the G.O.P. on these measures, laughed with anticipation:

"Well, the last straw was piled on the camel's back when the legislative leader said to the best minds:

" 'Keep off, keep off! You can get no credit for anything you have just mentioned. We fought every one of those things. . . . It is a matter of State history who fought the reorganization of the government. When we were in control in 1921 under Governor Miller we defeated it. It is a matter of history that when it went all over the State we said—"Keep off that amendment!" We tried everything we could to fight grade crossings. The chairman of the Finance Committee talked in all small communities against it and misrepresented it. Well, not only are we deprived of an issue against Smith, but there ain't anything we can say for ourselves.' "

Concluding, Smith portrayed the conference debating whether prohibition might be made an issue and dismissing the idea because it had been the policy of the party to "talk a little dry to the country people and then when we get to the great centers of population talk a little wet". Nor could the conference accept the threadbare issue of the menace of Tammany, since it knew that 14th Street had supported the welfare measures which he, as Governor, had advocated.

"Well," said Smith, "there ends the story of the conference. There is no issue and the conference could do no other thing but say to the candidate: 'Make your own issue'. So the candidate went out to make his own issue."

As he said this, Smith held up a cartoon of Mills that had appeared in a newspaper. He pointed to a black shadow that appeared in the background of the drawing.

"You know who that is! That is Hearst. Lowbrow, sinister looking creature that lurks behind the candidacy of

Ogden Livingston Mills, and he is the man that made the issue. Well, he made a regular Hearst issue. The business of the State of New York or the material financial prosperity or the betterment of the people does not mean anything to him and he invented the issue of milk.

"If I hadn't worked hard for the State, the little conference that has just suspended would not have been forced to drive the aristocratic and intelligent son of an aristocratic family out in the gutter to pick up Hearst for his issue.

"The conference could find no issue, because I have faithfully, honestly and solely given every minute of my time to the business of the State of New York. I have bettered its business side. I have bettered its human side. I have bettered every phase of it. I have never failed to tackle any problem that came up before it. With the help of New York and the help of citizens of all parties, I will go back to take up the job again on the first of January."

Chapter Eight

Al Smith will not, it is virtually certain, return to Albany again. The conclusion of his present term as Governor—no other man in the history of the State has been elected to this office four times—will mark the release of the prisoner. He will be glad that this is so, for the job has grown constantly more irksome. The small salary, $10,000, has made it impossible for him to set aside savings that any man, particularly when he has crossed the sad boundary line of fifty years, wishes to provide for his family. The work of the Governor's office is so great that only by rigid conservation of his strength has Smith been able to retain his health. He has had hardly a moment for rest or relaxation.

Ambitious as Al Smith is, and naturally, for the presidency, he will find much to console him if his party follows the usual practice of politicians and chooses a candidate dedicated to neutrality in all things and therefore without enemies; who is a Protestant and acceptable to the bigots who believe that a Catholic president would cable to the Vatican for approval of his Colonel House. Smith, as I have before suggested, is beginning to enjoy the fleshpots of life. He knows that as a private citizen he can earn a large salary from some big corporation. Free from the obligations of present or future public office, he will no longer have to pretend that his heart yearns for Oliver Street, although he dwells in the gilded splendor of the Biltmore Hotel. Mayor Hylan, until his political demise, was a faithful ornament of the middle-class Bushwick section of Brooklyn. But he has recently built himself a home at Forest Hills, one of the more select suburbs on Long Island. So Smith, perhaps, will move to Park Avenue.

Nine years have passed since he first went to Albany as Governor of the State of New York. They have been years filled with turmoil and have left their mark on both the man and the politician. The man, it is my viewpoint, is more inclined to impatience and is less tolerant when associates disagree with him. He is more austere now than at any other time in his life. He may be known universally to newspaper readers as "Good old Al", the hero of "The Sidewalks of New York". But strangers, and even men who know him fairly well, are learning to hesitate before they call him by his first name. He cares nothing for most of the amusements that men enjoy. He does not, for instance, play cards nor has he the slightest interest in racing, pugilism or baseball. He has taken up golf on the recommendation of his physicians and his game is mediocre. Swimming he really delights in, and when he is in the water his youth returns and he sheds the dignity that has so swiftly grown upon him. As for the politician, his attitude in the State convention of 1926 demonstrates his confidence that he and no other is the Boss. It is a theory of politics that the party's destiny is shaped by the voice of its members and its active workers. In New York, to-day, the Democratic Party is shaped by Al Smith, and those who disagree with him do so at their peril. And yet he is a phenomenon in that he has taken to himself all the power of a man who commands a personal machine, but uses his power chiefly in the interests of good government.

If Smith achieves the Democratic presidential nomination, his Republican adversaries will be forced to find, as best they can, some issues in his record as Governor. Their chief hope, as they are already making clear, rests in the charge that the expenses of the State have increased enormously since he has been at Albany. They are saying, even now, that he is disqualified on this ground, alone; as well as on others that they may be able to whip into publication form in due time. The budget during his first year was about $90,000,000 and had reached $200,000,000 by 1927. The G.O.P. strategists are pointing with horror to the increase in the public debt and are seeking some way to develop this issue so that too much emphasis will not be placed upon the fact that the bonds sold have been for hospitals, grade crossings, parks and other public improvements. At the close of the 1927 legislative session they chuckled with glee over Smith's inability to make good on the recommendation in his annual message to continue the 25 per cent income tax cut. The State, they said, was "back on a war-time basis of taxation". Smith's answer to accusations of extravagance will be, of course, the one he has made many times before: that the Republican Party controlled at least one house of the legislature during all of his terms and approved every cent that was appropriated. He can, and will, point again to the millions of dollars slashed annually by veto from the appropriation bills, and with his rare gift for the specific will show that these sums were to have been used for local improvements where the grass grows green and home-made wine makes formal support of the Volstead Act not too bothersome.

Occasionally one of "the two great political parties" will rise from the mud of mediocrity and will represent, because of the personality of its candidate, a principle that really means something. Woodrow Wilson, I think, gave the Democratic Party a standing that it had not had for decades. Even the obstinacy that wrecked his dreams, and cowardly leadership in the years that followed, could not quite efface it. But usually there is little to choose between the two organizations. The boast of Democracy that it stands uncompromisingly for liberalism is as silly as for the G.O.P. to deny that the income tax schedules devised by Mr. Mellon are arranged so that millionaires can afford to pay their alimony bills. The Republican Party, in office, appoints department heads approved by the House of Morgan. The Democrats, on the rare occasions when they are in that happy situation, select third-rate political leaders from the South. Any real question, like prohibition or the Klan, is as unwelcome to both parties as a chiropractor at a convention of the American Medical Association. Honesty has joined the tariff dodo, since the voters in 1924 endorsed the theory that public servants are expected to be crooked.

But I grow bitter. The record of Smith as Governor of the State of New York for four terms has in it much to indicate that here is another personality around whom discouraged idealists, so often called cynics, can rally. It is still within the realm of possibility that he will spoil that record before the 1928 convention is called to order. But it is more than probable that he will not, for Al Smith is watching his step very carefully these days. The danger is rather that he will be too cautious. His admirers hope, however, that he will resist pressure from such well-meaning gentlemen as former Governor Sweet of Colorado and will decline to protest that he has always been in favor of the Volstead Act.

Smith's record on prohibition will be discussed in a later chapter. Looking back to 1919, when he began his first term, there are a number of striking accomplishments to his credit. I have already described, almost lyrically, the theories of government that he expressed when the Red Menace was at its height in 1919 and 1920 and when he insisted upon the veto of 100 per cent Americanism laws. The measures that he forced down the throats of four Republican legislatures demonstrate his ability as a leader and are signs that, if President, he might have similar influence with Congress. The successful parts of his program might be summarized as follows, in the order, as I see them, of their importance:

Housing

From the start of his first term, then working through the Reconstruction Commission, Smith has had this problem under study and has won the approbation of social workers and other experts. The housing problem has been most acute, necessarily, in New York City where money is always available for large apartment houses and motion picture theaters, but where high rates of interest on mortgages make the construction of decent homes for poor people virtually impossible. The Governor supported the bills suggested by Samuel Untermyer, counsel to a legislative housing commission, which might have controlled combinations in building materials. Most of these were strangled by the Republican Party. He also supported rent legislation and bills permitting tax exemption to stimulate the building of homes. He urged, in 1926, a law which permitted corporations agreeing to limited dividends to issue bonds through a State Housing Bank, at low interest, and to condemn land for building purposes. Republican opposition, on the ground that it was Socialistic, forced Smith to accept a compromise bill which is less effective but which may still do much. It grants liberal tax exemption and tends to prevent speculation.

Education

As in the housing problem, Smith based his program on the findings of experts. He signed, early in his gubernatorial career, a bill giving equal pay to woman teachers, but has insisted that municipalities shall have the right to pass on other salary increases. During his first term the State contributed about $9,000,000 for education; for the fiscal year which ended June 30, 1927, it spent $82,500,000. Al can be criticized, however, for not interfering with continued Tammany meddling with the Board of Education in New York City, which has done much to undermine the morale of the city's school system.

Consolidation of Departments

When Smith took office the government of the State was carried on through almost 200 boards and commissions, many of them with authority to sign contracts obligating the State to large expenditures. Few of them were responsible to any one. The consolidation of these scattered bureaus into an orderly system of less than a score of departments was approved by leading Republicans in the Constitutional Convention of 1915. Smith's reconstruction commission gave further study to it four years later. Then the G.O.P. attempted to make a political issue of the subject, with the result that Smith was unable for years to accomplish passage of the necessary amendments to the statute and constitutional law. By appealing to public opinion he was successful in the end. The heads of the more important State departments are now responsible to the Governor and confer with him, as members of his Cabinet, every two weeks. For the first time in its history, New York has a scientific form of government. The system now in operation will be the subject of study by experts from all parts of the country.

The Executive Budget

State funds had for many years been appropriated by the legislature through a mysterious and appalling document understood by none except one or two of the leaders. This appropriation bill included, under various vague headings, items for local improvements. It was drafted behind the closed doors of committee rooms. The new Executive Budget places the initiative and the responsibility upon the Governor. At the beginning of the year he submits the list of necessary appropriations. The legislature may add to it, or subtract from it. But everything is done in the open. The G.O.P. majority, fighting this amendment, said that it made "a King of the Governor". It was approved at the polls.

Welfare Legislation

Smith's greatest services toward the protection of men, women and children in industry were accomplished while he was still a member of the legislature. But since he has been Governor he has used all of his influence to further such reforms as minimum wages and the 48-hour week for women. He has obtained an imperfect 48-hour week law. He has always opposed frequent Republican efforts to undermine the Workmen's Compensation Act. In 1925 he urged a referendum on the federal child labor amendment and said he felt sure that the people of the State favored its ratification. He did not, however, press the issue when the ancient war-cry of "state rights" was raised, by skillful manufacturing interests, against the amendment.

Parks

Smith began in 1923 the development of a State park system and obtained approval of a $15,000,000 bond issue for this purpose. He fought the Republican legislature which, in 1925, obeyed the mandate of a group of wealthy landowners on Long Island and attempted to prevent the establishment of public parks in the neighborhood of residential sections.

Water Power

I mention this at the end of the list for the reason that nothing has been accomplished, except negatively. The water-power resources of the State are still undeveloped and millions of dollars are being lost annually. Smith is entitled to credit, however, for the fact that the hydroelectric interests have as yet been unable to seize this natural resource under terms that are disadvantageous to the public. Both parties have injected politics into the issue. Smith has altered his program in some of its technical details at various times and does not, perhaps, regret that the issue has been preserved for presidential purposes. He seeks the creation of a quasi-public corporation which can sell its securities on a tax-exempt basis and build the power plants at lower cost than can private capital. Distribution of the current is to be accomplished through contracts with private companies. This has been defeated by the Republican Party. An alternative plan offered provides for private operation on long-term leases with the State. The State is to share in the earnings, can regulate the rates and can recapture the properties at the conclusion of the lease. In theory the Republican plan seems sound enough; in fact, rate regulation has never been fair to the consumer and recapture clauses are seldom workable.

BOOK FIVE

Presidential Yearnings

Chapter One

THE DEMOCRATIC NATIONAL CONVENTION OF 1924, which had convened on June 24 in high good humor, finally ended on the night of July 9 with every one except the members of the Republican National Committee, who had been watching the battle from a distance, plunged in gloom. These gentlemen, whose merriment had increased as the days had dragged by, knew that the nomination of John W. Davis meant the election of Calvin the Stuffy. They were aware, as at heart the Democrats must also have been aware, that the scarlet brand of "corporation lawyer" would do more to retain Coolidge in the White House than all the carefully staged sap-bucket toting and hay pitching of the Republican candidate. Davis would carry the South, of course. But in pivotal States such as New York his affiliations with the House of Morgan, the New York Telephone Company and the United States Rubber Company were certain to turn hundreds of thousands against him. It does not, ordinarily, matter to the Democrats of the nation that a candidate is a gentleman, intelligent and honest. Mr. Davis is all of these. But as a candidate he represented not only a compromise but also the conservative wing of the party. He could not play the rôle of Demagogue; and the Democrats, except under the most extraordinary circumstances, are lost unless they can thunder against the menace of Wall Street, banks, big corporations and the Standard Oil Company.

Another cause for chuckling at the headquarters of the Republicans was the history of the convention that had just ended. The Republican Convention, which had gathered at Cleveland merely to nominate Coolidge by acclaim and to select the discreetly profane Mr. Dawes as his running mate, had been smart enough to ignore the Ku Klux Klan. The Democrats, either more honest or unable to prevent it, had fought out this issue on the floor. The weary balloting between Al Smith and William G. McAdoo, with never a hope that either could do more than block the nomination of the other, had caused enmities that could never be patched up before Election Day, for all the enthusiastic statements and pledges of support that were given just before the tired delegates hurried to their trains. But what pleased the Republican strategists the most, particularly those who looked to the future, was their belief that Al Smith, whose candidacy they really feared, had been eliminated for all time as a presidential possibility. They knew that the issues between the Smith forces and those of McAdoo had not been settled. They felt certain that before 1928 arrived each man would have been commanded to withdraw in the interest of harmony and that the Democrats would again be forced to nominate some nondescript as their standard-bearer. They were in error, as it has turned out. But this was due to developments that none could have then foreseen.

The Democratic convention came to New York through the efforts of a group of citizens who felt that it would be an excellent thing to convince the rest of the country that the town was not the red-light menace generally conceived by the sticks. Such staunch Republicans as Frank Munsey assisted in the plans, first set in motion by Herbert Bayard Swope, executive editor of *The World*. The promise of enough cash to enrich the impoverished party treasury won the consent of the Democratic National Committee. During the weeks before the sessions began a gay spirit of boosting pervaded the city. The convention, it was declared, would be a great thing for business. The delegates and their wives would spend many a dollar at the shops and at the theaters. The hotels would do an enormous trade. Season tickets to the convention were in great demand and were exchanged for $100 contributions to the fund. Before it was over, however, the shopkeepers were growling that the delegates must have either left their money in the home-town bank or given it to the local bootleggers, who had not donated a nickel to the convention fund. Only the Follies and similarly frothy shows, which always flourish on rural patronage, did any business. Tickets to the convention, sought so eagerly before the opening day, were being scorned by chauffeurs and housemaids during the second week. The convention was a flop for the same reason that all nominating speeches and most political orations are a bore; it was far too long. The delegates finally left for their homes resenting the time and money that it had taken to nominate a candidate who could not win.

They were bitter, too, over the misguided enthusiasm that New York had shown for Al Smith and the degree to which his supporters had whooped up mechanical demonstrations in his behalf. Some went so far as to hint that holding the convention in Manhattan had been a plot on the part of Tammany Hall to nominate Al. The resentment was not, of course, unanimous. A few of the delegates were mannerly enough to appreciate the efforts made in their behalf and realized that the New York committee had established a precedent in convention cities by preventing profiteering on the part of hotels and restaurants. Half a dozen were bright enough to know that the deadlock which had occurred would have taken place irrespective of the convention city.

Only three years have passed, but the 1924 convention has been, happily, nearly forgotten. The old Madison Square Garden, scene of horse-shows, circuses and prize-fights and once notorious because on its roof Harry Thaw had shot Stanford White, has been torn down and its place is being taken by a building that will be merely another sky-scraper. Most of the days of the convention were dull and drab, but there were moments of high excitement, of color; even a few of courage. The sessions, on the whole, were monotonous and the delegates who clutched their State standards, paraded and screamed applause were puny figures whose votes were controlled by men scorning to come near the Garden. But there were exceptions:

. . . A morning session when the gay lanterns hung against the dim ceiling made, for the moment, a pretty thing of the Garden. The heat of the day was not yet and the flags and the bunting stirred in a breeze that somehow had found its way past the guards and the ticket takers. . . . Governor Brandon of Alabama, standing on his chair and screaming as the poll on each ballot started: "Twenty-four votes for Oscar-r-r W. Under-r-r-wood!" . . . White-lipped young patrolmen of the city force circulating through the aisles while the battle over the Klan plank raged and bloodshed was not far beneath the surface. . . . A frightened woman seated with the Georgia delegation, surrounded by chivalrous Southern gentlemen who gesticulated and shook their fists and forced her to change her vote and support the Klan, and thereby brand the Democratic Party lacking in courage. . . . A young man from Alabama, arising to place the name of Senator Underwood in nomination, and daring to name and damn the Klan. . . . Franklin D. Roosevelt, limping on crutches to the speaker's stand, smiling down and starting to say "Alfred E. Smith", but getting only as far as the first syllable. . . . A mad demonstration that began with happy spontaneity and lasted until only fire sirens and other mechanical devices were blaring a paid-for demonstration for Smith, who deserved a better tribute. . . . Al himself, appearing on the last night of the convention by unanimous invitation and making a speech that is better forgotten, because it proved that he was not then presidential in stature. . . . William Jennings Bryan, whose voice had once been the most resonant in the Democratic Party, attempting to speak and being booed by Tammany roughnecks; a man grown too old for the political arena and soon to die. . . . Consternation on the faces of Southern delegates when a well-meaning band leader played "Marching through Georgia" as a tribute to the Georgia delegation, beginning a parade.

In 1918, it will be recalled, when running for Governor for the first time, Smith received a letter from McAdoo endorsing his candidacy. Interesting in the light of subsequent events, this document meant nothing. It had been written at the request of the Democratic organization of New York, which was anxious to cloak its nominee with the respectability of Wilsonism, and thereby counteract the prejudice against Tammany Hall. Certainly McAdoo has never had any reason to feel friendly toward Smith. Two years later, at the Democratic convention at San Francisco, Al was a "favorite son" candidate from New York. Murphy, in charge of this maneuver, had not the slightest idea that Smith could be nominated and did not, probably, desire it. The purpose of advancing his name was a commonplace example of political strategy; to hold the wet delegates as a unit against the advances of the McAdoo prohibition forces. The scheme worked admirably. McAdoo could not get two-thirds of the delegates and when the break came the lads from New York were switched to James M. Cox, who was, at the least, moist. Cox was nominated and joined the ghostly procession of Democratic presidential nominees who have run for the Presidency without a chance of being elected.

The Democratic Party has dedicated itself by its system of nominations to lost, if any, causes. It is not, perhaps, wholly to blame for this because, unlike the Republicans who have no representation in the South and whose members are much alike from coast to coast in that they represent business interests and respectability, the Democratic leaders must curry favor with three different sections of the country, the East, the West and the South. The ideal Democratic nominee would be a Protestant and therefore not offensive to the South, a wet and therefore acceptable in the large cities of the East, a dry and therefore not obnoxious to the daughters and sons of wagon-train pioneers of the West who believe in, even obey, in some cases, the Volstead Act. He should, in addition, be somewhat liberal, but not enough so to alienate men of wealth whose purses must be opened for the campaign funds.

It is to prevent the nomination of a man who does not, in theory, combine all these virtues that the impossible two-thirds rule has been adopted. Thus when there are two leading candidates, possibly men of distinction, each able to control a third of the delegates, the nomination is virtually certain to go to one of the many dark horses ready to gallop up from obscurity. Smith, in 1924, was viewed with suspicion in the South because he was a wet and a Catholic. He had little or no support in the West. McAdoo was hated by the Wet-Irish-Catholic Democrats of the large industrial centers of the East. In 1924 Al, as runner-up to McAdoo, opposed the abolition of the two-thirds rule which gave him the power of veto. To-day the positions of the two men have been reversed. Smith has an excellent chance of getting a majority of the delegates and his managers therefore favor a nomination by the lesser margin. But McAdoo, of course, now supports the two-thirds rule with vigor.

Some day, perhaps, the Democratic Party will grow weary of defeat. It may then consider availability less and the ability of a candidate to win elections more. Continued loss of patronage, the South and West may decide, is even more lamentable than the specter of a wet or a Catholic in the White House. The old prejudices, however, are all too likely to be dominant again when the Democratic Convention of 1928 begins its deliberations.

Chapter Two

If there is anything as ludicrous, in most of its aspects, as the sessions of a national convention, it is the spectacle that goes on in each of the hotels where the delegates gather and where the hopeful candidates have established their headquarters. The Waldorf-Astoria was the principal rendezvous in the 1924 Democratic affair and certainly the staid old hotel had never appeared so strange. Not all of the candidates had their rallying grounds at the Waldorf; McAdoo was brooding by himself over at the Vanderbilt Hotel on Park Avenue. But nearly all of the delegates, alternates, political hangers-on and aspirants for ambassadorial jobs who had flocked to town thronged through the corridors.

The variety of peculiar methods by which visitors to a campaign city plan to nominate their candidate is amazing. Two or three days before the sessions started McAdoo supporters were handing out placards, bearing the magic words "Mc'll Do", to be tucked in the bands of straw hats. Smith's friends, apparently convinced that "The Sidewalks of New York" left much to be desired, had hurried around getting campaign songs which, they were confident, would stampede the convention for Al, once they were sung from the floor. I quote from one lyric, "Dedicated to Governor Alfred E. Smith":

AL, MY PAL

The nation's sad and things are bad
  While dark clouds fill the sky,
For evil men have triumphed in the land.
  But Justice soon their plans will ruin
And those that laugh will cry,
For better men will take command!

Chorus

Al, my pal, a nation's falling
In the war 'tween might and right,
Al, my pal, your country's calling,
  Lead us onward in the fight!
Al, my pal, to you we're turning,
Through dark clouds will shine the sun.
  Al, my pal, for you we're yearning,
  Lead us on to Washington!

Ten million men and women then
  Will march with eager eyes,
With ballots and not bullets in each hand.
  They'll strike for right with all their might,
And from that day will rise
A newer, better land!

Chorus: Al, my pal, etc.

It is not improbable that Smith, as late as mid-year in 1923, was scheduled to be used by the wet element of his party for the same purpose as in 1920: to wreck McAdoo. The former Secretary of the Treasury had made no secret of his intention again to seek the nomination and his candidacy was just as unwelcome to the wets of the East as it had been four years previous. Smith had, in effect, stopped him then. He could do so a second time. But by the time the Democrats of New York held their State convention at Albany, on April 15, for the purpose of selecting delegates-at-large to the national convention, his rôle had become far more important than that of a man who was merely to prevent the nomination of another. Long before the ballyhoo at the Garden began there were many who believed that he might actually be nominated. McAdoo, as counsel to Doheny, had fallen under the cloud of the oil scandals. He had obvious support from the Klan and did not repudiate that support. Smith, on the other hand, had surprised even his own backers by unexpected strength in distant parts of the country. In Wisconsin and Minnesota, for instance, he had been victorious in primary contests held to elect convention delegates. He had the definite pledge of George E. Brennan, Democratic Boss of Illinois, that the votes of that State would be his. Smith did not, it is true, have any definite newspaper assistance as his boom started to become a matter for serious consideration. Even the New York *World* questioned his entire fitness and protested that it had no candidate. Predictions were being made, however, that Al had an excellent chance, after salutes to favorite sons had been given, to get all or some of the delegates from New York, Connecticut, Rhode Island, New Hampshire, Massachusetts, New Jersey, Pennsylvania, Illinois, Wisconsin, Minnesota and Delaware. The forecasts, as it turned out, were not unduly optimistic.

As the convention drew near Smith, like the rest of the leading candidates, indulged in the usual windy and meaningless statements pointing out the certainty of his nomination and eventual election. But during the period from January to May in 1924 he held rigidly to his previously declared policy of declining to discuss the situation or to do anything personally to further his chances. I do not mean, naturally, that Al did not talk things over with Mrs. Moskowitz or other intimates. Democrats from friendly States were undoubtedly received with cordiality at Albany. But by far the greater part of his time he gave to the business of being Governor and so, when formally endorsed at the Albany State convention, he could say with entire honesty:

> "I want to step out of my character as Governor and have a personal word with you. . . . It would be a difficult task for any man to stand before an audience of this kind and be able adequately to express the appreciation

he would feel for the great compliment, the great honor and the great distinction that come to him to be spoken of as the choice of his party in the greatest State in the Union for the highest office in all the world.

"If I were to tell you that I haven't heard anything on this particular subject for the last year, you wouldn't believe it, because it wouldn't be true. I have heard a great deal about it; but in the frankness that ought to exist among friends and comrades together, let me say this to you: I have done absolutely nothing about it, either inside or outside of the State, and I do not intend to do anything about it.

"The man who would not have an ambition for that office would have a dead heart. But I stand exactly in the position to-day that I stood on the floor of the Constitutional Convention in 1915, when I said that the man who used one office and neglected it in order to climb to a higher one was not deserving of the one he had. I am going to do nothing about it, because there is nothing I can do. . . . If I fell down on this job, I would never forgive myself and I would not ask forgiveness from any one else. If the required number of delegates in the National Convention takes your view of it, I will be honored beyond the power of expression to lead the forces of my party in the next campaign."

Charles F. Murphy, Boss of Tammany Hall, was to have been the master mind, behind the scenes, of the plan to nominate Smith. He had confessed, it is said, that he considered the candidacy of Al the crowning achievement of a life filled with the victories that politicians call great. This time, he is reported to have told close associates, he would act unselfishly. Having a hand in sending a son of 14th Street to Washington would be reward enough. The miracle accomplished, he intended to sail for Europe and ask not a single favor. But Murphy died on the morning of April 25, ten days after the convention at Albany. It seemed, at the time, a terrific setback to the hopes of Smith, but I cannot see that it made the slightest difference in the end. Even Murphy's great talents in bargaining and strategy could not have changed the result. For Smith, I repeat, was doomed to defeat in 1924.

Franklin D. Roosevelt, who lives near Poughkeepsie, has some social position and does not bear the Tammany brand, was selected to act as Smith's manager and to counteract the prejudice against the Wigwam. The actual commanders were to be Brennan of Illinois and Norman E. Mack, national committeeman from Buffalo. Tammany was to remain very much in the background. Meanwhile, on May 18, Smith himself suffered grievous personal loss in the death of his cherished mother. But plans for the battle went on. Three weeks before the convention, on June 1, Roosevelt started the avalanche of silly predictions with the remark that Smith was certain to be nominated. His clairvoyance went as far as to include the remark that he "would have more than 300 votes in the Electoral College, well above the number necessary for a choice".

"I believe," said Smith himself, on the eve of the convention, "that when they get around to naming the real man, after distributing the complimentary votes, I'll be nominated."

"The rank and file of the people of this country want me nominated," he said, in another newspaper interview. "That constitutes the source of my strength. This statement may sound a bit chesty, but it isn't at all and it shouldn't be regarded that way. It's a mere statement of fact."

"Smith hasn't a chance," ruled William Jennings Bryan, cornered without difficulty at the Waldorf. "The Middle West does not know him and does not want him; and the South, of course, won't have Smith. And then you must remember that *I* come from Florida and we are for McAdoo."

And so, on the morning of June 24, the Democrats assembled in New York City for a national convention for the first time since 1868. It will be even longer, I suspect, before they come to Manhattan again. The weather on the opening session was hot enough, but before the convention finally adjourned it was suffocating. It was a wilted, perspiring and bedraggled assortment of President-makers who slumped to their hotels each night.

Before two days had passed, his name not yet in nomination, Smith found himself the leader of a cause vastly more important than the ancient issue of Wet *versus* Dry. The platform committee, meeting at the Wadorf and attempting to draft a document that would please everyone and offend nobody, was exhibiting the cowardice typical of such committees. The majority of its members insisted upon a Klan plank which did not name that mystic order, but disowned its practices. A more courageous minority held out for one that specifically declared war on the fraternity of intolerance. The only solution was to fight it out on the floor of the convention. Smith had naturally nothing but hatred and scorn for the kleagles and their small-town armies of third-rate tradesmen and other weak creatures needing white robes to cloak their impotence. Nor was this hatred due to his Catholicism, I am sure. It was in line with his entire outlook. As Governor of New York he had approved a bill which forced such secret societies to file their membership with the Secretary of State. But as a politician he might have now followed the example of other practitioners of expediency and dodged the issue. He did not do so. Several weeks before the convention began he was asked to state his position on the Klan.

"I had infinitely rather lose the nomination on an issue of principle," he said, "than be successful through resorting to subterfuge."

McAdoo, similarly questioned, said nothing. Thereby, in many cases falsely, his supporters were placed in the ranks of those who favored, even belonged to, the Klan.

The vote on the two Klan planks was scheduled for the night of June 29. The bitterness that attends all controversies of a religious nature was everywhere. The Madison Square Garden that night was an ominous place. So thin was the veneer of civilization, so black the thoughts in the minds of the delegates that it was a terrifying thing for onlookers to behold. The city police were on hand in added numbers. It was, in fact, only the presence of husky Irish patrolmen, who would as cheerfully have knocked in the head of a pugnacious Catholic as of a Protestant Klansman, that prevented rioting. If the smoldering enmities had flared into flame that night, the Democratic National Convention of 1924 would have ended forthwith and the party might never have recovered from the disgrace. Intolerance won, assisted by many delegates who felt that religious liberty and political freedom were less vital than votes in the Klan sections of the country, and who therefore cast their ballots for the milder of the two planks. The opponents of the Klan made a gallant fight, however, and for hours the result was in doubt. When the votes, fractional votes being allowed some of the delegates, were counted the tally stood 546.15 for the plank which straddled the issue and 542.85 for the one that had been written with courage.

This, beyond question, was a victory for McAdoo. The Smith men, if politicians ever are able to see the obvious, must have known from that moment that Al could not be nominated. Not all of the 546.15 votes cast to conciliate the Klan were McAdoo votes, of course. But all of them represented delegates who believed the Klan very powerful and it was unthinkable that they would nominate a Catholic. The real rôle of Al Smith became, then, that of a man who might defeat a candidate who had accepted the support of the Klan. His original objective, the elimination of a dry, had been lost sight of. Having accomplished his purpose, it was, perhaps, just as well for his friends that Smith was not nominated. With only a party torn by bitter strife behind him he would, beyond much doubt, have lost to the safe and sane Mr. Coolidge. This having occurred he would not now be available, a far stronger man, for 1928.

There were 1,098 delegates to the 1924 convention so that, under the two-thirds rule, 732 votes were necessary for a nomination. On the first ballot Smith received 241 votes and McAdoo 431½. On the 58th ballot, with which all records for duration of voting were shattered, Al had 331½ and McAdoo 495, not even a majority. Neither candidate ever received a majority. McAdoo's peak was 530 votes, while the most that Smith ever received, on the 76th ballot, was 368. These did not represent the actual strength of the two men, since from time to time delegations that did not desire the nomination of either voted for them for strategical purposes. Experts have placed McAdoo's real strength at about 420 and Smith's at not more than 300. Through 77 ballots, for the reason that they were held by primary instructions and the unit rule, 17 States never shifted their votes. McAdoo had twelve of these delegations; Smith none.

No Democratic convention in history had withstood so bitter and so stubborn a battle before. In 1860, at Charleston, S. C., 57 ballots were taken and then the convention split on the slavery issue, with one faction naming Stephen A. Douglas and the other John C. Breckenridge. The 1924 convention was, by July 5 with 77 ballots, well on the road to the destruction of the party. On one side were demands that Smith withdraw and leave the field to McAdoo, while from the other came frantic appeals that he stand fast and save the party from domination by the Klan. Smith readily consented to an agrement that the delegates were to be released from all promises, but he made the specification that McAdoo must also bow to this arrangement. Finally, and reluctantly, McAdoo did this on the night of July 9. Within four hours, on the 103rd ballot, John W. Davis was nominated.

"I shall lead in this campaign a united and militant and a victorious party," Mr. Davis told the delegates, who cheered out of sheer relief, simulated enthusiasm and rushed for their trains.

But before they did so a resolution was adopted calling upon Smith to address the convention. Few men have had a greater opportunity than this, and few have so completely fallen down. A nomination at last achieved, the delegates were glad to forget for an instant the bitter nature of the struggle. They had heard so much about Al that they were anxious to see him. They knew that he was dearly loved by the people of New York and they suspected that the love was based on a personality that was charming, gracious, humorous and typical of the city that had bred him. They wanted to laugh, probably no crowd of men and women had ever wanted to laugh so much as did the delegates to the dying national convention. Al started well enough. He begged them to forget the demonstrations in his behalf.

"If you have been annoyed in any way," he said, "by the various people with whom you have come into contact, in their zeal to explain to you why I am the greatest man in the world, overlook it."

But then he went on, with lamentable taste, to make a speech that might have been written for Mayor Hylan. He told of the great things accomplished during his régime at Albany by the State of New York; its soldier bonus, the hospitals for veterans, the appropriations for schools, the road program, the welfare laws. He said, in part:

"We have the most enlightened factory code in the world, bar none. We have the most progressive workmen's compensation act. We have gone as far as the Court of Appeals and the United States Supreme Court would permit us to go in legislation for the protection and the care of women and children who are engaged in industrial enterprises.

"I hope it has not been distressful during these trying days, but we have been for law enforcement. We have not given it a lip service. We have made it an actuality. [This statement brought one of the few laughs.]

"I was called to Washington in October of 1923 to talk with the President of the United States about the question of law enforcement, and I never heard such eloquent speeches in my life. The governors at that conference waxed eloquent. They talked about it, but I afterwards found out that two governors who attended that conference actually carried out the purposes of the conference; and I was one of them."

This was less than tactful, inasmuch as a number of the Governors to whom Smith referred were among the delegates. He then went on to boast that New York had been a pioneer "in the field of direct nominations" and that it had led the nation in prison reform. The State had attacked, "for the first time it has been scientifically attacked in any State in this Union, the question of housing and regional planning".

"We have made the most generous contributions to, and laid out the most comprehensive platform and program that could be imagined for the preservation of the public health. We have a widows' pension law, which, in spite of all it costs our taxpayers, leaves the fatherless child in the home of its own mother.

"We have helped agriculture. We have laid out a comprehensive plan for the development of parks and playgrounds and recreational places for the public of our State. And on top of it all we have reduced the taxes of the people by actual dollars and cents."

All of which, naturally, did not interest the delegates from South Dakota, Maryland and New Mexico in the least. It confirmed, in fact, their suspicions that these New Yorkers were extraordinarily well pleased with themselves and believed their State superior in every possible detail to the rest of the nation. It deepened their resentment over the boorish conduct of some of Al's supporters at the convention. They applauded, of course, as Smith concluded with a promise that, as "the leader of the Democracy of this State", he would work for the election of Mr. Davis.

During his speech Smith was watched with appraising eyes by hundreds of delegates. The members of the South Carolina delegation, it happened, had offered the hospitality of the floor to a former South Carolinian who had for some years resided in New York. While living there he had been won over to Smith and in letters to his friends in the South he had protested against the decision of the Democrats of the State to send a delegation instructed for McAdoo. But as he listened to Smith on this final occasion his face grew gloomier by the minute. As the Governor finished he turned to a friend.

"I take it all back," he said. "Al's not yet ready for the White House."

Chapter Three

THE CONVENTION OVER, AL SMITH SOON DEMONstrated the falsity of the theories that his presidential possibilities were at an end. He did so, in fact, during the campaign for Davis. Several speeches that he made in behalf of the Democratic nominee created a profound impression. An appearance in Boston, for instance, brought a mob of 15,000 people to the hall where he spoke. As he thanked the Democrats of Massachusetts, whose delegates had voted for him at the Madison Square Garden, there were many predictions that he would be nominated in 1928. Since then, as I have previously suggested, his position has constantly grown stronger while McAdoo has lost ground year by year. The victory of Smith over Mills in the fall of 1926 aroused nation-wide comment on the fact that no other man had been four times Governor of New York. His fight against Hylan in the Democratic primaries the year before had also been pointed to as indicative of his added strength and his greater independence of Tammany Hall.

Obviously, then, Smith's character must be studied in the light of the possibility that after the convention in 1928 he will be the standard bearer of the party. There are, I think, several specific points which must, if possible, be explained. It is these matters that are being debated in sections of the country as yet unconvinced that he should be nominated. What is his record as a Catholic? Is his judgment of policies influenced by the position of his Church? What of prohibition, on which subject he has recently been silent? Are statements by "persons close to him", and published as newspaper interviews, to be accepted? Does he favor revision of the Volstead Act? Repeal of the 18th amendment? What of the saloon? What of his fitness to be President from the angle, superficial in a sense but widely discussed, of breeding and poise? Is he, as the term is commonly used, a gentleman or is he a typical Tammany politician with a coating of polish acquired by years in public life? Will the nation be able to take pride in his appearance? What, finally, of his knowledge of national and international issues?

In making an effort to answer these questions I make no pretense of being, myself, a spokesman for the Governor. Those which have not already been answered by Smith will, inevitably, be the subject of explanatory statements long before the 1928 convention. My own answers are given with an effort to weigh the real value of assertions made for political purposes. They are based on careful examination of his public record, his messages and other papers and newspaper interviews over a period of many years. They are also based on interpretations offered by some of Al's intimates, enemies as well as friends, under pledge that I would not reveal their source. First, then, prohibition:

The Anti-Saloon League, with its usual faith in the power of money to do anything, has made preliminary plans to raise a large fund with which to prevent the nomination of Smith. The Women's Christian Temperance Union has also expressed hostility to his candidacy. The National Woman's Democratic Law Enforcement League, a more recently organized band of dry ladies, has launched a drive to block him, Governor Ritchie of Maryland or any other Democrat who does not bask in the sunny smile of Wayne B. Wheeler. All of these societies will place great emphasis on the wet record of Al Smith. They will, in fact, seek to spread the impression that the Smith who was an Assemblyman in 1904 is the man who now is receptive to the presidential nomination. And their blasts will undoubtedly worry the strategists nursing the Smith boom.

But Smith's remote saturation is, I submit, less important than the views he has expressed since he has been Governor of the State of New York. The historical aspect and his early actions are, however, illuminating to a certain degree. In fairness they must be considered in the light of changing social standards, just as Al's pronouncements about "the sacred responsibility of sustaining the Volstead Act" must be discounted because of the pressure of political expediency. Smith, it can be stated with flat and definite emphasis, does not desire the return of the saloon. He may have mourned its passing, although I doubt that he did so with any great depth of feeling. But he does not advocate its exhumation for two major reasons: the first, that he is socially minded enough to appreciate that its aggregate evils were probably as great as those caused by bootleggers, the second that it would be political suicide to hint seriously at the restoration of the brass rail and the free lunch.

This great truth was impressed upon Al all too painfully in 1923, as the result of an unhappy misunderstanding. On a warm day during the early spring of that year he was holding the afternoon conference with the legislative correspondents. There was little news and the conversation turned to reminiscences. Al, for the moment, felt that life had become less pleasant in some ways.

"Wouldn't you like," he mused, "to have your foot on the rail and blow the foam off some suds?"

The newspaper men agreed thirstily, but knew that the remark had been made in confidence, as are so many by Smith, and that nothing was to be written about it. It chanced to be repeated, however, to a reporter who had not been present at the conference and who, for some reason that has never been clearly explained, thought that he was at liberty to telegraph it to his paper. Smith was furiously angry when he saw the item, and even more so as clippings of editorial damnation began to pour in from dry sections of the country. William H. Anderson, prior to running afoul of the law and spending some months in Sing Sing prison, often threw the remark into Al's face in statements issued as Superintendent of the Anti-Saloon League. In a letter to United States Senator Simeon D. Fess, of Ohio, on March 26, 1923, the Governor gave his own explanation of the incident:

"You may have noticed recently in the newspapers a statement coming from me about bar rails. I think that on my record you will join with the people who know me well and do me the credit of believing that I have enough common sense and experience of life to understand that the saloon is and ought to be a defunct institution in this country. In an informal meeting with newspaper men, after several facetious remarks had been made about the promised introduction of a 3 per cent beer bill, I joined with the reporters themselves in joking about it, and took occasion myself to speak facetiously of the bar rail. My remark was intended for gentlemen with a sense of humor, and not for use by an intolerant and prejudiced adversary, spying for a chance to misrepresent the real meaning of a casual jest. There was present one such man. It is the only occasion in my public life on which

I have ever known a newspaper man to violate the ethics of his profession."

The militant drys have often made the charge that Smith pretends to stand for the right of the people to decide the alcoholic content of what they drink, but that as an Assemblyman he fought local option laws. These gave to communities the power to forbid the sale of liquor if a majority of the population so desired. The records show that Tammany Hall members of the legislature did oppose local option and that Al voted with them on this, as he did on nearly everything else. In 1906, in one of his earliest speeches, he charged that the Anti-Saloon League had collected $300,000 with which "to promote legislation". In 1915, as minority leader during the administration of Governor Whitman, he fought a local option bill. Wherever the sale of liquor was prohibited, he said, "hypocrisy reign". He told the members of the Assembly that he had recently spent the summer in a "dry town" where the village barber received double his usual rate for a shave for agreeing to treat his customers with "a special tonic" after the operation.

When Smith took office as Governor for the first time, on January 1, 1919, the most important matter before the legislature was ratification or rejection of the 18th amendment. In his annual message to the law-makers, the Governor asked "careful consideration of the pending amendment to the Federal

Constitution for national prohibition". He did not intend, he said, to review the arguments for and against the proposal. But he questioned whether the people of the State were "ready to surrender their inherent right to legislate upon the question".

"Are they," he asked, "prepared to forfeit any part of their police power? Are they reconciled to a policy of incorporating in the Federal Constitution a rigid restriction upon their personal liberty? I believe it is our duty to ascertain their will directly upon this subject. I believe we should consult them, and to that end I recommend to your honorable body that legislation be enacted submitting the question to a popular referendum in order that its determination might represent the expression of the will of the majority."

Mr. Anderson, of course, drew his shining sword to attack this proposal to consult the people and branded the proposed referendum "bogus and futile". The G.O.P. controlled both houses of the legislature and obeyed the orders of the Anti-Saloon League. The amendment was ratified on January 29, with Jimmy Walker, as a leading orator of Tammany, denouncing Anderson as the "most drunken man in the State, drunk with the power that he exercises over the Republican Party".

The Governor has no power of veto with respect to legislative ratification of a federal amendment, so Smith could only remark that it had been approved by the Republicans by the aid of a caucus and "by a strict party vote". He expressed regret that his appeal for a referendum had been ignored. There was nothing that, as Governor, he could do and he deplored that "the Republican majority in the legislature had denied the people the right to speak for themselves".

Before the end of the year, the Anti-Saloon League was demanding the passage of a State enforcement law to assist the federal agents in their task of making America sober by statute. Smith declined to commit himself on this. But how far he really was from favoring such a law was shown by his message to the legislature at the beginning of the 1920 session, a message that momentarily brought hope of relief to the unhappy wets of the land. In several States, Smith said, legislative bodies had ratified the amendment in the face of provisions in their constitutions that referenda were first necessary. Their action thus being illegal, it was at least possible that the 18th amendment had never been lawfully adopted by three-fourths of the States. The New York legislature had, he admitted, acted within the law. But constitutional experts agreed that a State might rescind ratification provided three-fourths of the other States had not already approved the amendment. This being so, should not New York hasten to withdraw its approval?

"Force is added to this suggestion," Smith went on, "because of the circumstances surrounding the passage of the resolution by the legislature of this State. The members of that legislature were not elected in view of any proposed amendment to the United States Constitution, that question had not been passed upon by the people of the State in their election. The resolution passed the legislature by a very narrow margin. The question was not a party one, but in order to enforce its passage it was made the subject of a party caucus, and members of the legislature whose personal views, and in some instances the well-known views of their local constituents, were opposed to such action, were coerced by the party lash to surrender their own convictions and vote for the resolution.

". . . in order that the true opinion and position of the State of New York in regard to the 18th amendment be ascertained and carried out, and made known to the people of other States, I recommend that the legislature rescind its prior ratification of the said amendment and submit the question to the qualified electors of the State at the general election in the year 1920."

The drys prevented without great difficulty any such scheme as this which would, in the event that enough other States had taken similar action, have permitted the voters to say whether the saloon was to be revived. Later during the same year both houses of the legislature, under the same Republican leaders who had maneuvered to ratify the amendment in 1919, passed a bill intended to pacify the wets. This permitted the sale of beer of 2.75 alcoholic content by weight, about 3.50 per cent by volume, in restaurants and hotels. The bill was an obvious fake, for the Volstead Act placed the voltage limit at .5 per cent and the United States Supreme Court swiftly declared that the New York law was unconstitutional. The highest court held that the "concurrent power" mentioned in the amendment was power on the part of the State to enforce the dry law, not to define what makes an intoxicant really intoxicating.

The Republican Party resumed, in the fall of 1920, its subservience to the Anti-Saloon League and justified, thereby, a remark made by Smith that it would be well for it to nominate Mr. Anderson as a gubernatorial candidate. The G.O.P. promised that it would enact a State enforcement law and when Nathan L. Miller became Governor he signed the Mullan-Gage act. This required the police of all the cities in the State to assist in suppressing the liquor traffic, provided for trial in State courts and for prosecution by district attorneys of the various counties. Whether it was effective or not is a question that will never be settled. Certainly it opened the door to grafting by many of the officials concerned, for the bootlegging profession was being organized on a business basis and bribery had been found to be the best means of obtaining the coöperation of patrolmen, constables and deputy sheriffs. In 1922 Smith was again a candidate against Miller.

By this time the Democrats were aware that the hooch issue was a dangerous one. The platform on which Smith ran did not pledge repeal of the Mullan-Gage law, nor did the candidate in his speeches make any promise that he would suggest it. The wet plank of the party called merely for modification of the Volstead Act to permit light wines and beers under the 2.75 limitation. Smith, in his first message to the legislature in 1923, was meticulously careful to go no further. This State paper recited the history of the 18th amendment and again set forth that its "history in our State does not indicate that a majority of the people are in sympathy with the existing Volstead Act". But on the dangerous subject of repealing the Mullan-Gage law, which was the chief topic of discussion, Al said not a word. The wets were disappointed, but not discouraged. Those with an understanding of the pitfalls of political life felt that Smith could do nothing else. They were confident that Al would not fail when the test came; that he would live up to under-cover campaign pledges they had presumed to make in his behalf:

"Vote for Al Smith and the cops will be called off prohibition enforcement!"

Chapter Four

THE POLITICAL LIFE OF ALFRED E. SMITH HAD been, until 1923, fairly free from extreme complications. He had had his battles, of course, with Hearst and had found on these occasions that courage brought both victory and added prestige. He had challenged Boss Murphy and the other practical men of Tammany Hall and had found that a refusal to compromise with decency also brought victory and prestige. In the main, however, the problems that he faced were limited in their complexity to New York State. He had fought, as an Assemblyman, against early inclinations to machine regularity and had, in the end, been won over by his native intelligence to a measure of independence. As Governor, during his first term, he considered problems in the light of the State alone, for he did not take seriously theories advanced by his friends that he had a political future beyond its boundaries.

But in 1923 the situation had changed radically. The most casual examiner of his public life cannot fail to be impressed with the sincere and honest efforts that he made to ignore, as Governor, the growing possibility that he would be the Democratic candidate for President. He was successful to an extraordinary degree, probably more so than any other man ever placed in a similar position. But from the time he defeated Judge Miller in the fall of 1922 he must, despite himself, have started to ponder policies and recommendations in the light of their national effect. In this, beyond doubt, he was encouraged by his new intimates. Prohibition was, of course, the most dangerous of all the issues. As a Democratic Governor, Smith could be moist without peril, even with profit. But as a candidate for the presidential nomination, passive though his candidacy was, he was constantly being warned that the South and its delegates were politically dry. Under these circumstances the wise course was to say as little as possible; at which Al Smith has become so proficient in recent years that he may, if nominated, succeed not only to Calvin Coolidge's job, but to the title of "The Silent Man in the White House" as well.

Thus, in 1923, he declined to agitate for the repeal of the obnoxious Mullan-Gage liquor law and veiled his eyes in a fishy stare when Albany correspondents made bold to ask him what he would do if the law chanced to be invalidated. He was obviously irritated, and anxious to escape, when a group of ladies calling themselves the Molly Pitcher Club waited upon him to protest that prohibition was a flop and that their husbands, sons and brothers were turning from mellow beer and sparkling wines to hard whisky and gin. Smith did not, naturally, go back on his suggestion that the legislature pass a resolution requesting Congress to soften the Volstead Act. Nor did he dodge a feeble Republican plot which required that he sign and personally forward a memorial containing this prayer. But a real crisis arose when, at two o'clock on the morning of May 2, the legislature passed the bill that nullified the Mullan-Gage law. Under the statute Al had thirty days to ponder whether he would approve or veto this act. He must have wished devoutly that it had been thirty years.

"How about the repealer?" the correspondents demanded twice a day.

"When I'm asked that," replied Al, "I always say, 'How old is Ann?'"

From time to time Smith insisted that he had not decided upon his course. Every speech that he made in the anxious interim was eagerly scanned for a clue, and an address at Coney Island on the night of May 19 plunged the wets into gloom. He then hinted, to an audience which had been yelling "Kill the Mullan-Gage bill" that he might "disappoint you in what I am going to say". He would do his best, he said, "to sustain the laws of the country and the Constitution". Eventually, having listened to lurid exhortations from Tammany Hall, he signed the bill. Before he had done so, however, the New

York *World* had published an editorial under the caption "Will Smith Wreck His Party?" The *World* pointed out that the Mullan-Gage law enforced the exact provisions of the Volstead Act and was therefore in direct contradiction to the light wine and beer resolution which Smith had signed and forwarded to Congress. It said, in part:

"Back of everything else, including the Governor's presidential ambitions, there is an issue of political sincerity. That issue cannot be dismissed by splitting hairs as to the exact meaning of a state platform that the voter accepted on trust. He took it for granted that the Democratic Party was opposed to the Volstead Act and consequently to the Mullan-Gage law. He did not try to measure the precise degree of that opposition. . . . To him Mr. Miller represented Volsteadism and Mr. Smith represented the opposition to Volsteadism and the election was a referendum.

"Governor Smith's position is embarrassing only as he makes it embarrassing. He can keep faith with the voters who elected him or he can break faith. If he breaks faith, the Democratic Party in New York is again headed to certain defeat."

News of Al Smith's approval of the repealer caused, as I indicated at the beginning of this biography, dancing in the gin-mills. And despite a long memorandum that the Governor issued explaining his decision, his act has always been held against him by Mr. Anderson and the other zealous drys. William Jennings Bryan was even moved to write a long article, of doubtful logic, criticizing the repeal.

"If I had been Governor," remarked Representative Andrew J. Volstead of Minnesota, "I would have vetoed the repealer."

Governor Smith's memorandum detailing his reasons is a 4,000 word document composed of equal parts of bunk, sincerity and specious reasoning. It reads as though it might have been written by a Judge of the Court of Appeals or a high-priced attorney. In it Al reviewed once more the history of prohibition in New York State, the efforts to pass the 2.75 beer bill and the position taken by the Democratic Party in 1922. He did not criticize, he said, the action of the 1921 legislature in passing the Mullan-Gage law. But he did take issue with the argument that any obligation rested upon the several States to pass or to maintain laws enforcing a federal statute. Here he went into an extended legal dissertation in support of his theory and concluded with the remark that although the duty of enacting State legislation did not exist, the States were forced, none the less, to see that their citizens obeyed the federal law.

"That means," he said, "that after repeal there will still rest upon the peace officers of this State the sacred responsibility of sustaining the Volstead Act with as much force and as much vigor as they would enforce any State law or local ordinance, and I shall expect the discharge of that duty in the fullest measure by every peace officer in the State. . . . In law and in fact there is no more lawlessness in repealing the Mullan-Gage law than there is in the failure of the State to pass statutes making it a State crime to violate any other federal statute.

"Let it be understood once and for all that this repeal does not in the slightest degree lessen the obligation of peace officers of the State to enforce in its strictest letter the Volstead Act, and warning to that effect is herein contained as coming from the Chief Executive of the State of New York.

"At this point, with all the earnestness that I am able to bring to my command, let me assure the thousands of people who wrote to me on this subject, and the citizens of the State generally, that the repeal of the Mullan-Gage law will not and cannot by any possible stretch of the imagination bring back into existence the saloon, which is and ought to be, a defunct institution in this country, and any attempt at its reëstablishment by a misconstruction of the executive attitude on this bill will be forcefully and vigorously suppressed."

The Governor got into difficulties when he took up the question of double jeopardy. First he praised the repeal because it removed the possibility that a citizen could be punished under the federal law and also under the State law. But then he remarked that forcing the State to prosecute violators was "wasteful and futile", because juries declined to convict. Practically speaking, he said, enforcement should rest with the federal government, since smuggling constituted the greatest source of supply.

The bootlegger had profited, he added, by the division of responsibility between the State and the federal authorities. Smith went on to object to statements attributed to President Harding that repeal meant nullification and savored of treason. He sharply called attention to the rights of the States in their own sphere and insisted that Washington must not encroach upon those rights. He denied, in conclusion, that his decision to sign the repealer had been prompted by expediency and again protested against the .5 per cent definition of booze contained in the Volstead Act. This, he said, "was written by the fanatical drys in defiance of the general experience of mankind and of actual fact".

From that time on, unless I grossly misread the evidence, Al Smith listened more attentively to his presidential advisers. He did not, of course, withdraw from his stand for modification of the Volstead Act. But most of the references that he made to prohibition were demands for law enforcement and repeated warnings that unless local authorities supported the 18th amendment he would consider removing them. He has not, I think, fired a single official, however. In October of 1923, as he boasted in addressing the Democratic National Convention some months later, he went to Washington with other Governors for a conference with President Coolidge on law enforcement. In February, with the convention still closer, he summoned the district attorneys of the State to Albany and told them that they must coöperate with the federal authorities and herd the bootleggers into jail. The various counties, he said, must give their enforcement officials the funds and assistance needed for this high purpose.

> "The 18th amendment is a part of the Constitution," he said once more, "and just as sacred as any other part. The so-called Volstead Act is just as sacred as any other law in the country—and we are here to discuss the best and most practical way of enforcing the amendment and the law sustaining it."

William Hayward, at the time United States Attorney for the New York district, was among those at Al's conference. The repeal of the Mullan-Gage law, he tactlessly remarked, had been the greatest blow that the federal enforcement agents had received since the 18th amendment became the law of the land. It was idle, he said, "to talk of real enforcement without a State law". But Hayward, of course, is a Republican and was probably out of sympathy with Smith's gathering. Concluding his harangue to the conference, the Governor pointed out that the men of the State constabulary were doing more to prevent smuggling over the Canadian border than previous to nullification of the State enactment. Similar demands for stringent local enforcement were publicly made by Al in his 1925 and 1927 messages to the legislature. Just before the 1924 convention he gave out a letter explaining his views. He stood, he said, for revision of the Volstead Act to permit 2.75 beer and was eternally and everlastingly opposed to the return of the saloon. He called attention in the letter to his zeal, at the Albany conference, in impressing upon the local constabulary bodies that they must rout the bootleggers. He again mentioned that he had been virtually the only Governor to take such vigorous action.

After the convention Smith returned to Albany in 1925 and 1927. It has become increasingly obvious that he is constantly being told to discuss prohibition, if at all, only in terms of law enforcement. But late in the 1926 session the legislature passed a bill which provided for a referendum on the whole question of prohibition. This exploded the nonsensical theory that the believers in light wines and beers would be satisfied with a 2.75 per cent alcoholic content. No good beer can be made on that basis and no good wine. The referendum called for revision of the Volstead Act to permit, if the several States so willed, the sale of "beverages which are not *in fact* intoxicating". The exact wording was:

"Shall the Congress of the United States modify the Volstead Act to enforce the 18th amendment of the Constitution of the United States so that the same shall not prohibit the manufacture, sale, transportation, importation or exportation of beverages which are not in fact intoxicating as determined in accordance with the laws of the respective States?"

Al Smith signed the bill providing for this referendum. The platform on which he ran against Ogden Mills in the fall urged an affirmative vote. A majority of 1,164,586 of the voters of the State spoke in the affirmative. Smith can no longer claim, as his friends are doing for him, that he believes in the 2.75 maximum. He believes in a maximum, or so he is on record, to be determined in some unknown manner by the various States. Before 1928 he will be urged, in fact he is already being so urged, to change his position, to say that he is not so very wet after all and to continue broadcasting statements about his passionate belief in the necessity for the enforcement of all laws, particularly the Volstead Act.

Chapter Five

The fact that Alfred E. Smith is a devout and sincere communicant of the Roman Catholic Church is still, it is greatly to be feared, the greatest obstacle to the realization of hopes that he may be elected to the highest office in the land. That this can be so, despite the frankness, courage and completeness of his now famous letter to Charles C. Marshall, is indicative of the degree to which a Christian nation, dedicated to freedom of thought and of worship, can deviate from the teachings of Christ. The Marshall-Smith correspondence, published this year in the *Atlantic Monthly* and almost universally reprinted in the newspapers, will prevent, it is probable, most of the open attacks on the Governor's religion. But bigots are immune to facts or reason. They will continue to whisper threats of Papal domination; and thunder publicly denunciations of Al's record on prohibition.

American politics is capable of swinish depths. This was demonstrated when Warren G. Harding was running for the presidency and the rumor was circulated, utterly without foundation, that he had a faint strain of Negro blood in his veins. In the corridors of a New York hotel, during the campaign, small white cards bearing a picture of the White House were passed out by mysterious strangers. Under the photograph were the words, "Uncle Tom's Cabin?". The attacks upon Smith's religion will be similarly underhand and cowardly. They will not, naturally, be sponsored openly by Democrats opposing his nomination or, in the event that he is chosen as his party's candidate, by the Republicans. They will be anonymous and as hard to trace as they will be slimy. They will take the form, perhaps, of circulars reprinting imaginary cable despatches setting forth that the Vatican is favorable to the candidacy and election of Smith. Intolerance will fight from behind a hood. It will not show its face.

A note of criticism may, perhaps, have crept into earlier sections of this biographical effort. I have said that Al Smith voted for many years under orders from Tammany Hall, that he considered the public welfare less than the good of the machine. It has been my unkind suggestion that in recent years he has permitted his strategists to create the impression that he has great sympathy for the Volstead Act and that his zeal for its enforcement is rivaled only by that of Dr. Wheeler. I have indicated that during a quarter of a century in public office he has been, at heart, little interested in problems outside of

New York City or New York State. I have deplored his distaste for reading and have commented upon the entirely barren nature of his intellectual life.

I recall all this to give emphasis, if I can, to a belief which a close study of his career has turned into a conviction: that Al Smith has never been influenced in any act or any policy by the fact that he is a Roman Catholic.

I do not, incidentally, subscribe to the theory that the Catholic Church would not interfere in temporal matters if it could do so; nor can Protestants or other sects plead that they are entirely innocent in this respect. I am convinced that the Catholics, as an organization, have frequently meddled in New York City through Tammany Hall. I think that the Roman Church has often taken a hand in politics in Massachusetts. I know that it has not hesitated, in New York, Massachusetts and elsewhere, to make known its desire for laws bringing a greater degree of censorship of books, theaters, motion pictures and magazines. It has fought movements toward the dissemination of birth control information. Governor Smith, in his answer to Marshall, denied specifically that any attempt had ever been made by his church, through priest or layman, to shape his views. If this is so, it acted wisely in refraining. After all, Al had defied Boss Murphy and Tammnay Hall on occasion. To a man trained as was Smith, in a district club on the East Side, it would have taken very little more nerve to defy a Cardinal or an Archbishop.

The Governor's letter to Marshall was welcomed as a confession of political faith and must have been vastly reassuring to the many people who believe sincerely, and perhaps not without cause, that the Catholic Church would attempt to influence a President who was its communicant. The most hardened anti-Catholic must admit, if he thinks at all, that the formally expressed convictions of an honest man are insurance enough against the nebulous possibility that an institution will exceed its rights. But Al Smith has demonstrated for years that he was not the political vassal of his church. He has opposed censorship in every form, knowing that the Catholic Church in New York City favored it. He has done nothing, I am assured by the American Birth Control League, to obstruct or oppose birth control legislation or propaganda, although both are prohibited by the tenets of his faith.

"Censorship in any form cannot be tolerated in a democratic government," he declared in an address in April of 1924.

This marked no departure from his philosophy of government. With the assistance of Jimmy Walker, also a Catholic and then majority leader of the State Senate, the Democrats defeated a hysterical movement in 1923 to purify literature through the so-called "Clean Books" bill. This measure, sponsored by John S. Sumner of the New York Society for the Suppression of Vice and inspired by the horror of an eminent New York jurist who caught his unmarried daughter reading an unsanitary book, made possible the burning of any work with a single passage that could be interpreted as smutty. Smith, it was known at the time, did not want the bill to pass and would undoubtedly have vetoed it had it been laid on his desk. In his first message to the legislature, that same year, he had called for repeal of the motion picture censorship law, saying:

"Censorship is not in keeping with our ideas of liberty and of freedom of worship or freedom of speech. The people of the State themselves have declared that every citizen may freely speak, write and publish his sentiments on all subjects, being responsible for the abuse of that right, and no law shall be passed to restrain or abridge liberty of speech or of the press. This fundamental principle has equal application to all methods of expression.

"The spoken drama has always had its place as an influence to educate. In many countries it is sustained as a national enterprise. In early days it was used to give expression to biblical history. Nobody will dispute that the invention of moving pictures opened the way for a new avenue of great education as well as amusement. We have looked too lightly on guarantees of freedom of speech and of the press when we selected from among our citizens three people who, before the fact, have the power to declare what is and what is not a violation of the statutes enacted for the protection of the morality of our people.

"Carrying this policy to its logical conclusion, everything written or spoken or thought might be subject to a censorship by public authority. We have abundant law in the State to jail the man who outrages public decency. If we have not, enact it. And we have jails enough to hold him after his conviction. I believe that the enactment of a statute providing for censorship of the moving pictures was a step away from that liberty which the Constitution guaranteed and it should be repealed."

The Governor has consistently maintained this position. In his annual message the following year he said:

"Censorship cannot exist without censors and no purely administrative body should have the right to impose its opinion of what should or should not be published or exhibited upon any citizen whose conduct does not transgress the law of the land. The power in one group of men to prevent the publication or exhibition of anything that does not transgress the law is a power which of necessity destroys initiative and shackles freedom of speech."

Likewise, in 1925, 1926 and 1927, he urged the abolition of motion picture censorship and in doing so reiterated his belief that indecency in books, newspapers, or on the stage or on the screen is best prevented through the enforcement of existing statutes against lewdness. Following the adjournment of the 1927 legislature, it is true, he signed the "Theatrical Padlock" bill which gives to the Commissioner of Licenses in New York City the power to revoke for one year the license of a theater where has been shown a play found in the courts to have been indecent. The law was the result of a particularly purple series of shows given on Broadway during the year. It was also, partly, the result of a sudden tendency on the part of the town to suppress a great many things that it had once ignored. My own view is that the bill is a stupid one, even a vicious one. It makes the punishment for transgression of the code so severe and so financially disastrous that theater owners will hesitate to rent their houses for any drama more bawdy than "Little Women". Signing this bill seems to me to have been a blunder on Smith's part. But it is in no way contrary to his opposition to censorship. The padlock can be snapped into place only after conviction in the courts.

Al Smith must know that his religion may, in the end, cause his dream of the presidency to remain that and nothing more. He must have known so for years; he has been presidential timber since approximately the middle of 1923. But he has never, so far as I know, attempted to dodge any issue or any situation that focused the attention of the entire nation upon the fact that he is a Roman Catholic. Expediency has whispered, and been heard, on other matters. But his place of worship and his manner of bowing down before his God are, he conceives, quite his own business. It never entered his mind, apparently, that it would have been wise to be "confined to his room with a cold" on the day in the summer of 1926 when eight Cardinals of the One True Church were received at the City Hall. He wanted to attend the Eucharistic Congress at Chicago the same summer and he did. And I think that Protestants who make noisy orations about freedom of thought and worship should be the first to give Smith credit for a personal belief in that thesis.

The visit of the Cardinals to the City Hall on June 11, 1926, was a splendid pageant. Among the eight was Cardinal Bonzano, Envoy of Pope Pius XI to the Eucharistic Congress. Thousands of people jammed into the plaza in front of the City Hall to catch a glimpse of the dignitaries and for an hour past Mayor Jimmy Walker, who had never before in his life been on time at a function, had been nervously rehearsing the speech of welcome that he was to make. The presence in concentrated form of so many prelates was a little too much for His Honor. Accustomed to speaking extemporaneously, he had this time prepared his address in advance. It lacked all of his usual charm and was dull stuff. But when Al Smith stepped up to say a few words he was as care-free as though addressing the Newsboys' Club. He mentioned, laughing, the extent to which "The Sidewalks of New York" had become his personal song.

"It is said this song is for me," he said with a

grin, "but the truth is I have two partners in it—one is Cardinal Hayes and the other is the Mayor of New York. The Cardinal was born north of the City Hall when it was a residential section. When you get to Chicago you will meet Cardinal Mundelein. He has a big claim to 'The Sidewalks of New York', too. He was born here. We are satisfied to give him a fourth part of the song."

The next week Al went to the Eucharistic Congress. Before his departure for Chicago, Bishop Adna Wright Leonard of the Methodist Church, a leader in the prohibition movement, issued a statement setting forth that "No Governor who kisses the Papal ring can come within gunshot of the White House".

Chapter Six

On the morning of March 25, 1927, all of the New York papers and many journals in other cities carried in full or in abstract an open letter addressed to Governor Smith by a previously obscure gentleman, Charles C. Marshall. Mr. Marshall, an Episcopalian, a retired attorney and a student of church law, asked in dignified and restrained language whether it was not true that the canons of the Roman Catholic Church were at variance with the principles of government insured by the Constitution of the United States. As a candidate for the presidency how did Governor Smith reconcile these canons with the laws of the nation? The letter was published in the April issue of the *Atlantic Monthly* and released by that periodical to the press.

Al's first reaction to the communication, it is said, was one of grieved shock and surprise that any one could believe, in the face of his long record, that the code of church or churchman could stand, in his conception, before the laws of the land. He is, it will be seen, slightly naïve with respect to Catholicism and the prejudice with which it is so often regarded. He had first heard of the letter from

Franklin D. Roosevelt, who had received proofs from Ellery Sedgwick, editor of the *Atlantic*. In sending them to Mr. Roosevelt, Mr. Sedgwick had suggested that some spokesman for the Governor might care to reply to the Marshall indictment. He indicated that the columns of his magazine were open, extremely open, to anything that Smith might say himself. Smith would undoubtedly have preferred not to answer the communication. Even his advisers, I am told, were momentarily divided on the matter. But they soon reached the conclusion that this was no yelp from a Bishop Leonard but offered, on the contrary, a great opportunity for lifting the whole subject of Catholicism out of the mud of prejudice. Thus when the Marshall letter appeared it was simultaneously announced that Smith would shortly make answer.

After paying tribute to Governor Smith's character, his justice and fair play in public office, and declaring that his candidacy had stirred great enthusiasm, Mr. Marshall said that "through all this tribute there is a note of doubt, a sinister accent of interrogation, not as to intentional rectitude and moral purpose, but as to certain conceptions which your fellow citizens attribute to you as a loyal and conscientious Roman Catholic". These conceptions, he said, "are irreconcilable with that Constitution which as President you must support or defend, and with the principles of civil and religious liberty on which American institutions are based".

"To this consideration no word of yours, or in your behalf, has yet been addressed," Mr. Marshall remarked. "Its discussion in the interests of the public weal is obviously necessary, and yet a strange reticence avoids it, often with the unjust and withering attribution of bigotry or prejudice as the unworthy motive of its introduction. Undoubtedly a large part of the public would gladly avoid a subject the discussion of which is so unhappily associated with rancor and malevolence, and yet to avoid the subject is to neglect the profoundest interests in our national welfare."

The conceptions to which he referred, the attorney said, "are of the very life and being of" the Catholic Church. The "more conscientious the Roman Catholic and the more loyal to his Church, the more sincere and unqualified should be his acceptance of such conceptions". He cited the thesis of Catholicism that all power not given by God to the State is given to the Roman Catholic Church and that no other sects have "divine sanction, and [are] therefore without natural right to function on the same basis—in the religious and moral affairs of the State". Thus, he said, the Church is "hopelessly committed to that intolerance which has disfigured so much of her history."

Marshall then quoted Pope Pius IX as having denied, in the Syllabus of 1864, that "national churches, withdrawn from the authority of the Roman Pontiff and altogether separate", could lawfully be established. The *Catholic Encyclopedia*, he said, declared that the Roman Catholic Church " 'regards dogmatic intolerance, not alone as her incontestable right, but as her sacred duty' ". He quoted Pope Leo XII as holding that the Church " 'deems it unlawful to place the various forms of divine worship on the same footing as the true religion' ", but that it did not condemn the States which permitted it.

"That is," concluded Mr. Marshall, "there is not a lawful equality of other religions with that of the Roman Catholic Church, but that Church will allow State authorities for politic reasons—that is, by favor but not by right—to tolerate other religious societies. We would ask, sir, whether such favors can be accepted in the place of rights by those owning the name of freemen?

"Furthermore, the doctrine of the Two Powers, in effect and theory, inevitably makes the Catholic Church at times sovereign and paramount over the State. It is true that in theory the doctrine assigns to the secular State jurisdiction over secular matters and to the Roman Catholic Church jurisdiction over matters of faith and morals, each jurisdiction being exclusive of the other within undisputed lines. But the universal experience of mankind has demonstrated, and reason teaches, that many questions must arise between the State and the Roman Catholic Church in respect to which it is impossible to determine to the satisfaction of both in which jurisdiction the matter at issue lies.

"Here arises the irrepressible conflict. Shall the State or the Roman Catholic Church determine? The Constitution of the United States clearly ordains that the State shall determine the question. The Roman Catholic Church demands for itself the sole right to determine it, and holds that within the limits of that claim it is superior to and supreme over the State. The *Catholic Encyclopedia* clearly so declares: 'In case of direct contradiction, making it impossible for both jurisdictions to be exercised, the jurisdiction of the Church prevails and that of the State is excluded'. And Pope Piux IX in the Syllabus asserted: 'To say in the case of conflicting laws enacted by the Two Powers, the civil law prevails, is error.' "

In this conflict, Mr. Marshall said, the Church cannot yield "by the very nature of her existence". The State cannot, for the reason that a great mass of her citizens are not Catholics. Although the Church makes no claim to matters "in her opinion" secular and civil, he continued, it is still true that "determination of jurisdiction, in a conflict with the State, rests solely in her sovereign discretion".

". . . no argument is needed," he said, "to show that she may in theory and effect annihilate the rights of all who are not Roman Catholics, sweeping into the jurisdiction of a single religious society the most important interests of human well-being. The education of youth, the institution of marriage, the international relations of the State, and its domestic peace, as we shall proceed to show, are, in certain exigencies, wrested from the jurisdiction of the State, in which all citizens share, and confided to the jurisdiction of a single religious society, in which all citizens cannot share, great numbers being excluded by the barriers of religious belief. Do you, sir, regard such claims as tolerable in a republic that calls itself free?"

In addition to all this, the letter to Governor Smith went on, the Roman Catholic church makes the claim that the sovereignty of the Pope is "not only superior in theory to the sovereignty of the secular State, but is substituted on earth in place of the authority of God himself". This brings another conflict between the fundamental law of the nation and the code of Catholicism. Mr. Marshall quoted the encyclical letter of Pope Leo on "The Christian Constitution of the State" to support this contention. The Church asserts that it is not legal for the State to hold all religious sects in equal favor, a doctrine expressed by Pope Leo XIII. The Constitution of the United States holds that it is not lawful to do anything else. The Supreme Court has so ruled.

"Is our law, then, in papal theory no law?" he asked. "Is it contrary to natural right? Is it in conflict with the will and fiat of Almighty God? Clearly the Supreme Court and Pope Leo are profoundly at variance. Is it not obvious that such a difference of opinion, concerning the fundamental rights between two sovereigns operating within the same territory, may, even with the best intentions and the most sensitive consciences, be fruitful of political offenses that are odious among men?"

"Citizens who waver in your support would ask whether, as a Roman Catholic, you accept as authoritative

Chapter Seven

"I AM GRATEFUL TO YOU FOR DEFINING THIS ISSUE IN THE open and for your courteous expression of the satisfaction it will bring to my fellow citizens for me to give 'a disclaimer of the convictions' thus imputed. Without mental reservation I can and do make that disclaimer."

"I recognize no power in the institutions of my Church to interfere with the operations of the Constitution of the United States or the enforcement of the law of the land."

"You have no more right to ask me to defend as part of my faith every statement coming from a prelate than I should have to ask you to accept as an article of your religious faith every statement of an Episcopal Bishop, or of your political faith every statement of a President of the United States. So little are these matters the essence of my faith that I, a devout Catholic since childhood, never heard of them until I read your letter."

From the reply of Governor Smith.

Several Catholic editors, deplorably impatient, could not wait for Governor Smith to issue his own answer to the communication from Mr. Marshall. The Catholic weeklies, *America* and *The Commonweal*, were among the publications that undertook to deny the validity of the lawyer's arguments and to declare either that his quotations meant less than he ascribed to them or that his hypotheses were fanciful. It would have been wiser for the editors of these publications to have restrained themselves, for in this instance Al Smith needed no spokesmen. Their haste did not add to the really lofty tone of the discussion, nor did statements from sources obviously so partisan convince non-believers in Catholicism.

Having decided to state his beliefs, Governor Smith held a number of conferences with the group of men and women upon whom he has come to lean most heavily during the last few years. Tammany Hall, obviously, could not be of much assistance in a matter which concerned a measure of profound thought. Only Smith himself, of course, knows the method by which his answer was drafted. Boss Olvany may have been consulted with respect to the political effect of what was to be said. But it is fairly safe to assume that Mrs. Moskowitz, Secretary of State Moses and two or three others were those who gave Al the assistance he needed. Father Francis P. Duffy, chaplain of the 165th Infantry during the World War, was called in to interpret the technical parts of the Marshall letter and to cite authorities in refutation. This last he did with singular success. The priest has since declared that

Smith wrote the answer in person. This being so, the Governor is entitled to great credit for clear, concise language; language that approached in many passages no small measure of brilliance and literary style. It is the high point among all his public papers, some of which have been drafted with the aid of others. An uneducated boy from the Fourth Ward had traveled far to be able to write as did Al Smith on this occasion.

The reply was awaited with extraordinary interest not only in New York but throughout the country, for by March of 1927 Governor Smith had become the leading candidate for the presidential nomination of the Democratic Party. The anticipation was heightened by premature publication in two newspapers which, with dubious ethics, had obtained advance proofs. As a matter of courtesy, since the original question had been propounded in the columns of that magazine, Smith had agreed to send his answer to the *Atlantic Monthly*, with the stipulation that it was to be released to all newspapers on the date that the magazine reached its subscribers and was placed on sale. The earlier publication by the two offending newspapers caused the date to be advanced. On the afternoon of April 17 editors were notified that copies of the communication would be given out at once at the Madison Avenue office of Mrs. Moskowitz. That night the Associated Press sent a 3,000 word story to its 400 member newspapers. All the other press associations carried similarly long despatches.

"Catholic and Patriot, Governor Smith replies," was the caption placed by the editor of the *Atlantic* over the text of the article. An editorial note declared the incident of the Smith-Marshall correspondence "historic for the country and for the Church":—

"Now for the first time in the republic's history, under a Constitution which forever forbids religious tests as a qualification for office, a candidate for the Presidency has been subjected to public questioning as to how he can give undivided allegiance to his country when his church restricts the freedom of his choice; and the candidate has answered—answered not deviously and with indirection, but straightforwardly, bravely and with the clear ring of candor. . . . The discussion has served its purpose. . . . The thoughts arising almost unbidden in the minds of the least bigoted of us when we watch a Roman Catholic aspire to the Presidency of the United States have become matters of high, serious, and eloquent debate."

The views imputed by his interrogator to American Catholics, the Governor said in opening his letter to Marshall, "would leave open to question the loyalty and devotion to this country and its Constitution of more than twenty million American Catholic citizens". He expressed gratitude for "defining the issue in the open" and for "the courteous expression of the satisfaction it will bring to my fellow citizens for me 'to give a disclaimer of the convictions' thus imputed". Without mental reservation, he said, he made such disclaimer. The convictions in question "are held neither by me nor by any other American Catholic, as far as I know". He denied, as Marshall stated, that he was a candidate for the presidency and quoted from his 1927 annual message to the State legislature in which he declared himself receptive to the nomination, but insisted that he would "do nothing to achieve it except give to the people of the state the kind and character of service that will make me deserve it".

"I should," he said, "be a poor American and a poor Catholic alike if I injected religious discussion into a political campaign. Therefore I would ask you to accept this answer from me not as a candidate for any public office, but as an American citizen, honored with high elective office, meeting a challenge to his patriotism and his intellectual integrity. Moreover, I call your attention to the fact that I am only a layman. . . . I am neither a lawyer nor a theologian. Whatever knowledge of the law I have was gained in the course of my long experience in the legislature and as Chief Executive of New York State. I had no such opportunity to study theology."

His first intention, Governor Smith said, was to answer "with just the faith that is in me". But "knowing instinctively that your conclusions could be logically proved false", he had later decided to take counsel "with some one schooled in the Church law". He had selected Father Duffy for this purpose, a man whose patriotism was above question.

"Taking your letter as a whole and reducing it to commonplace English," Smith continued, "you imply that there is a conflict between religious loyalty to the Catholic faith and patriotic loyalty to the United States. Everything that has actually happened to me during my long public career leads me to know that no such thing as that is true. I have taken an oath of office in this State nineteen times. Each time I swore to defend and maintain the Constitution of the United States. All of this represents a period of public service in elective office since 1903. I have never known any conflict between my official duties and my religious belief. No such conflict could exist. Certainly the people of this State recognize no such conflict. They have testified to my devotion to public duty by electing me to the highest office within their gift four times. . . . During the years I have discharged these trusts I have been a communicant of the Roman Catholic Church. If there were conflict, I, of all men, could not have escaped it, because I have not been a silent man, but a battler for social and political reform. These battles would in their very nature disclose this conflict, if there were any."

He had always regarded public education, he said, as a foremost function of government. He had supported in every way the State Department of Education. In addition he had fought for, and achieved, protection of men, women and children in industry. He had worked for improved conditions among the State's sick and insane. He had defended "freedom of speech and opinion against the attack of war-time hysteria" and had accomplished complete and scientific reorganization of the State government.

"I did not," he commented, "struggle for these things for any single element, but in the interest of all of the eleven million people who make up the State. In all of this work I had the support of churches of all denominations. I probably know as many ecclesiasts of my church as any other layman. During my long and active public career I never received from any of them anything except coöperation and encouragement in the full and complete discharge of my duty to the State. Moreover, I am unable to understand how anything that I was taught to believe as a Catholic could possibly be in conflict with what is good citizenship. The essence of my faith is built upon the Commandments of God. The law of the land is built upon the Commandments of God. There can be no conflict between them."

This, it might be remarked, is eloquent but inaccurate. Laws are not an elaboration of, for instance, the Ten Commandments. Taking the name of the Lord in vain is a sin, but not a crime. Adultery is a sin against God, and yet is not necessarily a crime. There is nothing in the penal law of any State requiring that children honor their fathers and mothers, although it may be required that they give financial assistance in case their parents are without other means of support. But so minor a lapse in logic is unimportant in comparison with the worth of the rest of Al's letter. It were better, he said, to cease "quarreling among ourselves over dogmatic principles" and inculcate "obedience to these Commandments in the hearts and minds of the youth of the country". More religion for youth, not less, is needed. The "bickering among our sects" was leading to doubt "whether or not it is necessary to pay attention to religion at all".

Smith then pointed out, as had been done by many others before him, "the long list of other public servants of my faith who have loyally served the State". Chief among these were Roger B. Taney and Edward Douglass White, both of whom were presiding justices of the United States Supreme Court. He might have added that Massachusetts, New York, Illinois, Minnesota, Missouri, Montana, Rhode Island, Louisiana, Idaho and North Dakota have elected Catholic governors or have sent statesmen of that faith to the United States Senate. The "tens of thousands of young Catholics who have risked and sacrificed their lives in defense of their country" also proved, Smith added, that the imputations by Marshall were false.

At this point the Governor departed from the general to the specific. Wishing "to meet you on your own ground", he addressed himself to the definite questions propounded. He critized the attorney for divorcing "sentences from their context in such a way as to give them something other than their real meaning". This had been done, Smith said, in the instance of the reference to the decree by Pope Leo XIII declaring the orders of the Church of England void. Mr. Marshall had given the impression that "the Pope gratuitously issued an affront to the Anglican Church". Actually, the ruling had been in response to a request made by the priests of the English church for a statement on the validity of their priestly orders. Mr. Marshall's quotation from the *Catholic Encyclopedia* stating that the church "regards dogmatic intolerance, not alone as her incontestable right, but as her sacred duty" did not mean intolerance toward other sects, Smith explained. It meant, as the whole of the article in question demonstrated, no deviation within the church "from complete acceptance of its dogma".

"Similar criticism," Smith went on, "can be made of many of your quotations. But, beyond this, by what right do you ask me to assume responsibility for every statement that may be made in an encyclical letter? As you will find in the *Catholic Encyclopedia* (Vol. V, p. 414), these encyclicals are not articles of our faith. The Syllabus of Pope Pius IX, which you quote on the possible conflict between Church and State, is declared by Cardinal Newman to have 'no dogmatic force'. You seem to think that Catholics must all be alike in mind and heart, as though they had been poured into and taken out of the same mould. You have no more right to ask me to defend as part of my faith every statement coming from a prelate than I should have to ask you to accept as an article of your religious faith every statement of an Episcopal Bishop, or of your political faith every statement made by a President of the United States. So little are these matters of the essence of my faith that I, a devout Catholic since childhood, never heard of them until I read your letter. Nor can you quote from the canons of our faith a syllable that would make us less good citizens than non-Catholics. In fact and in truth, I have been taught the spirit of tolerance, and when you, Mr. Marshall, as a Protestant Episcopalian, join with me in saying the Lord's Prayer, we both pray, not to 'My Father,' but to 'Our Father'."

Mr. Marshall's statements about the desire of Catholicism for an established church belonged, said Governor Smith, to what Archbishop Dowling had declared "the limbo of defunct controversies". The best Catholic thought, he said, quoting a number of authorities, admitted a "Catholic State" beyond the realm of actuality, even in Spain or the countries of South America. Where several religions had been firmly established, the State must insist upon complete religious liberty. Such, commented the Governor, "is good Americanism and good Catholicism".

". . . I stand squarely," he said, "in support of the provisions of the Constitution which guarantee religious freedom and equality."

The next point taken up in the answer to Marshall was the respective functions of Church and State and the hypothetical danger that the separate jurisdictions might conflict. Both the Catholic Church and the Protestant Episcopal Church, Smith insisted and again cited authorities, maintain that each is independent in its own sphere.

"Your church, just as mine," he said, "is voicing the injunction of our common Saviour to render unto Cæsar the things that are Cæsar's, and unto God the things that are God's.

"What is this conflict about which you talk? It may exist in some lands which do not guarantee religious freedom. But, in the wildest dreams of your imagination, you cannot conjure up a possible conflict between religious principle and political duty in the United States, except on the unthinkable hypothesis that some law were to be passed which violated the common morality of all God-fearing men. And if you can conjure up such a conflict, how would a Protestant resolve it? Obviously by the dictates of his conscience. That is exactly what a Catholic would do. There is no ecclesiastical tribunal which would have the slightest claim upon the obedience of Catholic communicants in the resolution of such a conflict. As Cardinal Gibbons said of the supposition that 'the Pope were to issue commands in purely civil matters':—

" 'He would be offending not only against civil society, but against God, and violating an authority as truly from God as his own. Any Catholic who clearly recognized this would not be bound to obey the Pope; or rather his conscience would bind him absolutely to disobey, because with Catholics conscience is the supreme law which under no circumstances can we lawfully disobey.'

"Archbishop Ireland said: 'To priest, to Bishop or to

Pope (I am willing to consider the hypothesis) who should attempt to rule in matters civil and political, to influence the citizen beyond the range of their own orbit of jurisdiction that are the things of God, the answer is quickly made: "Back to your own sphere of rights and duties, back to the things of God".'

"Bishop England, referring to our Constitution, said: 'Let the Pope and the Cardinals and all the powers of the Catholic world united make the least encroachment on that Constitution, we will protect it with our lives'."

Never in any office that he had held, said Governor Smith, had any man, "cleric or lay," attempted to exercise "Church influence on my administration" or "asked me to show special favor to Catholics or exercise discrimination against non-Catholics". It was well known, he added, that his appointments as Governor had been made on the basis of merit. He had never, he said, "asked any man about his religious belief". The Governor's Cabinet, created by the state reorganization amendments, had been selected by him. It consisted of two Catholics, thirteen Protestants and one Jew. His closest associate at Albany, George B. Graves, is "a Protestant, a Republican and a 32nd degree Mason".

"I have exemplified," he said, "that complete separation of Church and State which is the faith of American Catholics to-day."

You ask, Al continued in coming to the question of parochial schools, whether the Supreme Court would have defended the schools of the Catholic Church in the Oregon case had it been shown that theories in discrimination against Protestants were circulated. Both he and his children, he said, had attended parochial schools. He had never "heard of any such stuff being taught or of anybody who claimed that it was". The action of the Rota in annulling the Marlborough marriage, which Marshall had cited as indicative of the degree to which the Catholic church interfered in civil matters, had no validity under the laws of America or any other nation. All that the decree did was to define the status of the parties to the marriage contract as communicants of the church.

Taking up the Mexican question, where Marshall had declared that the Guthrie opinion had sanctioned the legality of armed intervention to protect the rights of Catholics in Mexico, Smith quoted in refutation the Pastoral Letter of the Catholic Episcopate of the United States. This flatly disavowed any endorsement of intervention in Mexico for the protection of the church.

"My personal attitude, wholly consistent with that of my church," said Smith, "is that . . . no country has a right to interfere in the internal affairs of any other country. I recognize the right of no church to ask armed intervention by this country in the affairs of another, merely for the defense of the rights of a church. But I do recognize the propriety of church action to request the good offices of this country to help the oppressed of any land, as those good offices have been so often used for the protection of Protestant missionaries in the Orient and persecuted Jews of Eastern Europe."

And then, in conclusion, Alfred E. Smith summarized his creed, as American and Catholic:

"I believe in the worship of God according to the faith and practice of the Roman Catholic Church. I recognize no power in the institutions of my church to interfere with the operations of the Constitution of the United States or the enforcement of the law of the land. I believe in absolute freedom of conscience for all men and in equality of all churches, all sects and all beliefs before the law as a matter of right and not as a matter of favor. I believe in the absolute separation of Church and State and in the strict enforcement of the provisions of the Constitution that Congress shall make no law respecting an establishment of religion or prohibiting the free exercise thereof.

"I believe that no tribunal of any church has any power to make any decree of any force in the law of the land, other than to establish the status of its own communicants within its own church. I believe in the support of the public school as one of the corner stones of American liberty. I believe in the right of every parent to choose whether his child shall be educated in the public school or in the religious school supported by those of his own faith. I believe in the principle of non-interference by this country in the internal affairs of other nations and that we should stand steadfastly against any such interference by whomsoever it may be urged. And I believe in the common brotherhood of man under the common fatherhood of God.

"In this spirit I join with fellow Americans of all creeds in a fervent prayer that never again in this land will any public servant be challenged because of the faith in which he has tried to walk humbly with his God."

Inevitably a document such as this one must have brought a deluge of commendation from all parts of the country. For the next week telegrams and letters poured into Governor Smith's office at Albany. Newspapers from coast to coast, in the South as well as in the North, voiced the opinion that he had spoken with honesty and with courage. Some editors felt that the answer would not satisfy the utterly narrow-minded, and added that nothing could do so. It was not long before it became apparent that Smith's enemies had swiftly changed their strategy. It was not his Catholicism that bothered them, they said. It never had. But how did he stand on the subject of prohibition? His wet views were the ones that needed clarifying.

Republican politicians, who beyond question fear the candidacy of Smith more than of any other man whom the Democrats may select to run in 1928, admitted in private that the letter was masterly. They were not too happy about it, for the reason that it might tend to bring harmony to the Democratic Convention. Charles D. Hilles, Republican National Committeeman and considered a crony of President Coolidge, declined to comment for publication. So did George K. Morris, Chairman of the Republican State Committee.

"Let Smith and Marshall fight it out; I have nothing to say," was the gallant remark from Sam Koenig of the Manhattan Republican machine.

"The letter was most excellent," said United States Senator William Borah, always more of a man than a politician.

Well, Smith has spoken. He will not again, I think, recite the catechism of "the faith in which he has tried to walk humbly with his God". It will be said, of course, that he could speak for himself alone and that his fine disavowals cannot be applied to less fastidious members of the Roman Catholic Church. If he is nominated, I have suggested, it will be found that there are a few whose intolerance has not been softened and who will still voice their prejudice against Catholicism. Some of those who will do so will be clergymen, men supposed to be consecrated to the theory that there is a brotherhood to which all men belong. These gentlemen of the cloth will be Protestants. Can they claim that their own church has never interfered in temporal matters? They have short memories, if they do. For Presbyterians, Baptists, Methodists and the rest have thundered in the past for prohibition, censorship and stricter divorce laws. They will do so again. Some of them have sought laws providing that the Book of Genesis be made the guide for the study of natural sciences.

The Protestant Church must also plead guilty to violating the thesis that the Church and State are ever separate in their jurisdictions.

Chapter Eight

THERE REMAIN FOR DISCUSSION, THEN, BUT TWO of the counts in the indictment which specifies that Al Smith is not qualified for the presidency. By far the more important of these is that as Governor of New York his outlook has expanded from the limits of the Fourth Ward merely to the boundaries of the State, that he has never pondered national or international problems. The other is that Al is still, after all, a crude sort of fellow, certain to stub his toe, metaphorically speaking, over the red plush carpets that would be unrolled before him were he to become Chief Executive of the nation.

Light on both these objections to his candidacy may have been found, I hope, in previous chapters of this entirely unauthorized biography. In general, I think, Smith must admit that his fundamental viewpoint has been chiefly local. Even as a private citizen he has been uninterested in such matters as the tariff, railroad consolidation, international debts and agriculture. He has, it is true, voiced theories concerning them on several occasions; when party obligations or his own ambitions made it necessary. Nor does the accusation that his interest is somewhat synthetic carry with it any thought that he will be unable to master these complexities should they become part of his official life. His intelligence, I think, is capable of demands even more severe than those already placed upon Smith. He has demonstrated many times that he is capable of growth.

The charge that he is deficient in poise or in necessary social smoothness has no longer, it is my belief, much foundation. Assume, for the sake of the argument, although it is not true, that all previous presidents have been gentlemen of culture, refinement and charm. Smith would not be found lacking in any of these. This would be so if only for the reason that the President of the United States lives in rarefied atmosphere, remote from the public. He is seen at state functions, being whirled through the streets in an automobile, making speeches and at infrequent White House receptions where he grasps the hands of the electorate with machine-like swiftness. At all of these Smith is already proficient. If underneath, when he is alone or with intimates, there persists a strain of the East Side, if he resorts to profanity, bad grammar and expectoration, it does not matter. Several who have been president have thus sinned; and the American public never sees its president with his coat off, his vest unbuttoned and his feet encased in house slippers. He is always the leader of a big parade.

Between now and the Democratic convention of 1928, perhaps by the time that this study has appeared, Smith will probably have found opportunities to air his beliefs, hastily formulated, on national issues. For a year past political leaders from widely separated parts of the country have been drifting into New York to demand that Al speak out on the woes of the farmer, on labor or on immigration. He has held, with admirable restraint, to his principle of not admitting that he is an active candidate and has insisted that these subjects are no concern of a man who is merely the Governor of the State of New York. But if the fiction that he is not a candidate cannot be maintained much longer, it will not be difficult for him to evolve policies on the matters that are of national interest.

Some of his advisers insist, in fact, that he has always had ideas regarding national problems. One of these, whose name it would be unkind to reveal, was connected with the campaign for Smith's nomination in 1924. Himself a man with a broad outlook, he told me that Al had asked him to assist in the contest. Before consenting, he said, he had demanded to know whether the Governor had considered the issues he would be called upon to face.

"To my surprise," he said, "I found that Al had thought about these things a great deal. Almost as though he were on the stump, he spoke for an hour. Regarding the League of Nations, it was his view, it would be better to urge that all of the friction of the past be forgotten. The thing he would seek to do would be to impress upon the people what the League had accomplished, what nations belonged to it and took part in its deliberations. He said that as President it would be a matter of no concern to him by what name the international organization was known. He would coöperate in any movement for world peace and would send unofficial advisers to sit around the table and discuss the problems before it.

"Smith has sound ideas with respect to the organization of the federal government. He thinks that his own experience in accomplishing consolidation of state departments in New York can be applied to the federal machine. He has thought about farm relief, too. He told me that it was his conviction that the prosperity of the agricultural interests depended upon a measure of scientific control of crops. He knew, for instance, that wheat had often been overproduced. He thought that excess crops might be controlled through the banks. The heads of these, he said, should refuse to extend credit to farmers who persisted in overproduction. He did not believe that subsidies from the government would provide a cure for an evil that was economic in its nature."

Other friends of Governor Smith are meeting the challenge that he is "a town-lot Sir Galahad" with the flat assertion that he is nothing of the sort. They have combed his record to show that instead of being interested in the State alone he has on many occasions given utterance on national and international affairs. Early in 1920, they point out, he criticized the Republican Party for wrecking the dreams of Woodrow Wilson that war might be prevented. In October of that year he issued an executive proclamation setting aside Sunday, October 24, as a day upon which the people of the State were to toss aside the comic sheets of their newspapers and familiarize themselves with the League of Nations covenant.

In February, 1923, it is now recalled, Governor Smith suggested that the President of the United States take office on January 1 following his election instead of in March and that members of the Senate have four-year terms running concurrently. In March of that year he declared himself opposed to literacy tests for immigrants. In response to a question regarding his position on five to four decisions by the United States Supreme Court, he said that it might be well to have more emphatic rulings when the question under consideration was a public health or public welfare law.

During the campaign for John W. Davis in 1924 Smith made several speeches in behalf of the Democratic candidate and these, naturally, concerned national issues. At Boston he criticized the foreign policy of President Coolidge, scored the tariff of the

Republicans and pointed out that the President had not openly attacked the Ku Klux Klan. He also berated the Republican administration for the oil scandals. At Manchester, N. H., he said:

"They say the Republican Party is not responsible for the breach of trust of its appointees. They didn't say that in 1920 when they were arousing the ranks of the people against a man who was dying so they could defeat the candidate of the party of Woodrow Wilson.

"No issues but Coolidge? Can they dodge the issue of seating Newberry and keeping him almost until his trial and conviction?

"When the Republican Party through somebody's cupidity and every one else's stupidity let the naval oil reserves get away it was striking a blow at the Navy. Is no one to answer for that? Why the whole Administration should have known about it. They either were in on it or they have no brains.

"The Republicans point with pride to Coolidge and say that he is the issue. They say that he is not a talker but a doer. Well, the last four years in Washington was no place for a silent man. It was the place for a leader and a leader never afraid to talk out."

Smith was, with reason, far from silent on national issues during the weeks just before the last Democratic convention. In an interview in the New York *Times*, prior to the Madison Square Garden débâcle, he discussed various subjects at length.

"Let us lead the nation back from 'normalcy' to 'honesty'," he said. " 'Normalcy' also prompts tariff extortion. The farmer has been cheated by the promise that high duties on agricultural products which are not imported would offset for him high duties on the articles he must buy. The laborer has been deluded by artificial inflation which gives him an apparent high wage, the real purchasing power of which is destroyed by the provisions of the Fordney-McCumber Tariff act. The business man has been misled by artificial interference with the course of commerce that enriches the favored monopoly at the expense of the average man. The restriction of foreign imports for the benefit of the tariff beneficiaries has impaired the ability of our foreign debtors to discharge their obligations to us.

"A nation stretching from Maine to California, which comprises metropolis and farm, foreigner and native, mountain and plain, with every variety of community and every habit of life, must retain that local self-government which our forefathers regarded as a foundation of our Republic. New York cannot impose local rules for Oklahoma, nor Montana for Florida. Reasonable differences of viewpoint in widely differing sections must be recognized if we are to preserve national unity.

"We must, therefore, revitalize the constitutional provision that powers not expressly given to the Federal Government are reserved to the States. We must stop the dangerous overcentralization of federal power. We must halt the march of federal commissions and bureaus and taxation and laws that are pressing on every locality. We must be not only for one, but for all.

"Our tradition condemns alike entangling alliances and unreasonable isolation. The vacillating policy following under the Republican administration is challenged not only by those who regard it as false to the American ideal of service to the world but also, with equal force, by those who regard it as destructive of our own self-interest.

"The arteries of trade reach through the civilized world. When Europe lies economically prostrate, the flow of our merchandise through these arteries stops short. In our western wheat belt, the greatest in the world, more than 200 banks have failed under the Republican régime. Our surplus agricultural products rot in storehouses because foreign nations, our legitimate customers, are without power to purchase. From us they have received no affirmative help, but even actual injury in our policy of aloofness.

"There is nothing partisan in these considerations. When the Republican Party spoke through the voice of its great statesmen and not through the voice of its small politicians that party, too, proclaimed the necessity of maintaining proper and reasonable contacts with other nations of the world. The matter is one both of aims and of economic policy. At the water's edge all partisan contentions should cease.

"But our party must lead the way where the Republicans have failed. We should enlist the ablest men of all parties to examine at first hand conditions and the actual functioning of the national and international agencies operating in Europe to-day, both from economic and governmental points of view. In the light of their recommendations we should act and act promptly, for the furtherance alike of American ideals and American prosperity, with the full knowledge of conditions as they are. Then we may be guided to action, not by partisan rancor, but by knowledge and wisdom.

"We must help build the machinery for peace. The hopes and fears of every father and mother in our land cry out for it. The same cry resounds from the parents of every land. . . . Let no man say that this is mere sentimentality. The broken heart of a stricken mother is the most real thing in life. We must come together with other nations to end war.

"It is the sacred right and mission of the party of Cleveland and Wilson to lead in translating into action the Biblical exhortation:

" 'Have we not all one Father? Has not one God created us? Why, therefore, should we deal treacherously, each with his brother?'

"In every activity of government, domestic and foreign, the Democratic Party must reëstablish what one of its great leaders proclaimed and exemplified—that 'Public office is a public trust.' "

I quote so extensively from these remarks not to indicate, as Smith's supporters in time will do, that he is deeply interested in such matters. I do not question their sincerity, but I hold to a suspicion that they were not entirely spontaneous. Whatever the purpose behind their utterance, however, they prove that Al can speak intelligently, even eloquently, on matters that have no bearing on his labors as Governor of New York. Despite his growing tendency toward caution Smith has, once or twice, insisted that courage is to be preferred to silence. The most recent example of this was at the New York State convention in 1926, when he demanded that the platform contain an endorsement of the World Court. Some of the principles, also, on which he has made himself heard as Governor are applicable in their essence to the nation as well as to the State. Among these were his scorn for loyalty tests among teachers and his opposition to the expulsion of the Socialist Assemblymen. His grasp of financial matters can be translated without great difficulty into national terms.

On at least two big problems, Governor Smith has been able to speak nationally without stepping out of his rôle. One of these is the development for the benefit of the public of water power. Virtually since the first day that he became Governor, Al Smith has worked energetically to prevent exploitation of this natural resource by private capital. He has, it must be admitted, shifted his policy in some details. But in the larger aspects his program seems sound and constructive. It has been one of his frequent pieces of political good fortune that the Republican Party has successfully blocked his recommendations, with the result that the issue is preserved for national consumption. It will be greeted with favor, undoubtedly, by the residents of the western states who are agitated over the Boulder Dam and other power projects. The other State problem of wide interest is the suggestion Smith made in March of 1926 that the State barge canal be made part of a ship canal connecting the Great Lakes with the Atlantic seaboard. His analysis of this contained in a letter to the members of Congress from New York is a refutation of the charge that he cannot assimilate details of the country's transportation puzzles.

A final word may not, perhaps, be out of place to reassure the sensitive souls who fear that Al Smith might not measure up to what they believe the social traditions of the White House. These can find comfort in the knowledge that Smith associates to-day with men of great wealth. He is momentarily, being Governor and receiving only $10,000 a year, short of funds. But the tastes that he has been acquiring during the last few years are those that go with private cars, yachts and large suites of rooms in the best hotels. Such is his innate self-assurance that he has rarely, at any time, felt out of place among the blue-bloods of the Social Register. But more recently he has acquired a polish that enables him, to an increasing degree, to say the right word. No one, I have said before, can find fault with his manner of dress or his appearance when he presides at functions. There have been few governors in the history of the State whose dignity and bearing have been as impressive. The austerity with which the office of President of the United States is surrounded will increase this dignity. Al Smith might become even more aloof, even more stuffy if you like, than he is to-day. If he were ever to spend a year or so in the White House, I predict, the melody of "The Sidewalks of New York" would be heard less frequently. It might be revived, of course, if he ran for a second term. But there is an excellent chance that it would fade into the misty realm of forgotten things, along with the dear, dead days when Al Smith wore a brown derby and called across to the barkeeper of many a tavern to scrape off the foam or to fill the glasses again.

Chapter Nine

Political prognostication has, obviously, no legitimate place in this volume. It is a pastime always fraught with peril, particularly with regard to the chances of any particular candidate for a presidential nomination. The 1928 Democratic convention is, as this is being written, almost a year off. At the moment Al Smith would seem to be leading the procession, a fact that in itself may spell his doom because it enables the opposition to concentrate its fire. Whether he will be chosen to lead his party is something written in the stars; and in the secret plottings of practical politicians. I do not know what the outcome will be. But it will not be out of place, perhaps, to analyze predictions being made by more reckless men and to summarize the attitude being expressed toward Smith in various parts of the country.

Almost from the conclusion of the 1924 convention Smith has been a national figure. At first, I have indicated, it was believed that he could no longer be viewed as a presidential aspirant. But this was quickly dispelled when he campaigned for Davis and drew crowds far in excess of the Democratic candidate. Newspapers throughout the country commented on the leading part that he played in the rejection of Mayor Hylan by Tammany Hall in 1925. But it was in November of 1926, when he defeated Ogden Mills and became Governor of New York for the fourth term, that even in the most unfriendly communities politicians began to remark on his extraordinary talents as a campaigner and to wonder whether he, more than any other man, might not be able to revive the forlorn prospects of Democracy. The West, officially dry, started to hope that Al would either keep silent on prohibition or, preferably, state in ringing terms his devotion to the Volstead Act. The South, also dry and in addition Protestant in its religious leanings, reflected that even a Catholic might be preferable to a permanent Republican in the White House.

It is not quite accurate to quote from the editorials of Julian Harris, owner and editor of the *Enquirer-Sun* of Columbus, Ga., as indicative of the viewpoint of the South. Mr. Harris, whose newspaper has already won the Pulitzer Prize for its distinguished courage, is not a typical Southerner. His beliefs are based on reason and not prejudice. He writes what he believes instead of what he thinks his subscribers believe. Despite all this, however, his journal has been financially successful and his influence in Georgia and in other parts of the South increases constantly. Early this year he wrote to me:

"I have been for Alfred E. Smith from the moment he was reëlected to the New York Governorship; not that I did not see him as an able man and a possibility before then, but his latest success makes him the *only* man for the Democrats to name."

In an editorial on November 7, 1926, Mr. Harris commented on the victory of Smith over Mills. Many things might happen before 1928, he warned. It was not unlikely, however, that in two years Smith would still be the outstanding personality in his party and the only nominee with whom the Democrats had a chance to win.

> ". . . it is well," he said, "that the Southern Democrats should begin to appraise the unusual executive ability of Alfred E. Smith, . . . begin to study open-mindedly his past record, and scrutinize with careful fairness during the next two years his administration of the affairs of the greatest State in the union."

This was, of course, before the Marshall correspondence. Mr. Harris, in his editorial, warned Georgians to remember the constitutional guarantees which relate to freedom of worship. He detailed the repeated victories of the Governor of New York as proving that more than mere local popularity was responsible for his success. But many Southerners, he admitted, "see him through the distorting fog of religious prejudice".

In the same issue of his paper, Mr. Harris quoted from the editorials of other Southern journals. The

Montgomery (Ala.) *Advertiser* defended Smith's impartiality in religious affairs and had praised his honesty and courage. The Macon (Ga.) *Telegraph* said that "unless there are tremendous upheavals between now and the convention he is almost in a position to force his nomination". The Chattanooga (Tenn.) *Times* remarked that were Smith a Protestant, his nomination would be "unanimously acclaimed". Despite his Catholicism, the paper said, he might be nominated and this would be an excellent thing, since it would furnish a test of whether the religious issue was to supersede constitutional guarantees. These newspapers, Mr. Harris commented, were unhappily not representative of the whole South. The Atlanta *Constitution* had intimated that a Catholic could not be nominated. "Face the facts," warned the Macon (Ga.) *News*; "Smith is a wet and the religious issue against him will be raised." The Jackson (Miss.) *News* insisted that the nomination of Smith "or any other wet aspirant would smash Democracy to smithereens in this commonwealth."

"The Democrats may as well be honest," Mr. Harris wrote on December 26, 1926. "Democrats—those of the South at any rate—are not particularly opposed to Smith because he is not a prohibitionist, because the Southern people are not greater prohibitionists than the people of any other section of the country; if they are, their practice fails to prove it. . . . The real opposition to Smith is based on the fact that he is a Roman Catholic communicant, and Southern Democrats who oppose him may as well be honest about it."

All of this was, I repeat, before Al Smith wrote his answer to Mr. Marshall. The newspapers of the South almost unanimously applauded this declaration, of course. There was no other course open to the most Klan-ridden of editors. Whether the letter has gone far to minimize the religious issue is a thing that can merely be pondered. It has been my theory that it will force the opposition to concentrate, in the open, on Al's prohibition views.

In the West, also, has come a definite change in the sentiment toward Smith. This is not so much, if I read the signs correctly, a drift toward Al as a defection from McAdoo. In 1924 the former Secretary of the Treasury drew heavily from the open spaces and from the South. To-day, there are indications, he will win few delegations west of the Mississippi. There will, of course, be any number of "favorite son" candidates who will be offered by the western commonwealths. Delegations to the convention will probably be uninstructed, instead of required to vote for Smith, McAdoo or some other candidate. Or they may be ordered to cast a few ballots for the figure who is the pride of their particular state. When it becomes apparent that he cannot win they will shift to the candidate who has a chance; Smith or some other. Thus Al has a chance of winning ultimately, although not as the convention starts, California, Arizona, Montana, Nevada, New Mexico, Oklahoma, Texas and Wyoming. All of these were McAdoo states in 1924. Western newspapers are looking askance at Smith's prohibition record. The Anti-Saloon League will, beyond question, send agitators to the corn and cow country to convince the clergy that Smith stands for nullification and the saloon. Meanwhile, it might be added, there are signs that some parts of the West are beginning to lose faith in the dry cause. Obviously, if this is so, Al will benefit. The newspapers have recently been filled with rumors that McAdoo is going to withdraw. But this, I think, is far from verification. That he is weaker than in 1924 seems to be true. But at the present time enough delegates might rally to him to veto the nomination of Smith.

All of which means, perhaps, less than nothing. Al Smith must go through another session of the legislature during which the Republican Party will ignore the business of the State of New York in order to disqualify him for the presidency. It will again resort, as it has done with small success in the past, to obstructive tactics. It will raise the issue of extravagance. Much will depend upon the 1928 session of the law-makers of New York. The strategists of the Democratic Party will, in the interval, perfect their plans to have Al Smith run, if he runs at all, on a platform which straddles the issue of prohibition. So astute a political observer as Frank R. Kent of the Baltimore *Sun* wrote in the *Nation* on March 30, 1927, that the plan of the Democratic leaders secretly favoring Smith was to encourage "favorite son" movements. These, as it happens, will take place in the states where once McAdoo was strong. They will, if the scheme succeeds, result in the elimination of the man considered, even now, Al's leading opponent and will prevent another costly battle such as that of 1924. It may work. It is, at all events, a plan far superior to those which the limited intellects of politicians ordinarily achieve.

Smith will, if nominated, receive the support of the Solid South. Talk that southerners will decline to vote for a Catholic is perfectly foolish. Some may remain away from the polls, of course. A few may mark their ballots for God and Protestantism. But the total of those who will do this will be so small as to be negligible. Will Al Smith be nominated? Does he deserve the nomination? The first question no one can answer. An answer to the second may, perhaps, have been found in the pages of this book. The Democratic Party has, it must be clear, passed through seven long, lean years of famine. In the last analysis it may choose a man, whatever his qualifications or faults, who can restore days of plenty, of prosperity and of federal jobs.

"It's just possible," one cynical politician has muttered, "that the party may get tired of finishing second in a two-horse race."

THE END

Index

Index

Index

V

W

Y

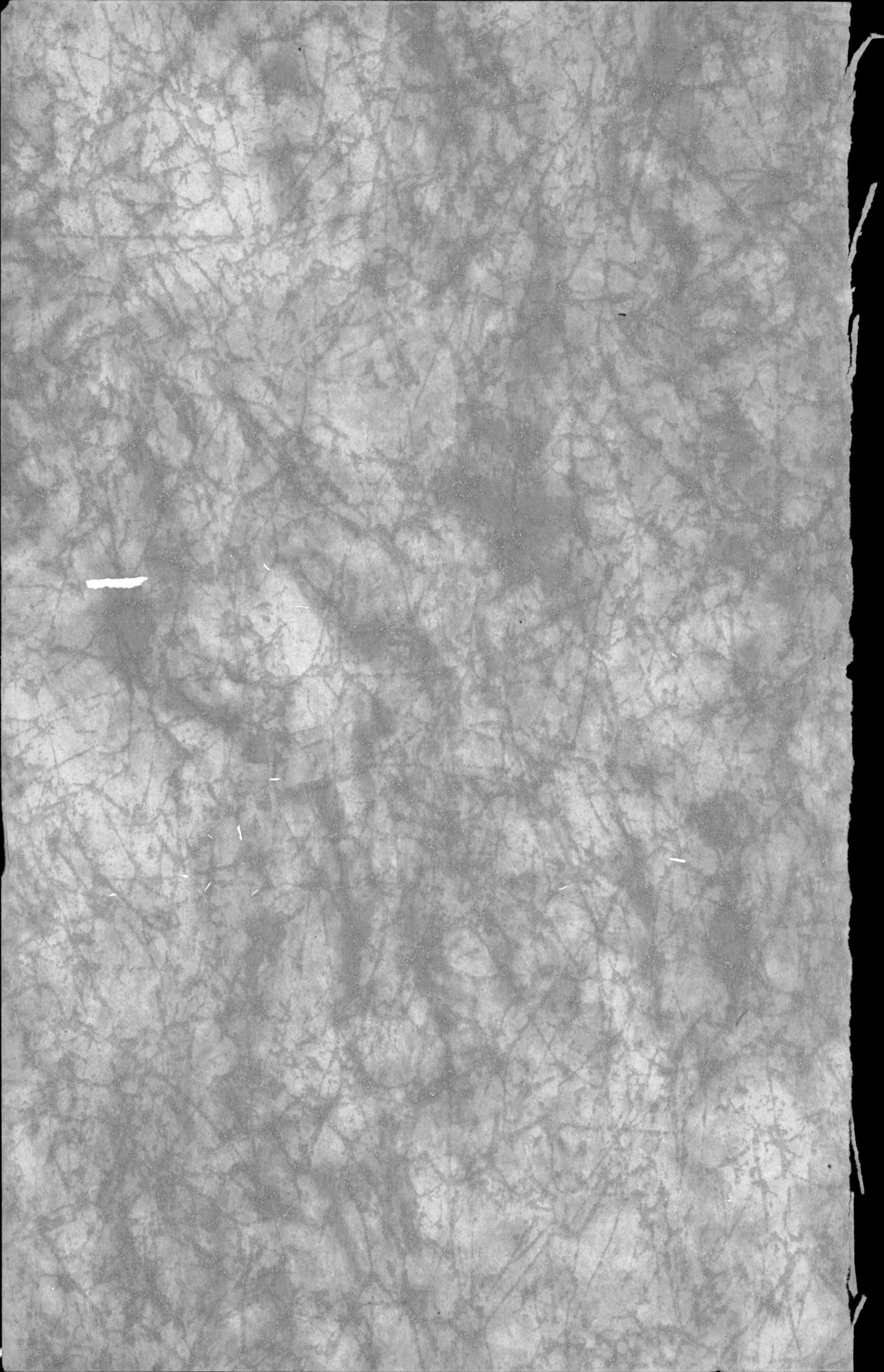